I0016844

# Building Expert Business Solutions with Zoho CRM

An indispensable guide to developing future-proof CRM solutions and growing your business exponentially

**Dominic Harrington**

BIRMINGHAM—MUMBAI

# Building Expert Business Solutions with Zoho CRM

Copyright © 2021 Packt Publishing

*All rights reserved.* No part of this book may be reproduced, stored in a retrieval system, or transmitted in any form or by any means, without the prior written permission of the publisher, except in the case of brief quotations embedded in critical articles or reviews.

Every effort has been made in the preparation of this book to ensure the accuracy of the information presented. However, the information contained in this book is sold without warranty, either express or implied. Neither the author, nor Packt Publishing or its dealers and distributors, will be held liable for any damages caused or alleged to have been caused directly or indirectly by this book.

Packt Publishing has endeavored to provide trademark information about all of the companies and products mentioned in this book by the appropriate use of capitals. However, Packt Publishing cannot guarantee the accuracy of this information.

**Group Product Manager**: Kunal Chaudhari

**Publishing Product Manager**: Alok Dhuri

**Senior Editor**: Storm Mann

**Content Development Editor**: Nithya Sadanandan

**Technical Editor**: Pradeep Sahu

**Copy Editor**: Safis Editing

**Project Coordinator**: Deeksha Thakkar

**Proofreader**: Safis Editing

**Indexer**: Manju Arasan

**Production Designer**: Joshua Misquitta

First published: July 2021

Production reference: 1160721

Published by Packt Publishing Ltd.

Livery Place

35 Livery Street

Birmingham

B3 2PB, UK.

ISBN 978-1-80056-466-4

www.packt.com

*To Victoria, Ethan, Olivia, and Isaac*

*– Dominic Harrington*

# Contributors

## About the author

**Dominic Harrington** has over 20 years' IT experience, specializing in helping business owners and managers to get the best value and results from their software. Dominic inspires his clients to learn, adapt, and succeed with the adoption of business applications by explaining technical to non-technical concepts to people in an easy-to-understand manner. Since 2015, through his successful consultancy business, Dominic has helped over 300 businesses adopt Zoho CRM in the UK across a wide range of business sectors, with businesses having anywhere from 1-1,500 employees and with turnovers from £30K to +£100 million. As a Zoho Development partner, his business has also released five applications on Zoho Marketplace to date – with plans for more underway.

# About the reviewer

With a career spanning nearly 40 years, **Chris Moran** has held senior roles in finance and sales across a variety of businesses. In 2021, Chris formed JCM and designed it to be an ethical, people-centered business. It rapidly grew to become a premier Zoho partner, serving clients across the UK and Europe.

# Table of Contents

# 6

# Game-Changing Workflows and Automations

# 7

# Essential Systems Administration

# 8

## Supercharge CRM with Marketplace Extensions, Custom Functions, and Integrations

# Section 3: Six of the Best Zoho Apps to Integrate with Your CRM

# 9

## Zoho Campaigns

# 10

## Zoho Forms

# 11
# Zoho Survey

# 12
# SalesIQ

# Section 4: Measure, Learn, Evolve

# 15
## Building Actionable Reports and Dashboards (CRM)

# 16

# Best Practices to Adopt and Evolve Your CRM

# Preface

Zoho CRM is one of the most popular CRM solutions on the market, with millions of users worldwide. You should think of Zoho CRM as a platform upon which you can configure your own CRM solution that is tailored specifically to your business. Established in 2006, Zoho continually develops new features, new designs, and new applications every year, which means it is a mature and stable yet innovative and future-proof system. Developed as a native cloud solution with multiple mobile applications available, with Zoho, you and your team can access, update, and review data from any place using any device at any time.

Having helped over 300 businesses implement Zoho in the last few years, I felt compelled to write this book to help others benefit from the journey that my clients and I have been on. I wanted to share the experience, lessons learned, and best practice so that you can make a great start to your Zoho journey and experience accelerated success.

I truly believe that implementing the processes and techniques in this book will be of tremendous benefit to you, and in doing so, you will develop a CRM solution for your business that is fit for the next 10 years of business growth.

## Who this book is for

If you're a business manager or a business owner interested in discovering how the Zoho platform can help transform your business, and are looking to gain a practical understanding of how to choose an app from the vast array of Zoho products, then this book is for you. Whether you're new to Zoho, or have basic experience and want to learn about its features and apps, this book can help you. Expert Zoho users who want to develop custom solutions for their business will also find this book helpful. Foundational knowledge of CRM concepts is expected to get the most out of this book.

# What this book covers

*Chapter 1, The Foundation Modules – Understanding the Building Blocks of Success*, will take you through the journey of building a successful CRM. Before you begin, you must decide on a destination by defining your *why*. In this chapter, you will learn how to define your *why* and will get a basic understanding of the foundation (or core) modules of Zoho CRM. Understanding these modules, the relationships between them, and their functionality will get you a huge step closer to realizing a successful solution. Getting this correctly aligned with your *why* gives you a solid foundation to build on.

*Chapter 2, Leads – Getting It Right the First Time*, will help you to understand which of the system fields you should keep, which ones you can lose, how to best define the picklists, and which custom fields you should add. A strong, well-defined Leads module sets you off on the best foot possible and sets the tone for how your team will use the system from here onward.

*Chapter 3, Deals – Sales Funnels to Fuel Your Business Growth*, will explore the singular most important module of Zoho CRM: Deals. This is your sales pipeline. It is the focus of most of your business development activities and the way that you build and use this module will have a huge impact not only on how successful you are with the system, but also on the future growth of your business.

*Chapter 4, Accounts and Contacts – The Beating Heart of Your CRM*, will give you an understanding of which fields you must have in these modules and how you will use them to interact with the rest of the system and also other Zoho and third-party systems. Whether you supply products/services to the general public, businesses, or both, the practical use cases in this chapter will help you understand how these modules should be optimized.

*Chapter 5, Working with Other System and Custom Modules*, will take you through the remaining system modules, including how and when they should be  used and how to set them up. You will learn how to develop additional modules that will streamline further business processes, improve internal and external communication, and involve more departments of your organization within the system.

*Chapter 6, Game-Changing Workflows and Automations*, will provide you with powerful insights and knowledge of arguably the most valuable aspect of Zoho CRM. Used well and often, the workflows in Zoho will greatly improve your efficiency time and again, and will really help take your CRM to the next level and get your users and team excited about how it can help them become more efficient and successful. We will go through some useful examples, such as notifying the sales team about a lead and assigning a task to give you a hands-on learning experience and to help you proactively manage opportunities and clients much more effectively.

*Chapter 7, Essential Systems Administration*, will explore the setup area of Zoho CRM. Everything within this area will help you service and maintain the CRM right from the initial build and throughout all the time you and your team use Zoho. Your business will evolve, the software will evolves your people will come/go and evolve. In this chapter, you will learn to use the core elements within the setup area correctly to allow you to tweak the system and adapt to changes. You will also go through some practical scenarios to jumpstart your CRM journey with the degree of security and flexibility required to suit your business.

*Chapter 8, Supercharge CRM with Marketplace Extensions, Custom Functions, and Integrations*, will give you an understanding of some of the best ways to supercharge your CRM system. Firstly, you will gain an understanding of Zoho Marketplace and an insight into some of the more useful and recommended extensions. Then you will learn about another key method of extending the functionality of Zoho CRM using custom functions – with some practical examples for you to try. Finally, you will discover some of the more popular third-party integrations and the different ways that they can be achieved.

*Chapter 9, Zoho Campaigns*, will cover Zoho Campaigns, which is an enterprise-level email marketing platform. It is similar in functionality to most other software in this sector – however, you could be missing a huge trick by not using this due to its powerful two-way integration with Zoho CRM. In this chapter, you will discover the key steps required to make sure you are effectively getting the right messages to the right people at the right time.

*Chapter 10, Zoho Forms*, will explore a powerful yet intuitive web form builder that requires no development. Zoho Forms can replace emails and spreadsheets for data-collecting purposes, and once integrated with the CRM can trigger workflows, thus unlocking the potential for more automation and saving your team a huge amount of time and effort. In this chapter, we will show you how to maximize this value to your business and will include real working examples from a business networking firm and a training company.

*Chapter 11, Zoho Survey*, will introduce you to Zoho Survey, which is an intuitive survey tool that makes capturing customer feedback fun and insightful. With a lot of overlap with Zoho Forms, sometimes the trick comes down to understanding which is the best tool to use out of Survey or Forms. Once again, the most powerful aspect of Survey is the ability to integrate with your CRM. Absorb the advice and tips in this chapter and you will never look back when it comes to gathering feedback and taking action on the results.

*Chapter 12, SalesIQ*, will look into a powerful and insightful tool, Sales IQ, that will allow you to engage with prospects and clients via a live chat tool and track website visitors so that you can better tailor communication to them. You will learn the basics of live chat that will help you convert leads and then also personalize some of the nurturing content once you know which pages have been visited, by whom, and when. As the saying goes – knowledge is power!

*Chapter 13, Zoho Analytics*, will cover Zoho Analytics, an enterprise-level **Business Intelligence** (or **BI**) tool. It is also one of the most underused tools among Zoho CRM users. This is partially down to the quality of the internal reports and dashboards, and sometimes there's also the misconception that this tool is overkill and too complex to use. In this chapter, that myth will be busted. Additionally, we will provide some practical examples of how this tool can be used to gain insights that would otherwise be missed.

*Chapter 14, Zoho Creator*, will look at another excellent application developed by Zoho that can further help the digital transformation of your business: Zoho Creator. In this chapter, we will provide an introduction to how you can create custom applications on your own without any prior coding experience or IT expertise using Zoho Creator's drag and drop interface.

*Chapter 15, Building Actionable Reports and Dashboards (CRM)*, will focus on the CRM capabilities where you will learn how to create list-based reports and schedule them to be distributed automatically to team members and also how to create visually appealing and powerful dashboards within minutes.

*Chapter 16, Best Practices to Adopt and Evolve Your CRM*, will help you to learn how to avoid common mistakes and set three early adoption milestones that will set you on the right path. As good as your CRM may be, if it is not adopted by your team successfully, you will never fully realize the potential it has to transform your business. Slow user adoption is frequently cited as the main reason for a CRM project to fail.

# To get the most out of this book

You will need access to the Zoho CRM Professional/Enterprise/CRM Plus or Ultimate edition. You will also need access to either the free or paid editions of the other Zoho applications used within *Section 3, Six of the Best Zoho Apps to Integrate with Your CRM*.

| Software covered within this book | System requirements |
|---|---|
| Zoho CRM | |
| Zoho Campaigns | Access to the internet using a popular browser such as Chrome, Firefox, or Microsoft Edge is required for all software covered within this book. |
| Zoho Forms | |
| Zoho Survey | |
| Sales IQ | |
| Zoho Analytics | |
| Zoho Creator | |

> **Note**
>
> Some of the features (including integration with CRM) may not be available using the free edition of the six other Zoho applications. Once you have read the chapter, implemented the suggestions, and completed the practical examples, you may wish to consider upgrading to unlock such features.

# Download the color images

We also provide a PDF file that has color images of the screenshots and diagrams used in this book. You can download it here: `https://static.packt-cdn.com/downloads/9781800564664_ColorImages.pdf`.

# Conventions used

There are a number of text conventions used throughout this book.

`Code in text`: Indicates code words in text, database table names, folder names, filenames, file extensions, pathnames, dummy URLs, user input, and Twitter handles. Here is an example: "In your website's source file, paste the code into your existing code anywhere before the `</body>` tag."

A block of code is set as follows:

```
leadinfo = {"Company":input.Company,"Last_Name":input.
Last_Name,"First_Name":input.First_Name,"Phone":input.Phone_
Number,"Email":input.Email,"Product":input.Product,"Partner_
Code":input.Partner_Code,"Lead_Source":input.Lead_Source};
response = zoho.crm.createRecord("Leads",leadinfo);
```

When we wish to draw your attention to a particular part of a code block, the relevant lines or items are set in bold:

```
leadinfo = {"Company":input.Company,"Last_Name":input.
Last_Name,"First_Name":input.First_Name,"Phone":input.Phone_
Number,"Email":input.Email,"Product":input.Product,"Partner_
Code":input.Partner_Code,"Lead_Source":input.Lead_Source};
response = zoho.crm.createRecord("Leads",leadinfo);
```

**Bold**: Indicates a new term, an important word, or words that you see on screen. For instance, words in menus or dialog boxes appear in **bold**. Here is an example: "You may obtain this code by navigating to **Settings | Brands | Your Brand Name | Installation | Website**."

> Tips or important notes
> Appear like this.

# Get in touch

Feedback from our readers is always welcome.

**General feedback**: If you have questions about any aspect of this book, email us at customercare@packtpub.com and mention the book title in the subject of your message.

**Errata**: Although we have taken every care to ensure the accuracy of our content, mistakes do happen. If you have found a mistake in this book, we would be grateful if you would report this to us. Please visit www.packtpub.com/support/errata and fill in the form.

**Piracy**: If you come across any illegal copies of our works in any form on the internet, we would be grateful if you would provide us with the location address or website name. Please contact us at copyright@packt.com with a link to the material.

**If you are interested in becoming an author**: If there is a topic that you have expertise in and you are interested in either writing or contributing to a book, please visit authors.packtpub.com.

# Share your thoughts

Once you've read *Building Expert Business Solutions with Zoho CRM*, we'd love to hear your thoughts! Scan the QR code below to go straight to the Amazon review page for this book and share your feedback.

https://packt.link/r/1-800-56466-X

Your review is important to us and the tech community and will help us make sure we're delivering excellent quality content.

# Section 1: Laying the Foundation

All successful and durable structures require a solid foundation. The same is true for Zoho CRM. In this section, you will learn about the key building blocks that, when assembled, will create a successful foundation. This foundation will become a platform for the future growth and success of your CRM, and your business.

This section comprises the following chapters:

- *Chapter 1, The Foundation Modules – Understanding the Building Blocks of Success*
- *Chapter 2, Leads – Getting It Right the First Time*
- *Chapter 3, Deals – Sales Funnels to Fuel Your Business Growth*
- *Chapter 4, Accounts and Contacts – The Beating Heart of Your CRM*

# 1
# The Foundation Modules – Understanding the Building Blocks of Success

Building a successful **Customer Relationship Management (CRM)** system is a journey. Before you begin, you must decide on a destination by defining your *why*. In this chapter, you will learn how to define your *why*, and you will also come to understand how to measure the success of your new CRM system. Furthermore, you will learn about the foundation modules of Zoho, understanding the purpose of each module and how they relate to each other.

Combining your *why* with a solid foundation will provide you with excellent building blocks to success. In doing so, you will be defining your destination, your expectation when you get there, and a clear route plan of how you are going to get there. These are all prerequisites of a successful CRM journey.

In this chapter, we will cover these topics:

- Exploring the need for a new CRM system
- Understanding why CRM is more than just a sales and marketing tool
- Defining key objectives and measures of success
- Introducing the foundation modules—**Leads**, **Deals**, **Accounts**, and **Contacts**

## Technical requirements

The requirements for not only this chapter but for the book as a whole are as follows:

- Basic knowledge of CRM concepts
- At least one license in one of the following Zoho Editions: Professional (CRM), Enterprise (CRM), CRM Plus, or Zoho One

## Exploring the need for a new CRM system

Before you begin to design and build your CRM, you need to understand *why* you are doing this. Understanding your reasoning and the need for a new CRM can help you make sure you prioritize the new system effectively to remove pain points and set clear goals. Consider some of the following reasons:

- Your sales team does not have a clear, well-defined process for generating new business.
- Your business is experiencing growth, and you need this growth to be scalable and more profitable.
- You have identified the need to improve how customer data is collected, managed, and used within your business.
- The sales team is missing out on opportunities from existing customers through not nurturing or following up with them enough.
- You have customer data in several different places and are using multiple systems that do not integrate with each other.
- You realize that your current CRM system is out of date or no longer fit for purpose.

You may be able to identify with more than one of the aforementioned reasons. Once you truly understand why you need a CRM system, we can begin to think about the next steps.

> **Tip**
> List the reasons because of which you/your team have decided that a new CRM is needed for your business. Doing so will provide a reference for later when it comes to defining success measures and also seeking *buy-in* from colleagues.

Now that you have identified a few reasons for change, it is also useful to consider how a CRM may also be of benefit to other areas of your business.

# Understanding why CRM is more than just a sales and marketing tool

Traditionally, the importance of CRM has been as a sales and marketing tool. However, some of the biggest gains for your business can come from other areas, such as operations, customer service, supplier management, and partner relationships. Listed next are some key business functions and how each one can benefit from a CRM system.

## Marketing

The marketing team will be able to segment prospects and customers and have visibility of every lead and deal—mapping out the journey from lead to sale. This will provide a clear understanding of the effectiveness of all marketing activities and help to measure the **return on investment** (**ROI**) by tracking leads and deals generated from each event or campaign.

## Sales

Sales managers will understand their pipeline much better and be able to forecast sales more accurately. The sales team will benefit from reduced admin, a better understanding of their clients, and the opportunity to spend more time selling and less time inputting data.

## Customer service

A customer might raise an issue via one channel such as Twitter or Facebook, but customer service may switch to email, phone, or live chat to resolve the matter. By pulling together the communication from multiple channels into a single platform, we provide the customer service team with all the information they need to resolve the query. We can ensure that whoever is speaking to the customer has access to the current status, next action, and notes, which will make the customer feel valued and well looked after.

## Customer success/account management

Having visibility of support requests, deals, and all communications history will enable the account manager to review all the information they need prior to making a call or visit to an existing customer. They will be prompted when the next call to each client is due and provided with structure to make sure they ask the right questions to measure customer happiness and retention and to identify opportunities to upsell or cross-sell related products and services.

## Operations

Once a deal has been *won*, we can automatically share these details with the operations/delivery team so that they can fulfill the order or job.

## Finance

We can use the system to notify the finance team when a deal has been *won*, an order fulfilled, or a job completed so that they can raise the necessary invoices.

We should also consider integrating the CRM with our accounting/invoicing software so that these processes may be streamlined and automated further.

## Supplier management and partner relationships

Using the CRM for tracking meetings, calls, and emails with suppliers and partners will help teams manage these relationships better.

Follow-ups can easily be created, and reporting enables a comparison of the efficiency of suppliers and also the success and activity of partners.

This inclusion of other business areas will help you deliver more value with the CRM, improve internal communication, and increase buy-in from the respective stakeholders.

So, having considered the areas we wish to improve with a new CRM, it is now time to be specific and to set some goals.

# Defining key objectives and measures of success

Now you have a detailed understanding of the business-wide drivers for change, it is time to set some objectives. This is often best achieved by defining specific ways in which you will measure the success of your new CRM system.

Examples of success measures include the following:

- To increase the conversion rate of lead to deal by 50% within 3 months
- To have the ability to measure our ROI on marketing
- To know how many times per year we have communicated with existing clients
- To have visibility of how many/which products each of our clients has
- All quotes, orders, and jobs paperwork will be replaced with electronic documentation
- Our operations team will be reminded when every service is due in advance so this can be scheduled and completed on time
- To increase first-year retention of members from 40% (current level) to 60% within 2 years
- To have the ability to measure where leads have come from
- To have the ability to measure conversion rates (from inquiry to customer)
- To provide the sales management team with complete visibility of the pipeline
- To provide senior management with a weighted forecast of the pipeline
- To have the ability to break down sales performance by territory/area and target areas for improvement
- To replace several spreadsheets and Outlook contact directories that are currently used in the business with a single central database accessible by all the team

> **Tip**
> Write down at least five specific ways in which you will measure the success of your new CRM system. This will help you to prove when your goals have been met.

Once you know what success looks like, you are ready to think about how to start designing your new CRM in Zoho and, specifically, the foundation modules.

# Introducing the foundation modules – Leads, Deals, Accounts, and Contacts

Firstly, let's consider the **foundation modules** and understand why they are named as such. When designing and building any structure such as a house, extension, or other building, it is critical that we include solid foundations to build upon. Failure to do this results in a structure that will not be fit for purpose or one that will not be long-standing.

The same is true of a CRM system and Zoho. We have four foundation modules, listed as follows:

- **Leads**
- **Deals**
- **Accounts**
- **Contacts**

In this section, we will discuss each of these modules, explaining the difference between them and the importance of using these modules correctly. Not knowing the difference between these modules is actually one of the biggest mistakes new users make—this often leads to building a system in the wrong way, meaning that for some, they may never truly realize the full potential that Zoho has to offer their business.

Let's start by looking at **Leads**.

## Leads

A **lead** in Zoho can be defined as an unqualified contact or sales opportunity in your business.

In the **Leads** module, we must capture all the information needed to help qualify a contact/possible opportunity as quickly and effectively as possible.

In short, the information we need to record in the **Leads** module is *who*, *what*, *how*, and *why* they have contacted us/we have contacted them, which can be detailed as follows:

- *Who*: The contact name and name of the organization (if **business-to-business**, or **B2B**)
- *What*: The nature of their inquiry; which product(s) or service(s) they are interested in

- *How*: The method by which they have contacted us—such as by phone or email; through the company website; via social media; referral

- *Why*: For what reason have they contacted us and made this inquiry

Once we have recorded the key data as per the preceding outline, the next important question to consider is: *How do we qualify a lead?*

While this varies from business to business and sector to sector, there are a few lead qualification methodologies/tools that can and should be applied—for example, **BANT** (**Budget, Authority, Needs, and Timeline**), SCOTSMAN (**Solution, Competition, Only Me, Timebound, Size, Money, Authority, Need**), or CHAMP (**Challenges, Authority, Money, and Prioritization**). To help decide which one will be a good fit for your business, a useful blog on this subject can be found here: `https://contactbase.net/sales-qualification-frameworks/`.

Once you have selected or adapted one that is a good fit for your business, then it is very useful to include fields that prompt our sales team with the best qualification questions to ask in our **Leads** module.

In *Chapter 2, Leads – Getting It Right the First Time*, you will learn how to add fields to capture all of the information discussed so far. So, let's now consider what happens once a lead has been received and recorded.

> **Tip**
>
> Capturing where the lead came from will provide us with the ability to understand which lead-generation activities generate the most leads, and of these leads, which generate the most revenue. Acting on these insights will have a significant positive financial implication on your bottom line. See *Chapter 15, Building Actionable Reports and Dashboards (CRM)*, for further details on this.

## Following up on leads

Once a lead is received and key information recorded, it is important to have a simple, clear, and well-defined follow-up process in place for you and the team to follow. The following table describes a typical process to consider:

| Lead Status | Description | Methods Involved |
| --- | --- | --- |
| Lead generation | Capturing leads or prospects from various sources | Referrals: word of mouth; inbound phone/email; website form; social media; paid advertising; networking |
| Lead nurturing and engagement | Lead qualification and conversion | Engagement over the phone, email, or video call |
| Lead qualification and conversion | Converting leads that qualify into genuine prospects that want to do business with you | Manual conversion within the CRM once they have met the qualification criteria AND we have booked an appointment with one of the sales team |

Table 1.1 – Following up a lead

As the **Leads** module is the starting point of our CRM journey for our new customers, it is also the first impression our users will have upon using the CRM itself. It is therefore very important that we consider that the **user experience** (**UX**) in this module will help define how they perceive and subsequently use the system in later modules. In short, creating a great first impression with users in the **Leads** module will have a significant impact on how well they use the CRM overall.

Once we have successfully qualified our lead, it is time to look at what happens next in deals.

# Deals

A **deal** is a qualified lead. If deal is not the correct term for you, don't worry—you can easily rename this to suit. Indeed, many users change this to **potentials**, **opportunities**, or whatever fits best within their business.

> Tip
> A useful glossary provided by Zoho can be found at `https://help.`
> `zoho.com/portal/en/kb/crm/getting-started/`
> `articles/understand-crm-account#Key_CRM_`
> `Terminologies.`

Deals can be defined as the business deals that generate revenue for your organization with other organizations (B2B) or with people (**business-to-consumer**, or **B2C**). A deal evolves through different sales stages such as **Qualified**, **Discovery**, **Quote**, and so on, before it is actually a deal, *lost* or *won*. **Leads** can be directly converted to opportunities that represent a potential sale.

The **Deals** module encapsulates your sales process. It will provide you and your team with the ability to view how many deals are in the pipeline, which stage each one is at, and what the potential value is. It also allows a sales manager to prepare an accurate revenue forecast.

Quite simply, when built and used correctly, this module transforms businesses and can provide an incredible platform for them to grow.

In *Chapter 3, Deals – Sales Funnels to Fuel Your Business Growth*, you will learn how to build your **Deals** module. However, before you do, it is important to define what the sales stages are that the sales team must go through in order to convert each deal into a sale in your business. Here are some sample sales stages:

| Sales Stage | Description | Methods Involved |
| --- | --- | --- |
| Discovery | During this 60-minute call/meeting the sales person will ask a series of questions. This will provide them with enough details of the project requirements so that they have enough information to be able to progress to the next stage | Online video call or face-to-face meeting |
| Additional Discovery Meeting | Sometimes a prospect will want another meeting to either see the system and/or as an opportunity for either party to provide feedback from the first meeting | Online video call or face-to-face meeting |
| Proposal | This involves providing a detailed summary of the scope of the project including deliverables, timescales and associated license and consultancy costs | Sending a templated document for electronic signature via email |
| Follow-Up | This involves obtaining feedback, answering any questions, and closing the deal | Phone/video call and email |
| Closed Won | The deal is accepted | Field update, call, or email to thank the customer for business and discuss next steps |
| Closed Lost | The deal is rejected | Capture the reason why and potentially add to a mailing list for future correspondence |

Table 1.2 – An example sales process

In *Figure 1.2*, we can see that our process has a distinct beginning, middle, and end. It avoids jargon and abbreviations and as a result, it should be simple and intuitive to follow. When defining your stages, ask yourself: *Would a new starter in my business understand when to apply each stage and what to do?* If the answer is *Yes*, then your process is intuitive.

> **Tip**
> List the stages that, when followed, will provide the most effective way to process a potential deal until it is **closed won** or **closed lost** within your business. Validate this with other sales managers or leaders in the organization to obtain early buy-in from these key stakeholders and influencers.

# Accounts

When converting a lead in Zoho, it will create a record in the **Accounts** module.

**Accounts** are the companies or departments within companies within which you have business dealings, often described as your customers.

This module will contain all of the organizational details that are needed for us to secure, retain, and service their business. The data recorded here will give us greater capability when it comes to reporting and gaining a deeper understanding of the demographics and traits of our customers.

How you create, manage, and use this module will have a significant impact on the success of your CRM. An **Accounts** module managed well will provide your business with the basis of accurate and insightful reporting. This will help you to fully understand not just what is happening right now, but the trends and progress being made to assist with the predictions and planning of future growth. In *Chapter 4, Accounts and Contacts – The Beating Heart of Your CRM*, you will learn how to set up this module effectively.

# Contacts

When converting a lead in Zoho, it will also create a record in the **Contacts** module.

**Contacts** are the people within the companies with which you have business dealings.

It is quite common and often recommended that these contacts also include suppliers, partners, referral partners, and other types of contacts with which you need to build and maintain relationships.

The **Contacts** module is key also when integrating with other Zoho and third-party applications such as Campaigns, Surveys, SalesIQ, and Emails, as people engage with your team using these channels.

How you create, maintain, and use the **Contacts** module will have a huge impact on how successful communication with your contacts will be. Successful communication helps to build trust, and increased trust builds stronger relationships. Stronger relationships help your business to grow, and this growth will be more sustainable. Learn how to best set up your **Contacts** module in *Chapter 4, Accounts and Contacts – The Beating Heart of Your CRM.*

> **Important note**
> The relationship between **Accounts** and **Contacts** in Zoho is one-to-many. Within one account (company) you may be dealing with several contacts (people), all of which will have their own record in Zoho. The benefit of this is that we can plan and track communication individually yet still have a summarized view within the **Accounts** record.

Having learned about each of the foundation modules individually, it's time to summarize them.

## Recapping on the foundation modules

So, now you understand the importance of each of the four individual core modules of Zoho CRM, it is useful to visualize the relationships between them. The following diagram illustrates this:

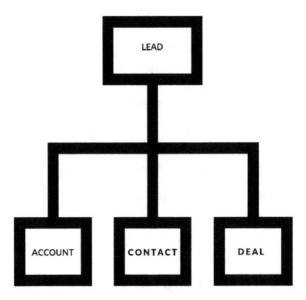

Figure 1.1 – Converting a lead

The general rule that is applied here is that when a lead is **Qualified**, it is converted into three records: **Accounts**, **Contacts**, and **Deals**.

With this knowledge and by setting our modules up to follow this process, everything should click into place, and we will understand how we can design our system in a way that gets the most out of the structure and functionality of Zoho CRM.

It is worth noting that new users sometimes challenge the difference between a lead and a deal. *Why not just use one module and have it all in the Deals module?* This is not an uncommon question.

The answer to this lies in the fact that *not all inquiries will ever be qualified* and, as it is only the **Qualified** leads that will turn into actual business deals and generate revenue, it is critical that we measure the number of leads that do/do not qualify and also make sure that our sales team are focusing their efforts in the right places (such as qualified ones). Quite often in businesses with a sales team, we find that one part of the team will be following up on inquiries, qualifying them, and booking appointments for one of the senior members of the sales team or the field sales representatives. Thus, splitting unqualified and qualified into two separate modules in Zoho lends itself perfectly to this process and division of labor and activity.

The second benefit of this approach is that we are not populating our **Accounts** and **Contacts** modules with lots of unqualified leads that will never progress, which in turn helps maintain the integrity and also the value of our database.

In *Chapter 2, Leads – Getting It Right the First Time*, we will explore the **Leads** module in a lot more detail; however, for now, it is useful to digest and understand that for most of our new business inquiries, this is the way we will process them in Zoho using the four foundation modules.

# Summary

You should now understand and have listed the reasons why you need a CRM system and be aware of the key drivers for change. You will have considered the needs of the business as a whole, and not just sales and marketing.

This will have enabled you to set clear objectives for the CRM and you will have defined some key measures of success for you and your team to aim for.

You have also learned about the four *foundation* modules of Zoho CRM, a definition and the function of each one, and how they relate to each other.

Now the building blocks of success have been laid, you are ready to progress. In the next chapter, you will learn how to set up the first foundation module: **Leads**.

# 2
# Leads – Getting It Right the First Time

Once you have understood the value, importance, and use of the **Leads** module (as described in the previous chapter), it is time to learn how best to set this module.

As **Leads** is the first contact point for all new business inquiries, it is important to build a strong and well-defined **Leads** module to set you off on the right foot.

The topics covered within this chapter are as follows:

- Which standard fields to remove and why
- Which standard fields to keep and why
- Creating custom fields
- Assigning picklist values
- Designing a user-friendly layout
- Using layout rules
- Mapping fields

Following the advice and instructions in the chapter will enable you to collect and manage data effectively for new inquiries. This success will set the tone for how users will interact with the system from here onward.

> **Note**
> The data captured in **Leads** drives some of the key reports. So, as you work through this chapter, make notes of the things you need to report on and make sure that this information is captured.

# Which standard fields to remove and why

When accessing your Zoho CRM for the first time, all the modules are enabled and within each module all the standard fields are visible. Your **Home** page will resemble the one displayed as follows:

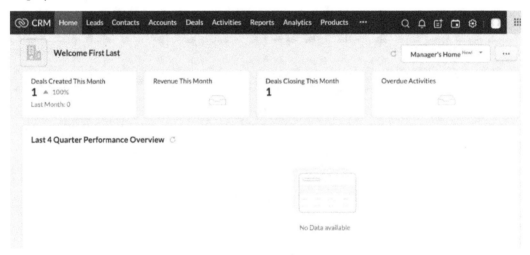

Figure 2.1 – Zoho CRM Home page when accessing the system for the first time

A standard field in Zoho in this context is defined as a field that is already present when we first access the system. Some of these fields record key data we need to capture, and others are needed as they link to other modules and functionality. However, there are several standard fields that may not be used by our teams and it is best practice to remove these fields so that the focus is on the ones that we do need.

A list and definition of all standard fields in the **Leads** module can be found at https://help.zoho.com/portal/en/kb/crm/sales-force-automation/leads/articles/standard-fields-leads.

Once you have reviewed this list of standard fields, identify which ones are not relevant to your lead qualification process. These are the ones you should remove. Keeping them in without a need will distract the user and also encourage bad habits such as leaving fields empty.

Suggested fields to remove and the reason(s) why are listed as follows:

- **Title**: This frequently gets confused with salutation, so if you wish to record the job title of your lead contact, it is better to create a custom field for this.

- **Industry**: While some users do keep this, it is often better understood and replaced with a more recognizable field called **Sector**.

- **Annual Revenue**: This is often replaced by a custom field with a picklist of ranges (if used at all). Otherwise, while this data may be correct at the point of entry, it will be out of date within 12 months. The exception to this is if you are linking your CRM to a third-party system that will keep this updated automatically, in which case you would keep this field.

- **Fax**: Rarely used within most offices.

- **Secondary Email**: In the **B2B** world, most business contacts possess only a single email address, thus rendering this field redundant. In **B2C** scenarios, it may be tempting to keep this field, so we have one email address for business and another for personal. It is not recommended to do this, however, as having two email addresses for a contact may hinder rather than help communication.

- **Skype ID**: This is rarely used; however, it should be kept if your team uses *Skype for Business* as a means of communication with leads and customers.

- **Rating**: This is rarely used as it is too vague and has been superseded by lead scoring rules.

- **Number of Employees**: This field is often replaced by a picklist of ranges if used at all. Keeping this field up to date over time presents a similar challenge to annual revenue, so the advice to remove it unless it can be automatically updated is valid for this field also.

- **Description**: This is too vague. A description of what?

The preceding list should be used as a guideline and if it contains any fields that you wish to keep once you have read the rest of this chapter, then feel free to do so.

Now that you have established which standard fields to remove and why, it is time to look at how we achieve this.

To remove a standard field from the **Leads** module, follow these four simple steps:

1.  From the **Home** page in CRM, access **Setup** by clicking on the icon displayed here:

Figure 2.2 – Setup icon

2.  Within the **Customization** menu, click on **Modules and Fields**.

3.  Click on **Leads** and then **Standard**.

4.  Identify a field you wish to remove, such as **Fax**, and then click on the settings icon (three dots) at the right, followed by **Remove Field**, as shown in *Figure 2.3*:

Figure 2.3 – Removing a field

If, for any reason, you wish to restore a removed field later, you may find it within the **Unused Fields** section and then drag and drop it back onto your page layout.

Once you have removed the fields you do not need, it is time to confirm the ones you need to keep and the reason(s) why you need them.

# Which standard fields to keep and why

The following is a list of the fields that you should keep and the reason(s) why. These fields hold some of the core data discussed in the previous chapter – including who the contact is, where they are from, and how they contacted us. Once the lead is qualified, this information forms the backbone of each of our **Account** and **Contact** records. Looking after this data will help build the value of the CRM system and help drive our progress toward our objectives and success measures:

- **Lead Owner**: This system field is assigned when a record is created and defaults to the user that inputs the record. It can be assigned to another user if needed. This field identifies which user is responsible for following up and processing the lead. It is also key when it comes to workflow automation and reporting later.

- **Salutation**: This key field is linked to the first name and cannot be removed. It contains a picklist of values such as **Mr**, **Mrs**, **Ms**, and **Dr**, which can be edited if required. It may be a useful field for users especially if the gender is not automatically clear from the first name.

- **First Name**: This is a key field for relationship-building purposes and will be used within document mail-merge and email templates later.

- **Last Name**: This is a system mandatory field and so cannot be removed or left empty when a user adds a record.

- **Company**: In B2B, this will be the name of the company the lead contact is related to/working at. In B2C, this field must be removed if you are not using the **Accounts** module. If you provide your goods/services to both B2B and B2C, then you will need to keep this field. The value entered in this field will become the account name when we convert the lead later, so it is important to get this right.

- **Lead Source**: This is one of the most important fields that allows you to record and measure where your leads come from. Make this field mandatory at all costs.

- **Phone**: Resist the temptation to replace this field with custom fields named **Landline**, **Office**, or similar as if you ever wish to integrate your CRM with a telephone system in the future, you will need to use this standard field.

- **Mobile**: Similar to **Phone**, you must keep this field futureproof for possible integration with telephone and/or SMS services.

Now we understand the system fields to keep, it is time to consider which custom fields to add to your **Leads** module.

# Creating custom fields

The standard fields alone will not completely allow your team to record everything that is needed to capture the details and qualify this lead effectively. For this reason, we have the ability to create our own custom fields. Custom fields are one of the most important ways that you can truly create a Zoho CRM tailored to your business.

In Zoho, we have the ability to add up to *155 custom fields* per module for *Professional Edition* and *300* for *Enterprise Edition*; however, it is easy to fall into the trap of adding too many fields.

So, follow the question *Can we add a field for X?* with subsequent questions such as the following:

- *Do we really need a field for X?*
- *What will we do with this information?*
- *Who is responsible for collecting this data?*
- *How often will we be able to obtain this data?*

The importance of this can be explained in a few ways:

- **Less is more**: Sometimes if we have too much information, we can be distracted from the key points by less valuable information.
- **Consider your sales team**: Salespeople generally do not want to be spending time on data entry. They want to do what they do best, selling. You need the sales team to love the CRM, not see it as a chore.
- **Encourage good habits**: There is nothing positive about viewing a record in the CRM that is 30%–50% empty because we don't have or cannot always obtain this data. As well as the user experience, we should also be aware that it can lead to bad habits being developed. If users see empty fields in lots of records, then *it won't matter if I don't always fill in others* is an attitude that may prevail under such circumstances.

Taking all this into consideration, however, you will need to add custom fields to ensure that the **Leads** module is tailored specifically to your business. Adding the right custom fields will improve the user experience by providing a look and feel of a system that is designed for them.

The following table provides examples of custom fields that you really should add:

| Field Name | Datatype | Description |
| --- | --- | --- |
| Referred By | Lookup Contacts | Allows user to select the contact name of the person/organisation that provide the referral |
| Interested In | Picklist or Multi-picklist | This is a list of the products or services the lead is interested in. Some users label this field products or services which is fine but we find "Interested In" is a little more intuitive |
| Initial Lead Notes | Multiline Text | If your lead is inbound phone then you absolutely must have this field to facilitate lead entry whilst on the call<br><br>If your lead is from a website this field can be mapped to the "Message" field on your webform<br><br>If your lead is a referral then use this field to capture the narrative that accompanied the referral, that is, "It's probably worth giving Bob a call from ABC Designs – he mentioned he needs a CRM for his growing business and is still using spreadsheets" is great insight we can record in this field |

Table 2.1 – Custom fields to add

The concise list of fields in *Table 2.1* is the bare minimum; however, the key to this module is that we should capture only the information we need to qualify the lead. As the lead is followed up, users will add notes to the record, which will maintain a narrative of the lead. The rest of the details can and should come later.

## Qualifying leads

So far, we have considered in detail the data we should be collecting and we are well underway to designing a very strong and robust module.

However, if we are in the B2B sector, then for our **Leads** module to be great, we need to add another dimension, such as a lead qualification tool or methodology.

In the previous chapter, we referred to a useful blog that you can access here for easy reference: `https://contactbase.net/sales-qualification-frameworks/`. You will find several more online if none of the frameworks in the blog meet your needs. When you have identified a framework that may suit your business and sales process, then it's time to include some fields in your **Leads** module to capture this information. In this example, we will use the *BANT framework* by adding a selection of custom fields as shown next:

| Field Name | Datatype |
| --- | --- |
| Budget – do they have one? | Picklist |
| Approximate Budget | Single Line |
| Authority – does the contact have authority to sign-off the deal? | Picklist |
| Who else is involved in the decision-making process? | Multiline |
| Need – What is the business pain our solution solves? | Multiline |
| Timeframe – When are they planning to buy | Picklist |

Table 2.2 – Custom fields to help qualify a lead

By adding the fields as per *Table 2.2*, we are providing prompts for the user. Not only are we prompting which questions to ask, but we are also making sure that their answers are structured correctly. These fields add a great deal of value to your CRM system.

Now that we have considered which custom fields to add and why, it is time to learn how to add them.

Before adding custom fields, please refer to the *Mapping fields* section toward the end of this chapter as it contains a time-saving tip.

To add a custom field, follow these steps:

1.  From the **Home** page in CRM, access setup by clicking on the following icon:

Figure 2.4 – Setup icon

2.  Within the **Customization** menu, click on **Modules and Fields**.

3.  Click on **Leads** and then **Standard** (layout).

4.  Identify the appropriate datatype from the top-left corner of this portion of the screen, as can be seen in the following screenshot:

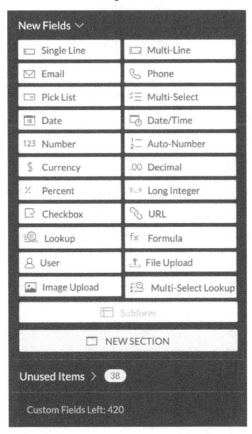

Figure 2.5 – New field datatypes

5.  Now, drag and drop your new field onto the appropriate section of your **Leads** form before naming the field in the highlighted label provided.

    In the following example, we are creating a custom URL field for a link to a LinkedIn profile, so we would drag and drop a new URL field into position and rename URL2 with a suitable label such as LinkedIn:

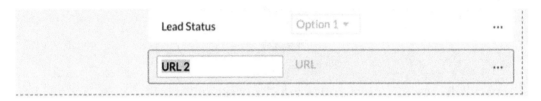

Figure 2.6 – Dragging and dropping new fields

> **Tip**
>
> Further details on adding custom fields and datatypes may be found at https://help.zoho.com/portal/en/kb/crm/customize-crm-account/customizing-fields/articles/use-custom-fields#Custom_Fields.

Some of the suggested fields to keep or add are of the **Picklist** or **Multi-Select** datatype, so let's now take a look at how we should assign these.

## Assigning picklist values

**Picklist** is a drop-down list where the user can select one of the values, and **Multi-Select** is a drop-down list where the user can select multiple values.

When defining these values, it is best to think about your reporting requirements. Take the following examples:

- *If you imagine a bar chart*, what would you want to see on the *y* axis (across the bottom)?

- *If you imagine a pie chart*, how would you like to see this divided up?

This is often an area that confuses many first-time CRM owners. So, the following are some detailed examples that are often used successfully:

| Picklist Field Name | Picklist/Multi-Select Values |
| --- | --- |
| Lead Source | Website<br>Inbound (Call/Email)<br>Self Generated<br>Campaign or Event<br>Referral - Customer<br>Referral - Partner<br>Referral - Other<br>Social Media<br>Networking |
| Lead Status | New Lead<br>Contact Attempted<br>Active<br>Contact in Future<br>Did not Qualify |
| Interested In | *This will be a list of your products or services, ideally no more than 20.*<br>*If you have more than that then try and use product category instead.* |
| Budget - do they have one? | Yes<br>No<br>Not Sure |
| Authority - does the contact have authority to sign-off the deal? | Yes - Complete<br>Yes - Partial<br>No<br>Not Sure |
| Timeframe - when are they planning to buy? | Immediately<br>Within 3 Months<br>Within 6 Months<br>6-12 Months<br>Not Sure |

Table 2.3 – Picklist and multi-select values

This recommended list in *Table 2.3* should be used as a guideline for defining your own tailored list.

Now that we have considered removing, keeping, and adding fields into the **Leads** module, it is time to understand how to organize the page layout.

# Designing a user-friendly layout

It is important to organize the layout of the **Leads** page so that it is easy to follow, logical, and intuitive.

One of the techniques that will really assist with this is to utilize sections. We may rename, add, and create our own sections as required. Using layout rules, which we will cover later in the chapter, we can choose to show or hide a section based on the values of the fields we have selected.

In *Figure 2.7* and *Figure 2.8*, you will see how we have grouped the fields into sections – with ideally no more than 10-12 fields in each one. Fields can be dragged and dropped within the layout.

The fields are grouped within sections with a name that describes the fields or context. Each section can comprise single or multiple columns and may be positioned in any order that is most logical for your users.

Be consistent with this approach throughout the CRM as a whole and you will design a system that will be user-friendly and intuitive. The following screenshots show examples of an intuitive layout. The upper part of the layout is as follows:

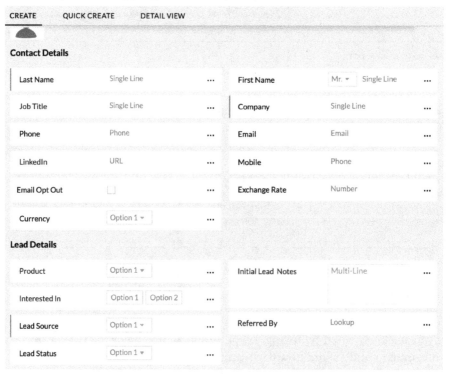

Figure 2.7 – Page layout of the Leads module (upper half)

The lower part of the image can be seen in *Figure 2.8*:

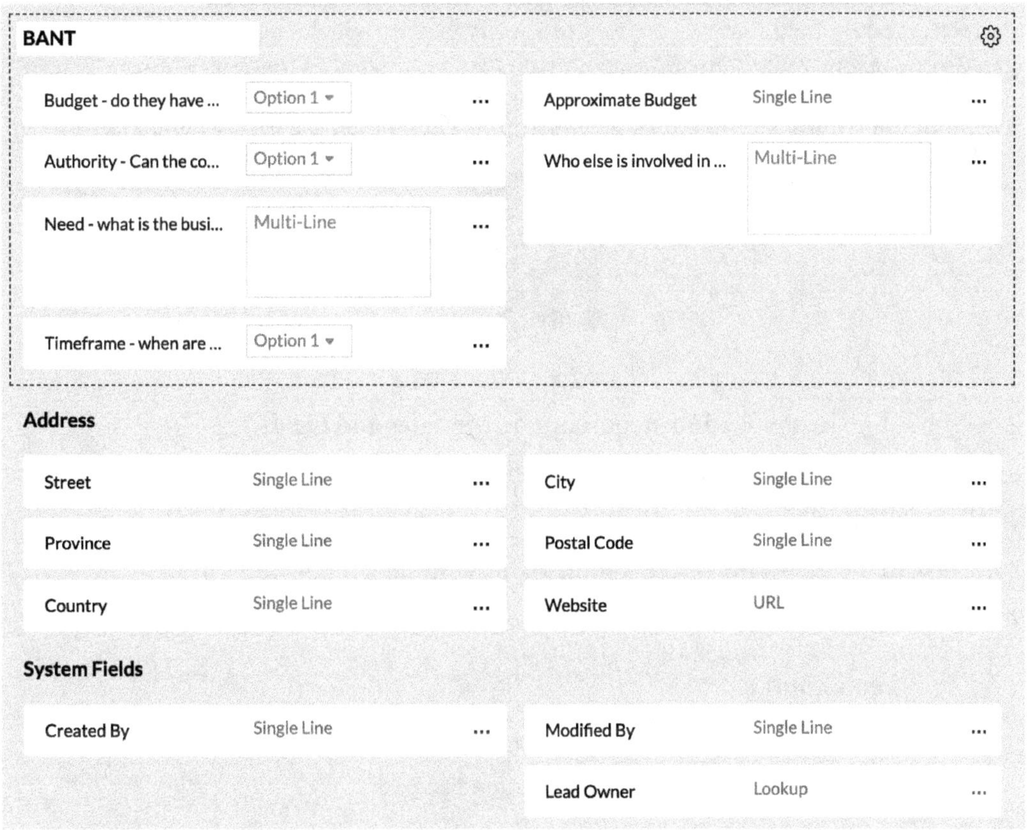

| BANT | | |
|---|---|---|
| Budget - do they have ... | Option 1 ▾ | ··· |
| Authority - Can the co... | Option 1 ▾ | ··· |
| Need - what is the busi... | Multi-Line | ··· |
| Timeframe - when are ... | Option 1 ▾ | ··· |

| | | |
|---|---|---|
| Approximate Budget | Single Line | ··· |
| Who else is involved in ... | Multi-Line | ··· |

**Address**

| Street | Single Line | ··· | City | Single Line | ··· |
|---|---|---|---|---|---|
| Province | Single Line | ··· | Postal Code | Single Line | ··· |
| Country | Single Line | ··· | Website | URL | ··· |

**System Fields**

| Created By | Single Line | ··· | Modified By | Single Line | ··· |
|---|---|---|---|---|---|
| | | | Lead Owner | Lookup | ··· |

Figure 2.8 – Page layout of the Leads module (lower half)

Once you have completed the page layout similar to *Figure 2.7* and *Figure 2.8*, you can further refine this by creating layout rules.

# Using layout rules

Layout rules in Zoho provide you with a way to hide or show fields based on the value of a field the user has already selected.

Let's illustrate this with an example.

If a user selects the **Lead Source** option of **Referral - Customer**, then we would need them to also add the name of the customer that referred them. In our **Leads** module, we have a **Referred By** field that will be used to specify exactly which customer (contact) referred your business to them. This layout rule may be created as follows:

1. From the **Home** page in CRM, go to setup by clicking on the following icon:

Figure 2.9 – Setup icon

2. Within the **Customization** menu, click on **Modules and Fields**.

3. Click on **Leads** and then **Standard** (layout).

4. Locate the **Lead Source** field.

5. Click on the three dots (more) on the right-hand side:

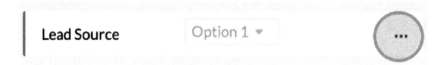

Figure 2.10 – How to edit a field

6. Click on **Create Layout Rule**:

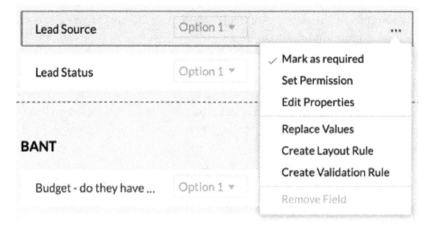

Figure 2.11 – Creating a layout rule

7. Give your rule a name – for example, `Show fields based on source`:

## New Layout Rule

**Show fields based on source**

Describe your rule

Figure 2.12 – Naming your new layout rule

8. Select the **Lead Source** values to include in our **Layout** rule:

a) **Referral - Customer**

b) **Referral - Other**

c) **Referral - Partner**:

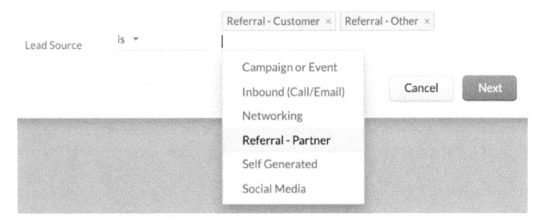

Figure 2.13 – Adding conditions to a layout rule

9.  Click **Next** followed by **+ Trigger Action**, then **Show Field**, type in **Referred By**, and then click **Save**:

## Edit Action

### Show Fields

Select the fields you would like to show.

Referred By ×

Save     Cancel

Figure 2.14 – Showing a field within a layout rule

10. Click **+ Trigger an action**, then **Set Mandatory Fields**:

Show Fields(1)

+ Trigger an action

Show Fields
Show Sections
Set Mandatory Fields

Figure 2.15 – Setting a field as mandatory within a layout rule

11. Enter Referred By and then click **Save**:

Figure 2.16 – Setting Referred By as mandatory

12. You will now be presented with an overview of the layout rule, from which you need to click on the arrow pointing left in the top left-hand corner:

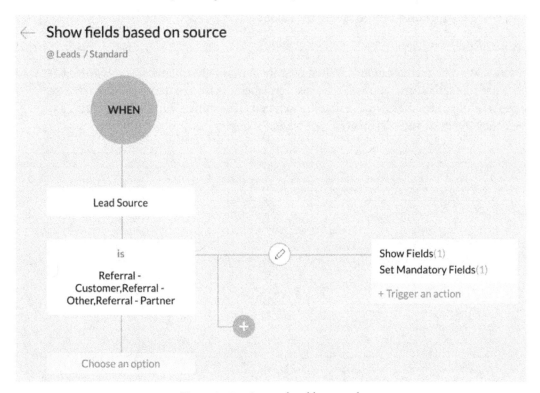

Figure 2.17 – A completed layout rule

13. If you wish to add more options for other lead sources, you would do so from the same screen as in *Figure 2.17* by clicking on **Choose an option**.

> **Tip**
> Layout rules are a very powerful way of only showing and/or making mandatory fields when a specific condition has been met. Frequent use of this technique throughout *all* modules will make your CRM user-friendly and intuitive while helping to maintain the integrity of your database.

When a lead is converted into a deal, account, and contact, we need to specify to which modules we want the data fields to be copied (otherwise known as **mapping**).

## Mapping fields

Fields that are already present in the initial system will automatically be mapped, so we have to instruct only for the custom fields we have created.

There are two ways to map a field upon lead conversion:

- On field creation – before saving the layout
- Within the lead conversion mapping table

Let's look at on field creation first. When creating a new field in **Leads**, scroll down to the bottom of this screen and you will see a section labeled **Also create for**. Check the box for the module or modules you wish to be mapped. This option will save you time as you create the field once and it is created for you and mapped in the other module(s):

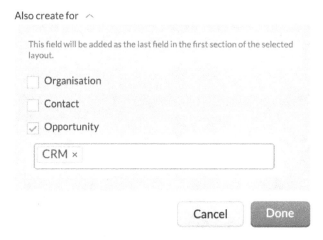

Figure 2.18 – Copying the fields from Leads to other modules

If for any reason we did not map a field as in the preceding screenshot or we wish to change the field mapping of a standard field, this can be done on the **Lead Conversion Mapping** screen:

1. From the **Home** page in CRM, access setup by clicking on the following icon:

Figure 2.19 – Setup icon

2. Within the **Customization** menu, click on **Modules and Fields**.

3. Click on **Leads** and then **Standard** (layout).

4. Click on the settings icon and then **Lead Conversion Mapping**:

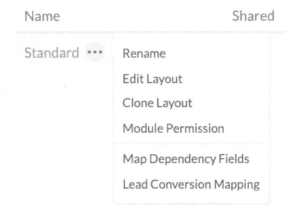

Figure 2.20 – Mapping fields from Leads to other modules

In the table that appears under the **Mapping Information** heading, for each field on the left under the **Lead** heading, select the field that you need to map to in the **Account**, **Contact**, or **Deal** module, as can be seen in *Figure 2.21*:

Layouts    Layout Rules    Validation Rules    Fields    Links and Buttons    Summary                    ⊙

## Lead Conversion Mapping

### Layout Mapping                                                                 * Custom Field

Map the lead layout to the layouts of account, contact, and deal to make lead conversion more specific to layouts.

| Standard ⇒ | Account | Contact | Deal |
|---|---|---|---|
|  | Standard ▼ | Standard ▼ | Standard ▼ |

### Mapping Information

Based on the layout mapping of modules, map the fields in the lead module to the fields in account, contact and deal module.
With the mapped fields, converting a lead will automatically transfer the information you have gathered to an account, contact and deal.

| Lead | Account | Contact | Deal |
|---|---|---|---|
| * Approximate Budget | -None- ▼ | -None- ▼ | Approximate Budget ▼ |
| * Authority - Can the contact sign-off the Deal | -None- ▼ | -None- ▼ | -None- ▼ |

Figure 2.21 – Lead conversion mapping table

In *Figure 2.21*, we can map **Approximate Budget** by selecting the drop-down menu in any/all of the **Account, Contact**, or **Deals** columns proving we have an available field of the same datatype (**Currency**) in that module.

# Summary

In this chapter, you have learned how to design and build the perfect blueprint for your **Leads** module. You will have defined which fields you should remove, keep, and add in order to ensure that your team can capture all the information needed on new inquiries or leads.

You have also learned how to use layouts to group and present the fields logically and layout rules to ensure that we capture the correct information all the time. This will help us to qualify leads more effectively in a shorter space of time.

In the next chapter, you will learn what happens when a lead is qualified and how to set up your perfect **Deals** module.

# 3
# Deals – Sales Funnels to Fuel Your Business Growth

The **Deals** module is the central hub of your business development activities and will comprise qualified leads from new and existing customers.

The records in this module will make up your sales pipeline, and the way that you set up and use this module will have a significant impact on the future growth of your business.

The topics covered in this chapter include the following:

- Mapping your sales process as stages
- Understanding standard fields
- Adding fields to quantify the deal
- Improving data entry using layout rules
- Adding depth by using subforms
- Additional best practices

So, let's begin, first and foremost, with probably the single most important objective in Zoho CRM itself – defining your sales process within the CRM.

# Mapping your sales process as stages

The most important and first aspect to consider in the **Deals** module is mapping your sales process. Once this has been defined, it will pave the way for the future growth of your business. The stages of the **Deals** module with supporting functionality (explained later in this chapter) will have a bigger impact on your business growth than any other field in the system. In *Chapter 1, The Foundation Modules – The Building Blocks of Success*, you saw an example sales process. You subsequently listed the stages of your sales process that, when followed, will provide the most effective way to process a potential deal until your prospect has agreed to purchase your products/services or otherwise.

If your business provides multiple services where the current sales process has different stages and terminology or you are struggling for inspiration, then you might be encouraged by the following use case.

One UK-based non-profit company with over 1,200 employees and 12 completely different business functions (divisions) made the decision to implement Zoho CRM across the whole organization.

One of the key deliverables was for the board and senior management team to be able to report on the volume and value of work and projects in the pipeline across the whole business. So, the implementation team stripped the processes down to basics and came up with a process that could be used by every single business development manager within each business unit.

The resulting stages were as follows:

1. **Qualified**
2. **Discovery**
3. **Proposal**
4. **Pre-Mobilization**
5. **Closed Won**
6. **Closed Lost**

With the exception of Pre-Mobilization, which is often named **Negotiation**, it's fair to say that the other stages could be used by many businesses around the world.

So, the moral of this story is that any organization that has multiple divisions and processes right now can consolidate them into one and thus simply report on and automate their workflows later.

Let's have a detailed look at how to set up the aforementioned stages:

1. From the **Home** page in the CRM, access **Setup** by clicking the following icon:

Figure 3.1 – Setup icon

2. Navigate to **Modules and Fields**, move your mouse over **Deals**, and then click on **Stage Probability Mapping**. You will see the following screen:

| Stage Name | Probability (%) | Forecast Type | Forecast Category |
|---|---|---|---|
| Qualified | 10 | Open | Pipeline |
| Discovery | 20 | Open | Pipeline |
| Quote Sent | 20 | Open | Pipeline |
| Follow Up | 40 | Open | Pipeline |
| Closed Won | 100 | Closed Won | Closed |
| Closed Lost | 0 | Closed Lost | Omitted |

Figure 3.2 – Stage Probability Mapping screen

3. On the **Sales Probability Mapping** screen, you will see the existing stages.
4. Click the **Add Stage (+)** link to add a new stage.
5. Click the **Remove Stage (-)** link to remove a stage.
6. For each stage, set **Probability (%)**, **Forecast Type**, and **Forecast Category**.

It is important to set **Forecast Type**, **Forecast Category**, and **Probability (%)** as they tie in with some of the standard reports and views of records and core functionality. These options are as follows:

**Forecast Type**: Options include **Open, Closed Won**, and **Closed Lost**.

**Forecast Category**: Select from **Pipeline, Closed**, and **Omitted**.

**Probability %**: Add your typical **Win Rate** value for each stage.

In addition to pipeline reporting, there is a **Forecasting** module in Zoho CRM that may add further value. Further details are available at `https://help.zoho.com/portal/en/kb/crm/sales-force-automation/forecasts`.

The stage names you create here will dictate how you measure your sales pipeline. You will measure the volume and value of deals at each stage of your *funnel*, an example of which can be seen here:

Pipeline

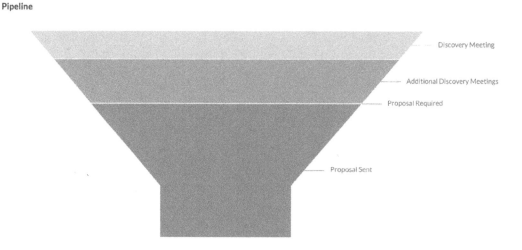

Figure 3.3 – An example sales funnel

Visualize your funnel as per the preceding example. Each of the labels will represent a key milestone stage within your sales process. Best practice includes making sure the stage names are clear, jargon-free, and intuitive. Ask yourself the following questions:

- Does this process provide the most effective route to close more deals?

- Would a future salesperson coming into our business understand what each of the stages meant and when each record should be progressed to the next one?

If you answer *Yes* to both of those questions, then your stages will most likely be good ones.

Once you have set up your stages, the following is a screenshot that shows how these milestone stages will appear when a user views a deal record:

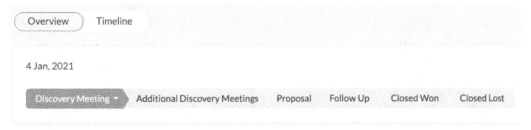

Figure 3.4 – The stages as viewed within a deal record, whereby the current stage is highlighted blue

Once these stages have been set, it is time to add additional fields that will help your team further clarify the customer's needs.

# Understanding standard fields

When accessing the **Deals** module for the first time, for the same reasons as in the previous chapter, we must review and remove any of the standard (pre-existing) fields that we do not need.

A list of these standard fields can be found here: `https://help.zoho.com/portal/en/kb/crm/customize-crm-account/customizing-fields/articles/standard-modules-fields#Deals`.

The following is a list of the fields you should keep along with the reason(s) why:

- **Deal Owner**: The name of the user to know the deal is assigned. This is also a crucial field when it comes to workflow automation and reporting later.

- **Deal Name**: This is a mandatory field and is used to give the record a name that summarizes the deal. For example, a prospect for booking 25 delegates on a first aid training course would be named `First Aid Training - 25 Delegates`.

- **Account Name**: This is a lookup of accounts that a deal is associated with. It is crucial that you keep this field as it will be mapped from the company name when a user converts the lead. Note also that if you have renamed the **Accounts** module, then this field will inherit the same name here. For example, if you renamed **Accounts** to **Companies**, this field will be named **Company Name**.

- **Lead Source**: This is a crucial field that will say where this deal came from (mapped from **Leads**).

- **Campaign Source**: If the lead source was **Email Campaign**, then this field will specify the name of the exact campaign this originated from.

- **Contact Name**: This is a lookup of contacts that a deal is associated with. It is crucial to keep this field as this will be mapped from the **Lead Name** field upon converting the lead.

- **Amount**: This is a currency field to contain the amount that can be expected after closing the deal. This is most often associated with revenue before tax.

- **Closing Date**: This date field should be used to specify the expected decision date and will then become the actual decision (or closing) date of the deal. It is important that we keep this field as it is used in key screens, reports, and workflows later.

- **Stage**: The single most important field within the **Deals** module as described earlier in this chapter. It is used to define our sales process and indicate which stage each deal is up to.

  **Probability**: Used to specify the probability of closing a deal (linked to **Probability %** from the stage).

- **Expected Revenue**: Provides a weighted forecast amount based on the stage probability. For example, if we had a **Stage Probability** value of 50% at the **Quote** stage and the amount of the potential deal was $100,000, then, based on the 50% chance of winning the deal, we would forecast $50,000 (50% of $100,000). If you find this beneficial, then keep this field; if not, remove this field (and **Probability**).

- **Created By**: The name of the user who created the deal as well as the date and time it was created.

- **Modified By**: The name of the user who last modified the deal along with the date and time of this modification.

Once you have reviewed the standard fields and removed the ones you do not need, it is time to add some custom fields that will allow the sales team to further detail the customer requirements.

# Adding fields to quantify the deal

The first stage of our deal process stage is often called **Discovery**, **Needs Analysis**, or **Design**.

Depending on the type of services and goods you are selling, your sales team will need to be asking questions to ascertain the exact requirements of your client. These questions, ideally, should be fields within the **Deals** module.

Consider these examples:

- A business providing IT hardware, software, telecoms, and general IT support will need to ask questions to find out the number of workstations and users and the names and types of software applications that will be supported.

- A CRM consultancy would need to ask questions about the number of users, configuration, training, and integration requirements.

- A training provider would need to know the name of the course, the number of delegates, venue, and catering requirements.

- A hospitality venue hosting events and conferences would need to know the number of visitors or delegates, timings, and the catering requirements.

> **Tip**
> List all the questions your salesperson will need to ask to obtain all the requirements of your prospective customer or client.

Once you have listed these questions, for each one, consider the data type of the field required in the CRM. Ideally, the fields to capture these requirements will be a mixture of **Picklist** and **Number** data types to make sure your team is quantifying correctly. You should avoid **Single Line** and **Multiline** text fields unless it is to capture any non-standard or additional requirements.

Now create all these required fields in the CRM, ideally locating them within a new, suitably titled section, such as **Discovery**, **Requirements**, or **Needs Analysis**.

Refer to `https://help.zoho.com/portal/en/kb/crm/customize-crm-account/customizing-fields/articles/use-custom-fields#Custom_Fields` for additional information on adding custom fields.

Note also that the fields that you mapped from leads as described in *Chapter 2, Leads – Getting It Right the First Time*, will also be present in **Deals**, so your layout will need to include these also. It is recommended that you position these fields toward the top of the deal form within a section named **Deal Details** or **Requirements**.

> **Tip**
>
> Organize all the fields in **Deals** in suitably named sections. Ideally, aiming for 10–12 fields maximum per section will keep our **Deals** records easy to read and intuitive.

# Improving data entry using layout rules

Layout rules in Zoho CRM are one of the best features to make your system intuitive and user-friendly and to ensure that users always capture all the relevant details at the right time.

In the **Deals** module, we can, and should, use layout rules at most if not all stages of the sales process. Let's consider one of the examples cited earlier: IT services at the **Discovery** stage.

*Example 1 – IT Services*: One of the questions may be to find out the number of office workstations to be supported. This will be followed by a question asking whether laptops will also be supported (Yes/No). If the answer is Yes, then we can create a layout rule that shows and makes mandatory a couple of additional questions to find out the number of laptops (**Number** data type) and what type of operating software is installed (**Multipicklist**).

This layout rule can be set up as follows:

1. From the **Home** page in the CRM, click on the following icon:

Figure 3.5 – Setup icon

2. Click on **Modules and Fields**, then click **Deals**.

3. Select **Standard** (layout).

4.  Locate the field that will be the *Parent* or *Trigger* for this rule – in this example,
    **Laptop Support Required** – and then access a menu by clicking on **…** to the right
    of the field:

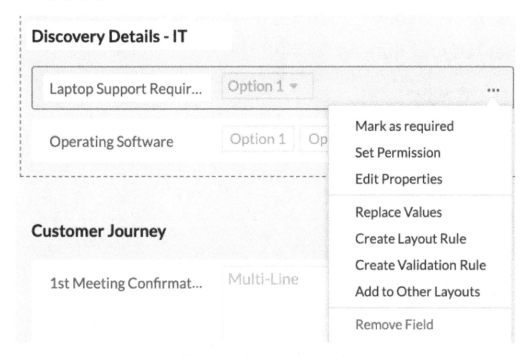

Figure 3.6 – Creating a layout rule

5.  Select **Create Layout Rule**.

6. Give the layout rule a name – for example, `Show additional laptop fields`. Choose a condition to initiate the rule – for example, **Laptop Support Required is Yes**:

https://desk.

# New Layout Rule

Show additional laptop fields

Describe your rule

**Choose the layout**

Standard ▼

**Choose a primary field that controls this rule.**

Laptop Support Required ▼

**Choose a condition to initiate the rule.**

| Laptop Support Required | is ▼ | Yes × |

Cancel    Next

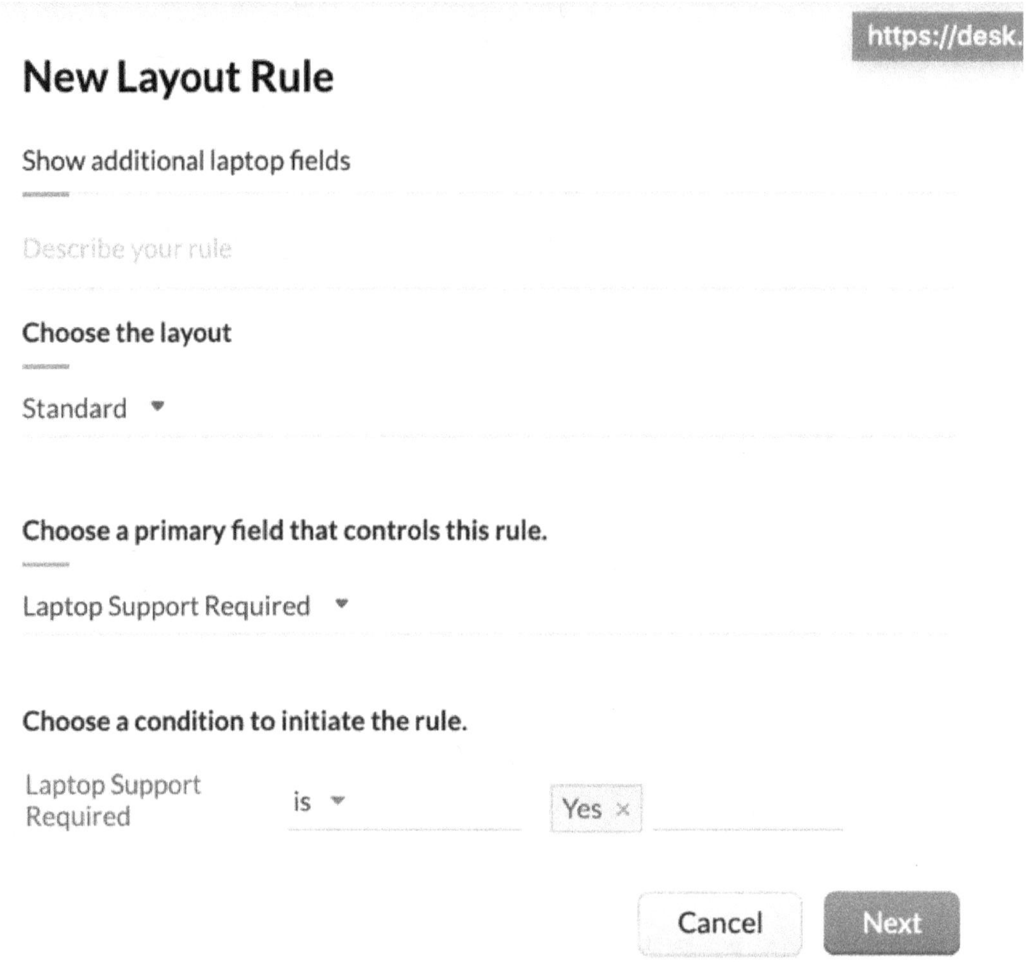

Figure 3.7 – Naming and initiating (triggering) your rule

7. Click **Next**.

8. Click on +**Trigger Action**.

9. Click on **Show Fields**.

10. In the **Create Action** section that appears on the right, locate (by scrolling or typing the name) the fields you now wish to show – for example, **Number Supported** and **Operating Software** – and then click **Save**:

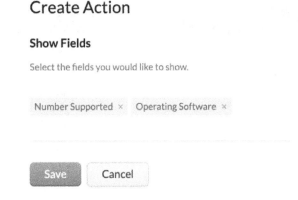

## Create Action

**Show Fields**

Select the fields you would like to show.

Number Supported ×    Operating Software ×

Save    Cancel

Figure 3.8 – Selecting which fields to show when the rule is triggered

11. If you also wish to make these fields mandatory (recommended), then repeat *steps 9, 10*, and *11* by clicking on **+Set Mandatory** (instead of **Show Fields**).

12. Repeat *steps 5-11* for any other layout rules you wish to apply in **Deals**.

*Example 2 – CRM Consultancy*: A salesperson may ask the prospect if any integrations to third-party systems are required (picklist Yes/No). If the answer is Yes, then we can create a layout rule that will show and make mandatory further fields that present the user with a multi-picklist of possible systems to integrate with – for example, Office 365, Xero, Google, and Sage.

> **Tip**
> List all the conditional questions that need to be asked of the salesperson based on the values of previous responses. This will keep your system streamlined and intuitive as well as help the sales team enjoy using the system. Create layout rules for each one.

# Creating layout rules triggered by stages

Most of the value in using layout rules in **Deals** is gained when they are triggered by a user updating the stage of a deal. As each stage is a milestone within our sales process, it follows that when these milestones are reached, we need to capture specific information.

Details recorded here should either validate that we have achieved a specific milestone *or* contain information to report on or share with other business functions.

The following table provides a few examples:

| Condition (Trigger) | Action(s) |
|---|---|
| Stage is Additional Discovery Meeting | Show and make mandatory fields that will force the user to record the reason for the additional meeting. This could be of type picklist and values could include: Senior Decision Maker Needed; Product Demonstration; Other Stakeholder Requirements Input. This will provide useful insight into why additional meetings are needed for which types of opportunity and which users need them most. |
| Stage is Proposal | Show and make mandatory fields such as Closing Date and Amount. This will force the user to enter details in here that will be used for pipeline reporting.<br>Another useful mandatory field could be a date field to capture the date of the agreed follow-up call or meeting. |
| Stage is Follow-up (or Negotiation) | Show and make mandatory the reason that the customer is not ready to purchase yet. Providing this field as a picklist will provide a useful reporting measure that may help improve your sales process, especially in the previous stages. It should also identify any training needs of your salespeople. |
| Stage is Closed Won | Show and make mandatory fields that will force the user to enter information that will be needed by Operations and Finance - to assist with delivering the goods/service and obtaining swift payment.<br><br>Huge value can be added here and you should liaise with these departments and confirm exactly what information is desired so that these fields can be factored in. |
| Stage is Closed Lost | Show and make mandatory a field that will force the user to select from a list of reasons (Reason for Loss) that the Customer did not purchase. This layout rule will ensure that the sales team and business can fully understand why customers did not purchase or renew. |

Table 3.1 – Examples of layout rules to be triggered at different deal stages

The examples provided in the preceding table are by no means an exhaustive list, so use these as a guideline and review your own process to identify which ones will add value to you and your team.

# Adding depth by using subforms

A **subform** is a secondary form or table where we can associate multiple items to a single record. In the **Deals** module, this can be very useful as it will allow us to record additional information about the product or service we are providing to our customers all within a single deal record. This will help keep our CRM user-friendly, effective, and efficient.

For example, let's consider a company that supplies mobile telephones and contracts to businesses and consumers. The deal record will hold information at the top level, including the customer name, contact, and the stage we are up to in the sales process. The requirement may be to supply multiple handsets on varying tariffs, each potentially with a unique serial number or IMEI, as it is known in the industry. To try and manage this in the usual way with sections and fields only could be time-consuming and potentially limiting, as we may not have enough custom fields/layout rules to manage it.

Here are the instructions for creating a subform to manage this scenario:

1.  From the **Home** page in the CRM, click the following icon:

Figure 3.9 – Setup icon

2.  Within the **Customization** menu, click on **Modules and Fields**.

3.  Click on **Deals** and then select **Standard** (layout).

4.  From the **New Fields** section, select **Subform**, and then drag and drop onto your deal form as shown here:

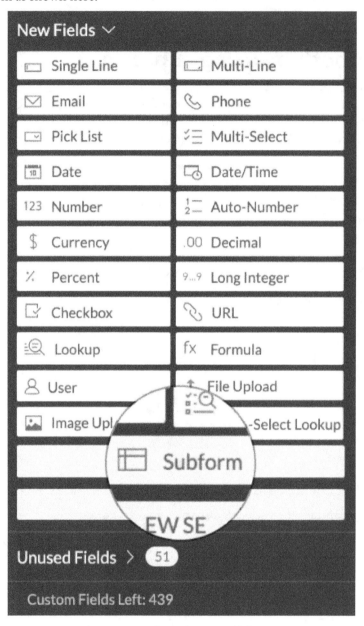

Figure 3.10 – Creating a new subform

5.  In the textbox provided, give your subform a title, something that describes what this subform will be used to record details of. In this case, use `Handsets`:

Handsets

+ Add Field

Figure 3.11 – Naming your subform

6.  Now click on **+AddField**, and then click on the data type of the first field you wish to add within your subform:

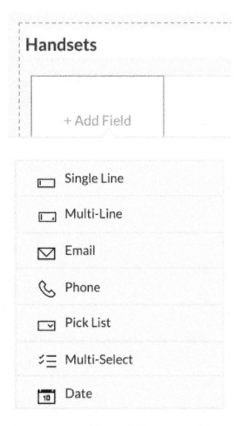

Figure 3.12 – Adding a field to your subform

7.  Now give the field a name and set any other properties as required (these vary by data type).

8.  Repeat *steps* 6 and 7 until you have created all the required fields (maximum of 10 per subform and 2 subforms per layout).

9.  Within **Setup**, your completed subform will resemble this example:

Figure 3.13 – Example of a completed subform within Setup

10. Sometimes we may need to aggregate the total of one or more of our subform fields. In this scenario, we will use an aggregate field to sum the monthly rental for all the handsets and display this for the user. This is achieved as follows:

a) Click on +**Add Aggregate Field**, then in the popup that appears, set **Field Label**, set **Aggregate Function** (choosing from **Sum**, **Average**, **Max**, and **Min**), confirm the field to aggregate, and then click **Done**:

Figure 3.14 – Adding an aggregate field to calculate total monthly rental

11. Within a deal record, your subform containing entries will look like this:

**Handsets**

| Model | Network | Tariff | IMEI | Monthly Rental Cost (£) |
|---|---|---|---|---|
| iPhone 12S | EE | Unlimited Data | 09091018002880 | 75.00 |
| Samsung Galaxy | O2 | 40G Data | 99898918181991 | 60.00 |

Figure 3.15 – Example of a subform containing multiple entries with an aggregate total

For additional information on subforms, please refer to `https://help.zoho.com/portal/en/kb/crm/customize-crm-account/managing-subforms/articles/build-subforms`.

If you do not identify a need for a subform within your **Deals** module, this is not uncommon, so simply do not create one at this time.

So far in this chapter, we have provided guidance on *what you need to*, *why*, and *how*. However, there are also a few other tips and suggestions that may help improve the setup of the **Deals** module.

# Additional best practices

By following the guidance detailed in this chapter, you are well on your way to having a powerful, intuitive, and successful **Deals** module. However, here are a few more suggestions that may enhance performance even more:

- *Try not to have too many stages*. Ideally, there will be 6–12 stages in your sales process. Too few stages may result in details either missing or being contained within fields further down, which will make things not as intuitive as they would be if the details were visible on the milestone/timeline. Too many stages will make it harder to focus and effectively measure our progress. Sometimes, however, it is beneficial to have more stages to help manage the process after someone has placed the order.

- *Do not have more than one unsuccessful outcome*. In the example earlier in this chapter, we had just one unsuccessful outcome – **Closed Lost**. When selected, this would trigger a layout rule to show and make mandatory an additional field, **Reason for Loss**. This method is far more intuitive and easier to report on than having multiple stages, one for each unsuccessful reason.

- *Avoid adding an On Hold stage.* There are many scenarios where a salesperson may cite that a deal has not been *Won* or *Lost* due to the fact that the client has just had to push back the purchase for one reason or another. While technically, this may sound like a credible reason to have an **On Hold** stage, it is not really necessary as the user could change the (expected) **Closing Date** value and add a note and a follow-up task to re-engage at a later date. Another reason for not using **On Hold** is that this stage is often misused and can lead to procrastination and/or offer the user an easier way out than admitting the deal is lost. Either way, having deals at this **On Hold** stage will often distort reports and clutter the pipeline.

- *Concede a loss much earlier.* One common pitfall is that salespeople don't like admitting defeat, especially when a deal has simply gone cold or a customer has become unresponsive. Failure of the sales team to mark deals as lost will distort reports, clutter the pipeline, and distract focus away from deals that are still on the table. The best advice here is to agree on a timescale of inactivity/no response from a customer – for example, 6 months – and then mark the deal as **Closed Lost** manually or automatically using a workflow rule (refer to *Chapter 6, Game-Changing Workflows and Automations*).

- *Avoid too many fields.* Salespeople in general do not enjoy data entry. If we add too many fields in the deals module, then we can put the user off using the CRM or encourage bad habits by explaining that they don't always need to fill them in. The best way to manage data entry is by using layout rules as mentioned earlier. The purpose of fields in the **Deals** module is to make sure we can accurately understand our customer's needs and also record details of the solution we will be proposing.

# Summary

In this chapter, you have learned how to set up and optimize your **Deals** module effectively to create the perfect pipeline for your business.

You have gained confidence from the example of the business with over 1,200 employees across 12 divisions. If they can successfully adopt a sales process with just 6 stages that will work for all their sales teams, then it is achievable for all Zoho users to have a streamlined common process.

You should now         have an understanding of the important standard fields and should have learned how to use layout rules to ensure that we capture the correct information at the right time. You should understand that doing so will help improve the discipline of the sales team and enforce consistency. You will be also aware of best practices to keep this module lean, streamlined, and intuitive.

Finally, you should have an understanding of the most common pitfalls that you should avoid when setting up this module.

In the next chapter, you will learn how to best set up your Accounts and Contacts modules, which will conclude the remaining foundation modules and also *Section 1, Laying the Foundation*, of this book.

# 4
# Accounts and Contacts – The Beating Heart of Your CRM

The **Accounts** and **Contacts** modules contain all the key organization and contact details of your prospects and customers.

In this chapter, we will recap on the relationships between **Deals**, **Accounts**, and **Contacts** before taking a detailed look at the **Accounts** and **Contacts** modules separately. You will learn which fields should be kept (and why) and will be provided with examples of custom fields to add that will help you build a highly effective customer database. This will help you to successfully set up your customer database and to add value not just to your **Customer Relationship Management** (CRM), but to your business overall.

Topics covered within this chapter include the following:

- Recapping the module relationships
- Keeping standard fields in **Accounts**

- Adding custom fields to **Accounts**

- Keeping standard fields in **Contacts**

- Adding custom fields to **Contacts**

- Best practices for **Accounts** and **Contacts**

By the end of this chapter, you will have optimized the perfect **Accounts** and **Contacts** modules for your business and future-proofed them for working well with other CRM modules and other system integration.

## Recapping the module relationships

Before going into detail on both **Accounts** and **Contacts** modules, it is worthwhile recapping how they relate to the other foundation modules **Leads** and **Deals**. This relationship is illustrated in the following diagram:

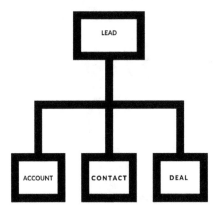

Figure 4.1 – Foundation modules: relationships when a lead is first converted

The general rule that is applied here is that when a lead is qualified, it is converted into three records: **Account, Contact**, and **Deal**.

Let's take the following scenario as an example:

A health and safety training  company using Zoho CRM specializes in the delivery of a range of training courses for manufacturers of food and drinks.

They receive an inquiry from **Bob Brown** from **ABC Foods** who is interested in finding out more about the training courses they provide. These details are recorded initially within our **Leads** module.

Once the **Lead** has been **Qualified**, it will be converted as follows:

- An **Account** record will be created under the name of **ABC Foods**, which will be used to record all the organization details as required.

- A **Contact** record will be created for **Bob Brown** containing his personal contact details.

- A **Deal** record will be created to contain details of the actual training requirement, including the name of the course(s), location, venue details, and delegates. This record will be linked to both **ABC Foods** and **Bob Brown**.

While *Figure 4.1* depicts the relationship when the original lead for **ABC Foods** was converted, during their customer lifetime there may be additional contacts that are involved in communications as well as additional deals (repeat business).

When this occurs, the relationships change, as follows:

- An **Account** may have many **Contacts.**

- An **Account** may have many **Deals.**

- A **Deal** may have many **Contacts.**

This can be illustrated as follows:

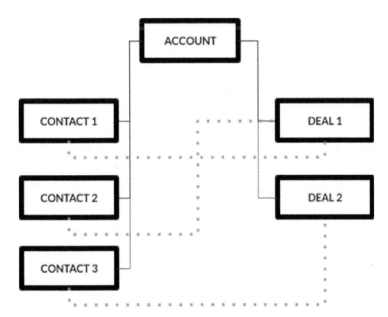

Figure 4.2 – Many-to-many relationships: Accounts to Contacts in blue and Deals to Contacts in red

Once this structure is understood and implemented, your business will have established a solid foundation. Let's now look at how we should set up the **Accounts** module.

# Keeping standard fields in Accounts

When accessing the **Accounts** module for the first time, for the same reasons as in the previous chapters we must review then remove any of the standard (pre-existing fields) that we do not need.

A list of these standard fields can be found here:

```
https://help.zoho.com/portal/en/kb/crm/sales-force-automation/
accounts/articles/standard-fields-accounts
```

The following is a list of these fields *you should keep* along with the reason(s) why:

- **Account Name**: This field is used to record the company name and is mandatory.

- **Account Owner**: The name of the user to whom the Account is assigned. This may be a useful field when it comes to Roles and Data Sharing Rules, Workflow Automation, and Reporting later.

- **Website**: The **Uniform Resource Locator** (**URL**) of the company's website.

- **Parent Account**: This field is used to associate the Account record with a parent account. This is essential when you need to link a head office address with a satellite office or branch. The rule is that if different contacts are in different locations, we must use this parent account to link them all together.

- **Phone**: Used to record the landline telephone number for the Account. It is important to keep this field and not replace it with custom fields as this may limit the ability to integrate with telephone systems later.

- **Standard Industrial Classification (SIC) Code**: The SIC code of the Account could prove useful in reporting and segmentation at a later date.

- **Created By**: The name of the user that created the Account as well as the date and time it was created.

- **Modified By**: The name of the user that last modified the Account, along with the date and time of this modification.

The following standard fields are used to capture the address to which you will be sending invoices or postal communications.

## Billing address fields

The billing address fields are listed as follows:

- **Billing Street**
- **Billing City**
- **Billing Province** (or **State**)
- **Billing Code**
- **Billing Country**

It is vital that you keep all these standard address fields as they will be needed if we are using any of the *Quotes – Orders – Invoices* modules at a later date. Another reason to keep these fields is to validate and maintain the address details for which you may find address lookup/validation tools available on the Marketplace. See *Chapter 8, Supercharge CRM With Marketplace Extensions, Custom Functions, and Integrations.*

The following standard fields are used to capture the address to which you will be shipping goods to your customer.

## Shipping address fields

The shipping address fields are as follows:

- **Shipping Street**
- **Shipping City**
- **Shipping Province** (or **State**)
- **Shipping Code**
- **Shipping Country**

If you are shipping products to addresses that may be different from the billing address, then you must keep these standard address fields. Otherwise, remove them.

# Adding custom fields to Accounts

In keeping with other modules, it is important that we keep the **Accounts** module concise. A best practice is to populate as much of this information as possible when converting a lead and keep manual research and data entry to a bare minimum.

It is important that data held within an account record be static, meaning that it is not something that will change regularly. If there is a requirement to record transactional data (for example, number of units sold), this needs to be recorded elsewhere. Refer to *Chapter 5, Working with Other System and Custom Modules*, for further details.

Here is a selection of custom fields that many Zoho CRM users find valuable:

| Field Name | Datatype | Description | Suggested Picklist Values |
|---|---|---|---|
| Status | Picklist | This is a replacement for the standard field - Rating | Prospect<br>Client<br>Partner<br>Lapsed Client<br>Other |
| Sector | Picklist | This is a replacement for the standard field - Industry<br>Add only values for the sectors if your current and target future clients | As required |
| Number of Employees * | Picklist | This is a replacement for the standard field - Employees | 1-10<br>11-50<br>51-100<br>101-250<br>251-500<br>Over 500 |
| Company LinkedIn | URL | The link to the Company page on LinkedIn | - |
| Lifetime Value | Currency | The total revenue received from this client<br><br>*Custom function for this within Chapter 8* | - |

Figure 4.3 – Custom fields in Accounts module

Once you have removed and added the fields as required, it is a best practice to organize them in suitably named sections as this will ensure that records in this module are intuitive and easy to read.

An example of how we might do this is shown as follows:

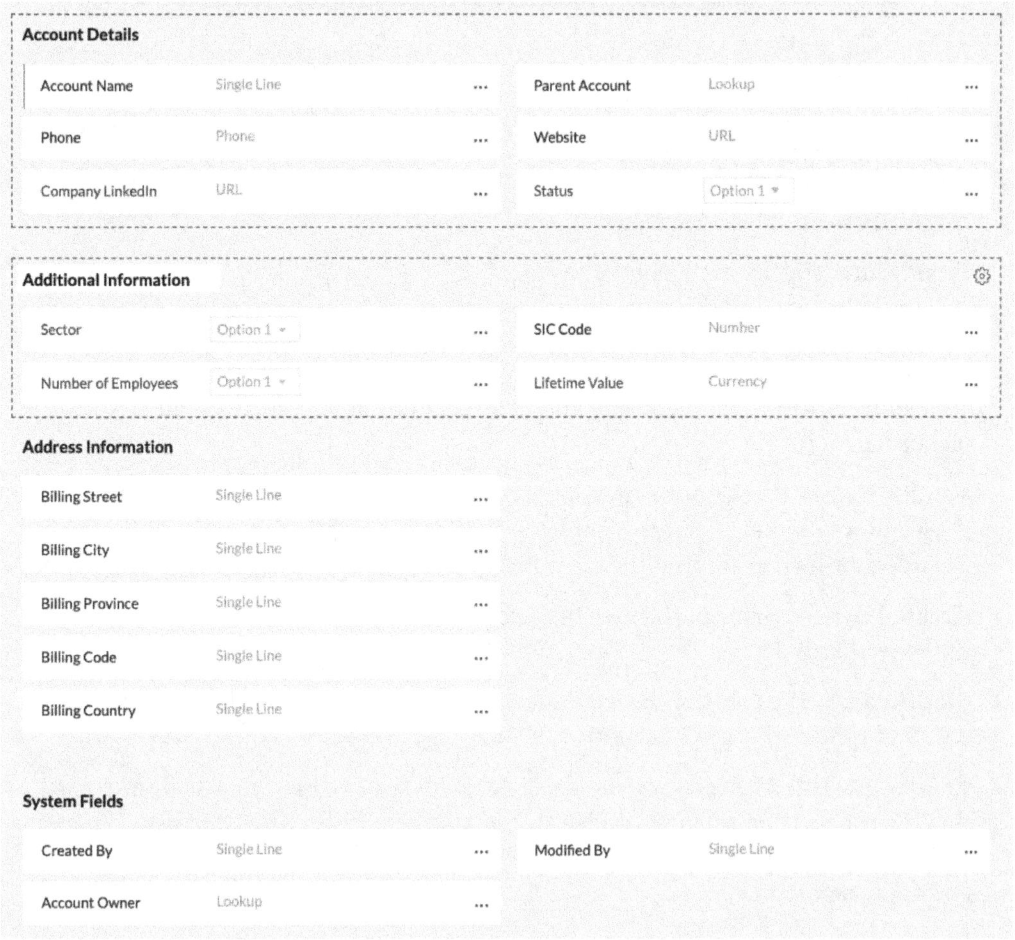

Figure 4.4 – Example of how to lay out your Accounts module

With this completed, you are ready to set up the fourth and final module of the foundation: **Contacts**.

# Keeping standard fields in Contacts

When accessing the **Contacts** module for the first time, we must review and remove any of the standard (pre-existing fields) that we do not need.

A list of standard fields can be found here:

`https://help.zoho.com/portal/en/kb/crm/sales-force-automation/contacts/articles/standard-fields-contacts`

Here is a list of these fields *you should keep*, along with the reason(s) why:

- **Contact Owner**: The name of the user to whom the Contact is assigned. This may be a useful field when it comes to Roles and Data Sharing Rules, Workflow Automation, and Reporting later.

- **First Name**: The first name of the contact.

- **Last Name**: The last name of the contact. This is a mandatory system field.

- **Account Name**: The Account name related to this contact. If you are providing goods/services to consumers only, then the **Account name** (and module) will not be needed.

- **Vendor Name**: The vendor name of the contact. Only needed if you are using the **Vendors** module. Refer to *Chapter 5, Working with Other System and Custom Modules,* for further information.

- **Created By**: The name of the user that created the Contact, as well as the date and time it was created.

- **Modified By**: The name of the user that last modified the Contact, along with the date and time of this modification.

- **Email Opt Out**: A checkbox that, if selected, will remove the contacts from a mailing list and they will not receive any emails from Zoho CRM. See also *Chapter 9, Zoho Campaigns,* to understand how this field updates across CRM and Campaigns.

- **Phone**: The landline or office number for the contact. It is important to use this standard field (as opposed to creating custom fields) to future-proof your CRM for any possible integration with a telephone system.

- **Mobile**: The landline or office number for the contact. It is important to use this standard field (as opposed to creating custom fields) to future-proof your CRM for any possible integration with a telephone or **short message service** (**SMS**) system.

- **Email**: The primary email address of the contact.

- **Mailing Street**: The mailing street of your contact.

- **Mailing City**: The mailing city/town of your contact.

- **Mailing State**: The mailing state, province, or county of your contact.

- **Mailing Zip**: The mailing zip or postal code of your contact.
- **Mailing Country**: The mailing country of your contact.

> Tip
>
> If you are providing goods and services to businesses, it is recommended that you remove all mailing address fields as they will be already present in the related Account record.
>
> If you are providing goods and services to consumers only, it is recommended that you keep the mailing address fields exactly how they are.

Once you have reviewed the **Contact** standard fields, you may need to add some custom fields specific to your business.

# Adding custom fields to Contacts

It is also important that we keep the **Contacts** module concise. A best practice is to populate as much of this information when converting a lead and keep manual research and data entry to a bare minimum. Here are some custom fields that many Zoho CRM users find valuable:

| Field Name | Datatype | Description | Suggested Picklist Values |
| --- | --- | --- | --- |
| Contact Type | Picklist | Used to record the type of contact as a more intuitive field name for an existing field named Status which is recommended to remove. | Prospect<br>Client<br>Partner<br>Vendor<br>Network<br>Other |
| Job Title | Single Line | This is a replacement for the standard field - Title and should be used to capture the job position of the contact. | |
| Sector | Picklist | Having this picklist field will prove invaluable when it comes to mailing list and segmenting contacts later | As required - will be the same values as used in the Leads, Deals, and Accounts |
| Additional Information | Description | Often used to capture things such as family, hobbies and interests. This is very important when it comes to relationship building. | |

Figure 4.5 – Custom fields to add to your Contacts module

In the preceding screenshot, **Contact Type** and **Sector** will be crucial for us to segment our contact list for reporting and marketing purposes.

> **Tip**
> Liaise with the marketing team and discuss the fields and picklist values that will help marketing communicate the right messages with the right contacts through segmentation. This will help the marketing function and add internal value to your CRM.

Once you have removed and added all the required fields, you will need to organize the layout similar to the example provided in the following screenshot:

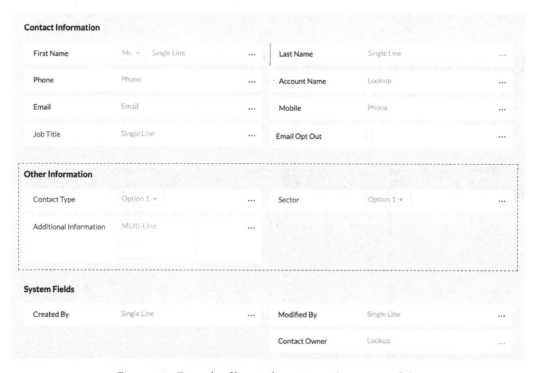

Figure 4.6 – Example of how to lay out your Contacts module

With the layout complete, you will have a **Contacts** module that will be a key hub for all communication and the value of complete, well-managed **Accounts** and **Contacts** modules will be clear for all to see.

One of the biggest issues with any CRM system is record duplication, which we will consider now.

# Avoiding duplication using unique fields

Having duplicate account or duplicate contact records is one of the biggest issues any CRM user can face. It can lead to inaccurate reporting and communication and can be potentially damaging to customer relationships.

However, this can be easily be avoided with just a few simple settings within the **Accounts** and **Contacts** modules.

Let's consider **Accounts** first, as follows:

1. From the **Home** page in CRM, access the setup by clicking on the spanner icon displayed here:

Figure 4.7 – Setup icon

2. Within the **Customization** menu, click on **Modules and Fields**.

3. Click on **Accounts** and then on **Standard (Layout)**.

4. Click **...** next to the **Account Name** field then click on **Do not allow duplicate values**, as shown in the following screenshot:

Figure 4.8 – How to avoid duplicate accounts

The system will no longer accept two account names with the same value.

Now, let's complete a similar action in the **Contacts** module, as follows:

1.  From the **Home** page in CRM, access the setup by clicking on the spanner icon displayed here:

Figure 4.9 – Setup icon

2.  Within the **Customization** menu, click on **Modules and Fields**.

3.  Click on **Contacts** and then on **Standard (Layout)**.

4.  Click **...** next to the **Email** field then click on **Do not allow duplicate values** , as shown in *Figure 4.10*.

5.  Repeat *Step 4* for the **Mobile** field as an additional measure.

    The process is illustrated in the following screenshot:

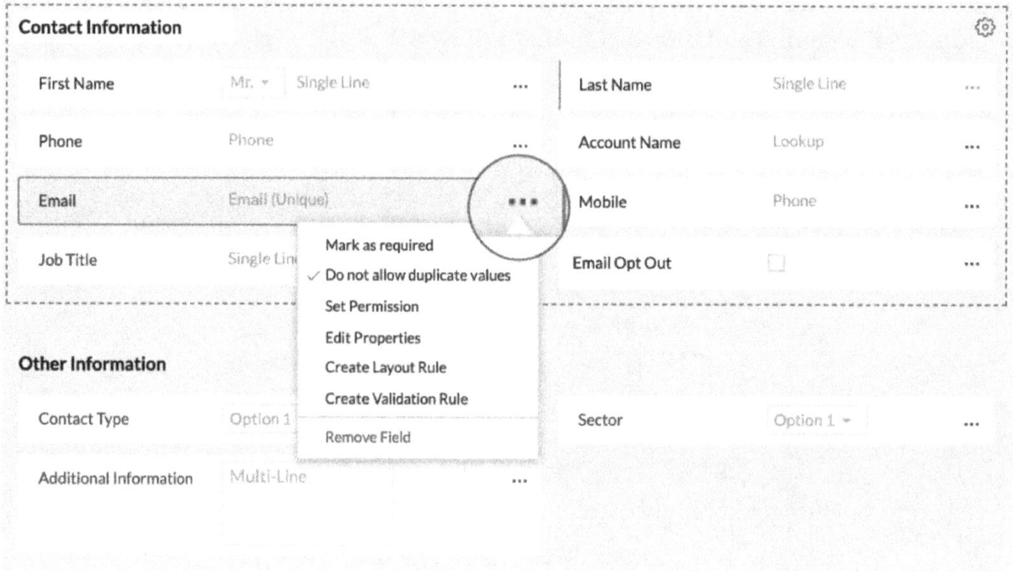

Figure 4.10 – How to avoid duplicate contacts based on email

As shown in the preceding screenshot, we can avoid duplicates on the **Email** field only. It is possible for two contacts to share the same name, and this is also on rare occasions possible for two people from the same company. Therefore, **Email** is a unique field that may be applied to a contact.

In addition to the unique fields discussed here, there a few other best practices you should be aware of.

## Best practices for Accounts and Contacts

The following guidelines will help you to manage and maintain the integrity of your core customer database and should be adhered to as much as possible:

- The relationship between **Accounts** and **Contacts** is one-to-many. For example, our **Account name** may be **ABC Foods** and the **Contacts** linked to that Account will be **Bob Brown**, with a separate **Contact** record for **Susan Smith**. Both of these will be linked to **ABC Foods**. It is crucial that all users add any related contacts to the correct Account.

- If your Account has a main head office in one city and other offices at different locations, then it is highly recommended that you add each of the other locations as a separate Account and link to the parent Account. This will enable your team to relate the contacts to each address properly.

- Where possible, validate information held in **Accounts** and **Contacts** by integrating with a third-party application or platform. Often, the other platform will have an **application programming interface** (**API**) that will support this integration, or in some cases may have developed a Marketplace extension to simplify this process. Refer to *Chapter 8, Supercharge CRM With Marketplace Extensions, Custom Functions, and Integrations,* for further details. This will add a great deal of value to your CRM, boosting confidence and adoption by its users and helping to reduce human error and avoid record duplication.

- A valid email address is the most important single piece of contact data in our CRM, so these should be collected, managed, and treated accordingly. All departments within your business will require this information to be present and correct, be it marketing, sales, operations, and finance. It is highly recommended that these be validated using a Marketplace extension—see *Chapter 8, Supercharge Your System With Marketplace Extensions, Custom Functions, and Third-Party Integrations.*

# Summary

In this chapter, you have learned how to set up and optimize your **Accounts** and **Contacts** modules.

You now have an understanding of the important standard fields and custom fields to ensure that we are building and maintaining a great customer database.

The integrity and accuracy of both these modules will provide your team with the confidence that the CRM is helping them in their roles and supporting your future aspirations as a business. You now understand the need to avoid duplication of Account and Contact records. In addition, you learned some best practices to follow to protect your system from duplication.

Now that you have reached the conclusion of *Section 1, Laying the Foundation* of the book, you should have a comprehensive understanding of the foundation modules and how they are the building blocks of success.

In *Section 2, Take Your CRM to the Next Level*, you will begin with *Chapter 5, Working with Other System and Custom Modules*.

# Section 2: Take Your CRM to the Next Level

In this section, you will learn how to build upon the foundations of your CRM and utilize the other key modules. This will facilitate more of your team to engage with the system, adding more value and enabling you to build a world-class CRM ready to help grow your business.

This section comprises the following chapters:

- *Chapter 5, Working with Other System and Custom Modules*
- *Chapter 6, Game-Changing Workflows and Automations*
- *Chapter 7, Essential Systems Administration*
- *Chapter 8, Supercharge CRM with Marketplace Extensions, Custom Functions, and Integrations*

# 5

# Working with Other System and Custom Modules

Now that you have designed and configured the foundation modules, it is time to discover which other modules can provide additional value. In this chapter, you will learn about the remaining system modules, including how and when should they be used and how to set them up.

You will learn how to develop additional custom modules that will further streamline additional business processes, improve internal and external communication, and also involve more departments of your organization using the **Customer Relationship Management (CRM)** system.

The topics covered within this chapter include the following:

- Working with the **Products** and **Quotes** modules
- How and when to use the **Sales Orders** module
- How and when to use the **Invoices** module
- Other essential modules you must keep
- Adding further value by creating custom modules

By the end of this chapter, you will have developed an understanding of which of the other modules you should use, how they will add value to your CRM and business, and how to best set them up. You will gain skills and knowledge to extend your CRM benefits beyond just sales and marketing and unlock insights and benefits that otherwise would have been missed.

# Working with the Products and Quotes modules

Outside of our four foundation modules (**Leads**, **Accounts**, **Contacts**, and **Deals**), the module that often adds the most value is **Quotes**.

Within a **business-to-business** (**B2B**) sales process, the seller always has to provide a price to a potential customer for the delivery or supply of their products and/or services. Depending on the nature of the deal that is being agreed upon, we will have different ways to describe and quantify this deal. Sometimes, we may be able to provide this quote within a simple email, but sometimes a document template within the **Deals** module will suffice. However, there are many times where a detailed line-by-line breakdown is required.

This is where the **Quotes** module can really help your Sales team. Let's consider a few examples of when the **Quotes** module will be of value, as follows:

- If you are selling products and need to list the product name, description, quantity, individual price, sub-total, and total costs
- If you are selling a combination of products and services
- If you are providing a bundle of services as part of one deliverable package of work—such as configuration, training, data migration, and systems integration

If your quotes or proposals match the criteria described in the list, then the **Quotes** module will be of benefit to your organization.

However, before you start to set up **Quotes**, you must consider the **Products** module.

# Products module

The **Products** module will allow you to record details of all the products and services that your organization provides. If you are using **Quotes, Sales Orders,** or **Invoices,** you will need to use this module as at least one product must be added when creating a record in any of these modules. It is recommended that you remove any unwanted fields, to make it easy for your users to administrate and update the products.

To establish which fields to keep or add to this module, think about the end result. Anything product-related that you will need to display on a quote will need a field, and also anything that you need to group by or filter by on reports will need a field within products.

Examples of this are discussed later in the *Quoted Items* section.

Further details are available at the following link:

```
https://help.zoho.com/portal/en/kb/crm/manage-inventory/
products/articles/working-with-products#Standard_Fields_in_
Products
```

> Tip
>
> The **Quotes** module is one of several modules that Zoho collectively describes as an **inventory module.** The other inventory modules are **Sales Orders, Invoices, Products,** and **Purchase Orders.**

Now that we have set up the **Products** module, let's look at how we can best configure our **Quotes** module.

# Setting up your Quotes module

The first step to complete when setting up the **Quotes** module is to remove the fields you do not need and understand which fields you should keep.

A list of standard fields in the **Quotes** module is available at `https://help.zoho.com/portal/en/kb/crm/manage-inventory/quotes/articles/standard-fields-quotes.`

Most of the fields in this list will be required; however, it is important that we remove any that are not required.

# Removing standard fields

Here is a list of standard fields that you should consider removing:

- **Carrier**: Unless it is important to specify which carrier or courier will be shipping the goods, this field should be removed.

- **Shipping**: Unless you need to add text describing the shipping type, this should be removed.

- **Inventory Manager**: Unless you need to add the name of the person responsible for arranging the shipping, remove this field.

- **Description**: This is too vague—description of what? When adding line items to a **Quote**, each item will have its own description field. If you need to add a further detailed description to the Quote in general, it is better to create a custom field that is more specific.

- **Terms and Conditions**: Using this system field does not allow us to apply formatting in our template documents and will allow the user to manually amend the content of this field. As many Zoho users have consulted legal firms for guidance in creating these terms and conditions, possibly the worst thing that can happen with a **Quote** is for a salesperson to make any changes to these.

  For this reason, it is recommended that you remove this field and either hold the terms and conditions as static text within the **Quote** template *or* provide a link to review the terms and conditions on your company website.

- **Quote Number**: This standard field will generate a non-user-friendly 16-digit reference number. It is recommended you replace this with a custom auto-number field named **Quote Ref:** where you can define the prefix and appearance of this number.

Once you have removed these fields, it's then time to consider adding custom fields.

# Adding custom fields

Custom fields will be specific to your requirements. Compare your existing **Quote/Proposal/Letter of Engagement** template and check which fields are missing from the **Quotes** module. Add these missing fields to the **Quotes** module.

Consider not only the services/products you are supplying but also the questions that the prospective customer may add. The best quote documents are the ones that are approved without any questions at all.

Once you have added the fields that you require, it is time to take a detailed look at how we can configure the section where a user will be adding line items—otherwise known as **Quoted Items**.

## Quoted Items

In 2021, a great new feature was added that, for the first time, allows an Admin user to configure how they add Products to a record in any of the inventory modules (including **Quotes**). This sub-form is named **Quoted Items**. An example of this is shown in the following screenshot:

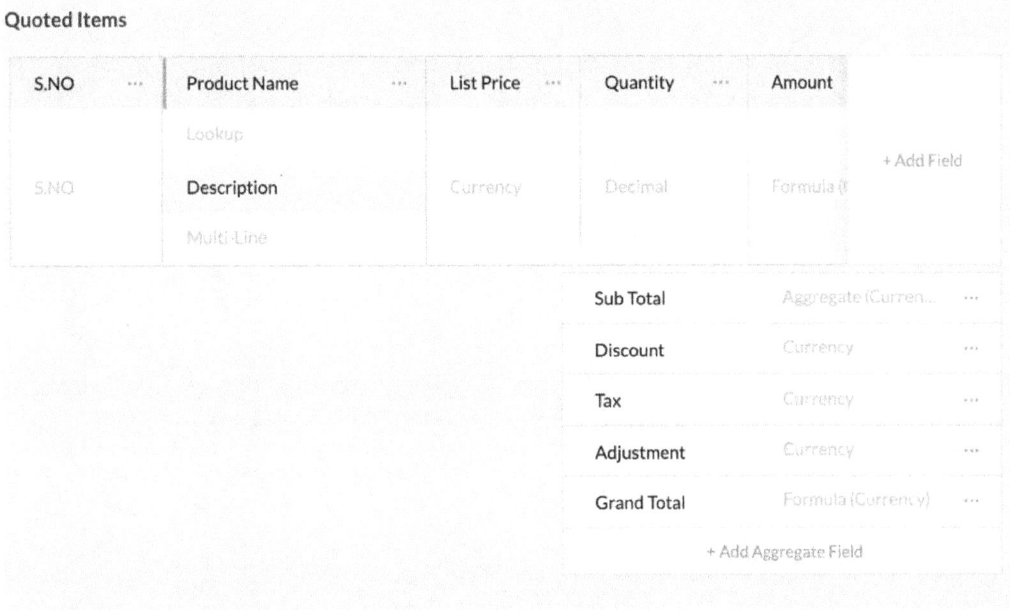

Quoted Items

| S.NO | | Product Name | | List Price | | Quantity | | Amount | |
|------|------|------|------|------|------|------|------|------|------|
| | | Lookup | | | | | | | + Add Field |
| S.NO | | Description | | Currency | | Decimal | | Formula (l | |
| | | Multi-Line | | | | | | | |

| | | | | | Sub Total | Aggregate (Curren... | ... |
|--|--|--|--|--|------|------|------|
| | | | | | Discount | Currency | ... |
| | | | | | Tax | Currency | ... |
| | | | | | Adjustment | Currency | ... |
| | | | | | Grand Total | Formula (Currency) | ... |

+ Add Aggregate Field

Figure 5.1 – Quoted Items table before any changes have been made

This works very much the same as sub-forms in other modules and, except for **Product Name** (system mandatory), we can remove any of the other sub-form and aggregate fields.

The main benefit of this feature is that it allows us to pull through any field from the **Products** module and display this on our **Quotes**. Let's illustrate this with an example.

In our **Products** module, we have a **List Price** field, which is the price at which we wish to sell an item. We also may have the price at which we purchased the item or the total cost of labor and/or materials, which is often referred to as a cost price. We can now add a field in the **Quoted Items** sub-form that will pull through this cost price, and furthermore, we can create a **Formula** field that will calculate our margin for each line item and also a margin for the overall quote, as follows:

1.  Click on + **Add Field** located on the right-hand side of the screen, as seen in *Figure 5.1*.

2.  Select the **Fields of Lookup** tab, then select the field we wish to add—in this case, **Cost Price**, as seen in the following screenshot:

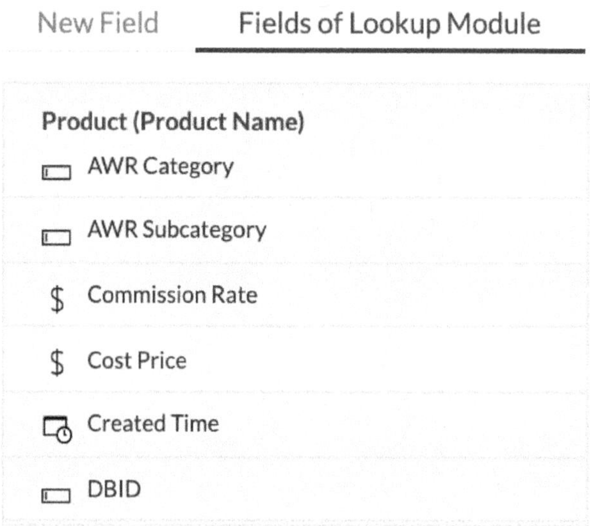

New Field        Fields of Lookup Module

**Product (Product Name)**

▭  AWR Category

▭  AWR Subcategory

$  Commission Rate

$  Cost Price

▭  Created Time

▭  DBID

Figure 5.2 – Adding a field of a lookup module to our Quoted Items sub-form

3.  Now, give your field a label—in this case, `Cost Price`.

4.  Within a sub-form in Zoho, we have a maximum number of 10 fields. So, before we create our formula field, we must remove one of the existing fields that we do not need. Review the fields and remove ones that you will not need. In this example, we will remove **S.No**, which is a field that only numbers each line item and as such is of limited value. You can remove a field by clicking on **...** then **Remove Field**.

5.  Now, let's add a field to calculate the margin. Click on + **Add Field** located on the right-hand side of the screen, as seen in *Figure 5.1*.

6.  Select **New Field | Formula**.

7.  Give your field a label—for example, `Margin`—and set the return type to **Currency**.

8.  Add the formula as shown in the following screenshot, and then click **Save**:

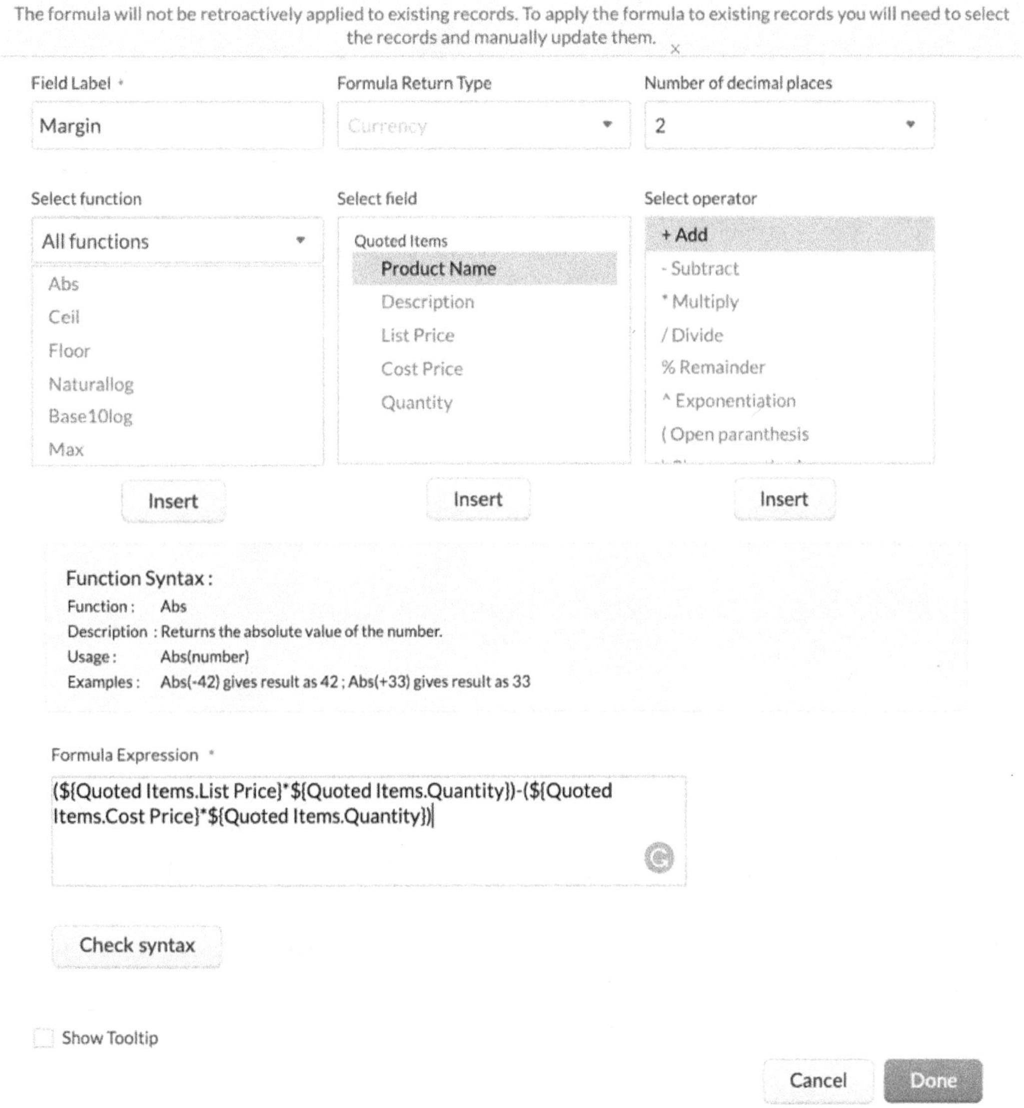

The formula will not be retroactively applied to existing records. To apply the formula to existing records you will need to select the records and manually update them. ✕

| Field Label * | Formula Return Type | Number of decimal places |
|---|---|---|
| Margin | Currency ▾ | 2 ▾ |

| Select function | Select field | Select operator |
|---|---|---|
| All functions ▾ | Quoted Items | + Add |
| Abs | **Product Name** | - Subtract |
| Ceil | Description | * Multiply |
| Floor | List Price | / Divide |
| Naturallog | Cost Price | % Remainder |
| Base10log | Quantity | ^ Exponentiation |
| Max | | ( Open paranthesis |

| Insert | Insert | Insert |

**Function Syntax :**

Function :    Abs
Description : Returns the absolute value of the number.
Usage :      Abs(number)
Examples :   Abs(-42) gives result as 42 ; Abs(+33) gives result as 33

Formula Expression *

(${Quoted Items.List Price}*${Quoted Items.Quantity})-(${Quoted Items.Cost Price}*${Quoted Items.Quantity})

Check syntax

☐ Show Tooltip

Cancel        Done

Figure 5.3 – Creating a field to calculate the margin based on the cost and unit price of the products

9.  Next, we are going to want an **Aggregate formula** field to sum the margin (calculate the profit) for all the items contained within the Quote. Begin by clicking **+ Add Aggregate Field** located in the bottom-right corner of the sub-form.

10. Set up this **Total Margin** field, as shown in the following screenshot:

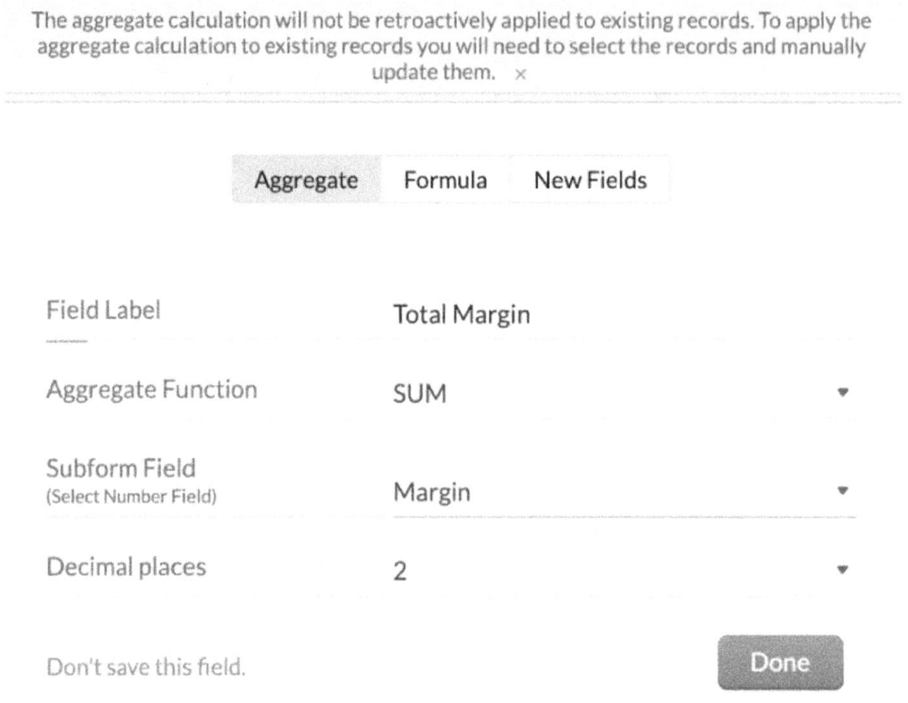

The aggregate calculation will not be retroactively applied to existing records. To apply the aggregate calculation to existing records you will need to select the records and manually update them.  ×

|  | Aggregate | Formula | New Fields |
|--|--|--|--|

| Field Label | Total Margin |
|--|--|
| Aggregate Function | SUM ▾ |
| Subform Field (Select Number Field) | Margin ▾ |
| Decimal places | 2 ▾ |

Don't save this field.                                             Done

Figure 5.4 – Creating an aggregate formula field

11. Finally, remove any of the other remaining unwanted sub-form and aggregate fields. Note that you may need to first remove the reference from the aggregate field before removing the field itself. The system will prompt you if this is needed.

12. Once you have completed all these steps, then an example **Quote** record with your customized **Quoted Items** table should resolve the following:

**Quoted Items**

| Product Name | List Price (£) | Cost Price (£) | Quantity | Amount (£) | Total (£) | Margin (£) |
|---|---|---|---|---|---|---|
| Product A | 250.00 | 75.00 | 2 | 500.00 | 500.00 | 350.00 |

|  |  |
|---|---|
| Sub Total | £ 500.00 |
| Total Margin | £ 350.00 |

Figure 5.5 – Example of a customized Quoted Items table in the record within the Quotes module

Now that we have set up the **Quotes** module as required, it's time to create a template document.

# Creating Quote templates to share as a PDF file or for electronic signature

Within Zoho CRM, there is an existing Quote template that you may amend and use. This template, however, is not fully customizable. So, in order to future-proof your template and have a fully flexible document, it is recommended that you create your own template(s).

We can create a new **Inventory (Quote)** template in one of the following ways:

- Inserting **HyperText Markup Language (HTML)**/plaintext
- Using one of the five templates in the gallery
- Using a blank template

While HTML/plaintext may be a good option if you have HTML skills or resources available, the most user-friendly and flexible option is to use a blank template, described as follows:

1.  From the **Home** page in CRM, access the setup by clicking on the following icon:

Figure 5.6 – Setup icon

2.  Within the **Customization** menu, click on **Templates**.

3. Click on **Inventory** and then click on the blue button named **+ New Template**, as illustrated in the following screenshot:

Figure 5.7 – Creating a new Quote template

4. On the next screen, the **Quotes** module will already be selected, so click **Next**.

5. You will now see five templates with one labeled blank on the left. Hover over this, then click on the **Select** button that will appear, as illustrated in the following screenshot:

Figure 5.8 – Selecting a blank template

6. Now, give your template a name in the top-left corner—for example, New Quote, followed by a suitable subject instructing the recipient what the message contains, as illustrated in the following screenshot:

Figure 5.9 – Naming your template and subject

7. Drag and drop the required components onto your blank canvas from left to right. You will need to add a **Text** component, at least to start drafting your message, and others as you wish, to amend the look and feel.

8.  To insert a merge field, firstly type #, which will present the following drop-down menu, and then select the field(s) from the module(s) as required. Merge tags are useful as they make your message more personal and relevant to the recipient. You can see a merge field being added in the following screenshot:

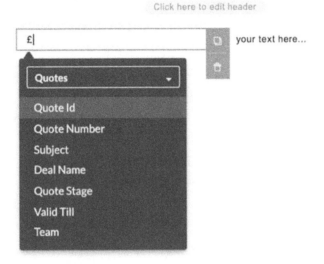

Figure 5.10 – Adding your merge field

9.  Preview and save your template.

Further details on creating a Quote template can be found at `https://help.zoho.com/portal/en/kb/crm/customize-crm-account/customizing-templates/articles/inventory-templates`.

Once you have drafted a template that you are happy with, you can look at the next module: **Sales Orders**.

# How and when to use the Sales Orders module

In a - model, the **Sales Orders** module is *only* to be used if you are shipping out actual goods and/or you are sending out members of your team to undertake any work onsite, such as installation, servicing, or maintenance as a result of a customer accepting the Quote.

If you are shipping goods, then the main use of this module is to create a **Delivery Note**, using the **Sales Order template editor**. The methods used to create this are identical to creating a Quote, so please refer to the previous section for further details on this.

Alternatively, if you are using a different software application for the actual delivery of products/services, then you may not need to use this module.

However, if your business is selling products via an e-commerce website to business users and/or consumers, then the **Sales Orders** module is critical to your use of Zoho. For the value of this to be achieved, it is a prerequisite that you integrate your website with Zoho CRM.

> **Tip**
> Integrating an e-commerce website with Zoho CRM is a specialist activity that should be carried out by your website developer and/or a Zoho Partner or an integration specialist.

## Setting up the Sales Orders module

In keeping with setting up other modules, you should firstly remove the existing standard fields you do not need before adding custom fields that will enable your operations and customer service teams to fulfill the order effectively.

Some example fields to consider adding are listed as follows:

- **Site Contact**: Either a lookup of **Contacts** or a single-line text field.
- **Delivery Date/Time**: The date and time you will be delivering your products/ services. Consider also having a **Required date** field to record the customer's initial requirements.
- **Access Instructions**: A multiline text field that will provide information to your team that will instruct them where to park and whom to report to on arrival.

If you added any custom fields and/or customized the **Quoted Items** sub-form in the **Quotes** module, you will also need to replicate this customization in **Sales Orders**.

It is important to map the custom fields you created in **Quotes** when converting a **Quote** into a **Sales Order**. This can be achieved by using either of the following methods.

### Method 1 – Upon creating a custom field in Quotes

When first creating a custom field in the **Quotes** module, you have a single chance to also create this field in other inventory modules (**Sales Orders** or **Invoices**) before you save the layout. Once a new field is added, you can take advantage of this time-saving tip by doing the following:

1. Click on ... to the right of the new field.

2.  Select **Edit Properties**.

3.  Now, check the box corresponding to the module you also wish to copy this field to—either **Sales Orders** or **Invoices** or both of these. This will create a field in the associated module(s) and map the data upon conversion.

If you do not always remember to do this, it is not a problem as you may use the second method, which we will see in the next section.

## Method 2 – Using the Quote conversion mapping table

If you missed an opportunity to map the fields as described in the preceding *Method 1*, you may follow the process described next at any time, as needed:

1.  From the **Home** page in CRM, access the setup by clicking on the icon displayed here:

Figure 5.11 – Setup icon

2.  Within the **Customization** menu, click on **Modules and Fields**.

3.  Move your cursor slowly over **Quotes**, and you should see the **Quote Conversion Mapping** menu appear, as follows:

Layout

Rename

Fields

Module Permission

Quote Conversion Mapping

Map Dependency Fields

Set Validation Rules

Figure 5.12 – Quote Conversion Mapping

4.  Click on **Quote Conversion Mapping** to reveal the following screen:

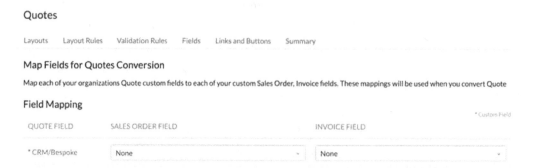

Figure 5.13 – Map Fields for Quotes Conversion screen

5.  In the screen shown in *Figure 5.13*, your custom fields will appear in the column on the left marked **QUOTE FIELD**. From the drop-down menus in the adjacent columns, select the field you wish to map in the **Sales Order** and **Invoice** modules. Note that the field must already exist in the other module(s) and be of the same data type as the field in **Quotes** for it to appear in the list.

With the fields set up and mapped (from **Quotes**) in **Sales Orders**, we are now ready to consider the **Invoices** module.

# How and when to use the Invoices module

As the heading suggests, it is not always the case that you should use the **Invoices** module. In fact, it is a best practice that the **Invoices** module *should only be used* if you are planning on integrating Zoho CRM with another cloud-based accounting software platform.

If you are planning on such integration, this may add huge value to your CRM, as follows:

- It will allow a user to simply convert a **Quote** or a **Sales Order** into an **Invoice** with just a click of a button, thus saving a huge amount of time in double-entry on both systems.

- It will also allow such users to create and send an invoice to the client without having to access the accounting software.

- It will facilitate a smoother and quicker invoicing process—workflow automation can be used to create an invoice based on a field update in the **Quotes** or **Sales Order** modules.

If this sounds as though it will work for your business, you should use this module, and setting it up will be similar to setting up **Quotes** and **Sales Orders**, as mentioned earlier in this chapter. To set up the **Invoices** module, follow the sequence listed as follows:

1. Remove unwanted standard fields.

2. Add required custom fields.

3. Map the fields from **Quotes** and **Sales Orders**, should you require the values in the Invoice record.

4. Replicate any customization that you made in **Quotes | Quoted Items**.

5. Plan the integration with your accounting software.

> **Tip**
> Integrating accounting software is a specialist activity that should be carried out by a Zoho Partner or the accounting software or a software integrator that has developed a plugin or connector.

Having considered the value of three—**Quotes**, **Sales Orders**, and **Invoices**—it's now time to gain insight into some of the other modules within Zoho CRM and the value they can potentially add.

# Other essential modules you must keep

There are five modules that you must keep as they are essential to managing the activities and measuring the performance of your team and many aspects of your business.

The way that you and your team use these modules will have a huge impact on the success of your CRM. These modules are listed as follows:

- **Tasks**: A task is a piece of work or activity that is due/completed with a specific subject, due date, and owner. A task will be related to another record in the CRM system (for example, **Lead**, **Contact**, **Account**, or **Deal**).

- **Meetings**: A meeting is a diary event that has a planned start and end time, a host, a location, and at least one participant(s).

- **Calls**: If you will be integrating your CRM system with a **Voice over Internet Protocol** (**VoIP**) system, then calls may be logged automatically against the record and user. If you are using the mobile application to place calls to clients/prospects, then this includes an option to log the call, which can be very useful to measure.

- **Reports**: This will allow users and management to provide and schedule list-based summary reports (see *Chapter 15, Building Actionable Reports and Dashboards (CRM)*, for further details).

- **Analytics**: This will allow users and management to create a visual representation of **key performance indicators** (**KPIs**) (see *Chapter 15, Building Actionable Reports and Dashboards (CRM)*, for further details).

## Additional modules to keep in mind

Within Zoho CRM, there are several other modules provided for us to configure and use, such as the following:

- **Campaigns**
- **Forecasts**
- **Cases**
- **Solutions**
- **Products**
- **Price Books**
- **Invoices**
- **Vendors**
- **Purchase Order**
- **Sales Orders**
- **Tasks**
- **Analytics**
- **Documents**

Each of these modules will be listed along the main menu across the top or beneath the ….

One of the keys to a successful CRM system is using only the modules that will add value to your business process. So, in this section, we advise why you should consider using others.

Firstly, we will consider the remaining inventory modules, as follows:

- **Purchase Orders**: This module can add a lot of value if you are selling goods and using the **Sales Orders** module of Zoho, especially if the goods you sell are not held in stock and are ordered by your team, then shipped straight to the customer. Ideally, you would need to create a custom button that would trigger a script to create a **Purchase Order (PO)** from within the **Sales Order**. This is something with which you need to seek assistance from Zoho or a partner. It is highly recommended, however, that if you do use the **Purchase Order** module in Zoho CRM, you integrate this with your accounting software to avoid duplication or reconciliation issues.

- **Vendors**: If you are using POs, then you will need to use the Vendor module to record the name, address, and contact information of each **Vendor** (or **Supplier**).

Now that we have considered the inventory modules, let's summarize how a few of the remaining modules may add further value to your CRM, as follows:

- **Campaigns**: This is possibly one of the most commonly misunderstood modules of Zoho CRM. The main benefit will be realized if you are also using Zoho Campaigns (email marketing campaign software). Enabling this module will synchronize certain Campaign data across **Leads** and **Contacts** so that your Sales team will have visibility of how engaged their prospects and clients are with the content. The campaign activity (opens, clicks, and bounces) pushed into CRM can also be a very useful input when it comes to lead scoring. See *Chapter 9, Zoho Campaigns*, for further information on Campaign integration and *Chapter 7, Essential Systems Administration*, for details on lead scoring.

- **Feeds**: The **Feeds** module is a way for users to *follow* key accounts, contacts, or deals as they progress. While this is not widely used, the module needs to be switched on to utilize its best feature—*tagging a user into a note*. For example, if a user wanted to update a colleague on a conversation they just had with a client, then while adding a note into that Contact record in CRM they could type @ followed by their colleague's username, and it will tag that user into the conversation. This user/colleague will receive this as an email notification. This is a great way to instantly update a colleague at the same time as entering a note.

  See here for additional information: `https://help.zoho.com/portal/en/kb/crm/collaborate-and-increase-team-productivity/feeds/articles/collaborate-using-feeds#Understanding_Feeds`.

Having now considered all of the core, essential, and optional modules already present within Zoho, it is now time to consider creating custom modules and the value they can bring.

# Adding further value by creating custom modules

So far in this book, we have talked only about the standard modules of Zoho CRM—that is, modules that are enabled and built into the system for us to use and configure as required. However, one of the standout features within the system is the ability to create our own *custom* modules. Note that the ability to create custom modules is available in CRM Enterprise, Zoho One, CRM Plus, and Ultimate editions.

In many cases, a business will have a successful CRM by using only standard modules; however, in certain businesses, they do not meet all of the requirements and there will be other processes or people that we require to manage within the system.

Let's consider a few examples of business types using Zoho, whereby a custom module will add huge value, as follows:

- **Training company**: This would need a custom module for delegates to record the name of each person that attended their course and other details including date/time and venue.

- **Private hospital/clinic**: This would need custom modules to record details of doctors, patients, and nurses.

- **Vehicle leasing company**: This would need custom modules to record details of all their funders and suppliers.

- **Software developer/supplier**: This would need a custom module to record details of all their agreements with clients. This would hold information such as terms of contracts, the number of users, monthly cost, and key contacts.

- **Mobile phone supplier**: This would need a module to hold all contracts, including the number of handsets, a price plan, and the duration of the contract.

- **IT network/infrastructure supplier**: This would need a module to record details of all service contracts with their client.

- **Wealth management company**: This would need to record fees related to each client (due and paid).

- **Energy consultancy**: This would need to record commission payments (due and received).

- **Insolvency practitioner**: This may need to record **County Court Judgments (CCJs)** and **Company Voluntary Arrangements (CVAs)**.

- **Caravan park**: This would require recording gas and electric readings.

The list of possible use cases is endless. What they all have in common is that they meet one or more of the following criteria:

- They help manage a key business process linked to clients.
- They help the team manage client relationships.
- They contain transactions that need to be linked with clients.
- They contain information/data that needs to be collated and reported upon, grouped by client.
- The processes being managed will be streamlined and automated by being managed within the CRM system.

Another thing in common is that they are often triggered or required when a deal is won and we have a customer to manage. As such, custom modules often serve as a bridge between sales, operations, and finance. When done correctly, there are huge gains to be had by using a custom module.

Consider also that we can create a custom module that can be integrated with a third-party system that populates the records automatically. This will add significant additional value.

If integration is not possible or feasible, then it is also easy to import data straight into the custom module on a daily/weekly/monthly basis as required. Just match the columns and data types in your file to the names of your fields.

> **Tip**
>
> Traditionally, a lot of this information listed previously has been/is stored on spreadsheets. Identify which spreadsheets in your business can be replaced with a custom module(s) in the CRM system.

Having considered examples of when and why we should create a custom module, let's now look at how we create one.

# Setting up a custom module

A custom module can be created as follows:

1. From the **Home** page in CRM, access the setup by clicking on the icon displayed as follows:

Figure 5.14 – Setup icon

2. Click on **+ New Module** located on the right-hand side of the screen, as illustrated in the following screenshot:

Figure 5.15 – Creating a new module

3. Now, replace the word **Untitled** with a suitable name for your new module in the top-left corner of the screen, as illustrated in the following screenshot:

Figure 5.16 – Naming your custom module

4. If you need to change the (Record) Name of the first field listed or change the data type to an **Auto-number** type, you must make either of those changes first before saving the module. This may be achieved by clicking on **...** then **Edit Properties**. See the tip at the end of this list.

5. Several fields will appear in the gray section in the center of the screen. Remove the ones you do not need.

6. Add the custom fields required using the drag-and-drop interface, dragging the data type from the top left into your form in the center.

7. Create sections to group fields together logically to make your module easy to read and intuitive.

8. Click **Save**.

> **Tip**
>
> Follow these next guidelines to help to decide what to do with the record name based on how the data will be entered into this custom module:
>
> If the records are to be created manually and there is a logical name, the user can type in here to identify the record then leave this field as **Single Line** (renaming if required). Otherwise, change it to **Auto-number**, as per *Step 4* of the preceding instructions.
>
> If the records are to be created by import or integration with a third-party system, a text field exists already that identifies the record then leaves this field as **Single Line** (renaming if required). Otherwise, change it to **Auto-number**, as per *Step 4* of the preceding instruction.

It is also important to note that the records in a custom module can be created automatically by creating a workflow rule. See *Chapter 6, Game-Changing Workflows and Automations*, for details of how to trigger workflows and then use the Instant Action named `Create Record`.

Remember, custom modules can be a game-changer for businesses. They may open up a stream of possibilities for marketing and operations, as well as enabling reporting and workflow automation opportunities that did not exist before.

# Summary

In this chapter, you have gained an understanding of some of the other modules within Zoho CRM.

You will have understood that you should consider adding these modules *only* when they add clear value to your business and help improve your business process. If in doubt, leave them out or consider them as a possible *Phase 2* for your CRM deployment/roll-out.

You have also considered the types of scenarios that may require you to add a custom module(s) and identified if this will help your business.

The skills learned in this chapter will give you the confidence to explore some of these additional modules now or at a future date and will be sure to make your CRM work better for all customer-facing departments of your business.

Once you have enabled and set up these modules, it is time to discover how you can really start to accelerate the benefits your CRM system will bring with the next chapter—*Chapter 6, Game-Changing Workflows and Automations*.

# 6
# Game-Changing Workflows and Automations

This chapter will provide you with powerful insight and knowledge of workflow automation, which is arguably the most valuable feature of Zoho CRM.

Used well and often, the workflows in Zoho will deliver huge efficiency time and again. They will take your **Customer Relationship Management (CRM)** system to the next level and get you and your and team excited about how it can help you become more efficient and successful.

In this chapter, we will work through practical examples that you may use straight away and also act as a stimulus for other ideas. These workflows will save you countless hours and help your team proactively manage opportunities and clients much more effectively.

Topics covered within this chapter include the following:

- Introducing workflow rules
- How to trigger a workflow with single and multiple conditions
- Using instant single, multiple, and scheduled actions
- Use cases and examples

By the end of this chapter, you will have learned how, why, and when to trigger workflows, set up some examples, and be inspired to create many more.

# Introducing workflow rules

**Workflow rules** are a set of actions that are executed when specific conditions are met. Upon these conditions being met, the rules automate the process of sending emails, assigning tasks, and updating fields.

Workflow rules consist of the following elements:

- **Basic Details**: To specify the module, rule name, and description.
- **Rule Trigger**: To specify when the rule should be triggered. Examples of such triggers are outlined as follows:

  **Execute based on a record's action**: Rules will be triggered when a record is created, edited, deleted, or if certain fields have been updated.

  **Execute based on date field's value**: Rules will be triggered either before, on, or after any date field in the record.

  **Execute based on the record's score**: Rules will be triggered when the score of a record is increased, decreased, or updated.

- **Workflow Condition**: It is possible to specify single or multiple conditions in a workflow rule. We may apply the rule to all records or only to certain records based on a condition(s) being met.

- **Actions**: Specify the actions to be automated for records that meet the criteria. The different types of actions are outlined as follows:

  **Instant Actions**: This includes sending an email, assigning a task, updating a field, pushing data to another system (webhook), customizing functions (script), converting a record, or creating a record.

  **Scheduled Actions**: All the same possible actions as with Instant actions, but this time they are scheduled to be actioned at a later date/time.

While this may sound alien at first, it is important to familiarize yourself with these elements as they apply to each and every rule that we set up in Zoho. As with most new skills, with practice comes experience and with experience comes more confidence, and in time they become simple to understand and execute.

Let's now consider each of these elements individually within an end-to-end process, starting with how to trigger a workflow.

# How to trigger a workflow with single and multiple conditions

With some knowledge of the basics, it is only by creating your first few workflows that you will start to master them. So, let's start with a simple example. We will create a workflow rule that will create a task, with a reminder and an email notification for a user to follow up when a new lead is created via the website. Proceed as follows:

1. From the **Home** page in CRM, access the setup by clicking on the following icon:

Figure 6.1 – Setup icon

2. Within the **Automation** menu, click on **Workflow Rules**.

3. Click on the **+ Create Rule** button.

4. Now, select a **Module**, then add a **Rule Name** and **Description**, as shown in the following screenshot. Then, click **Next**:

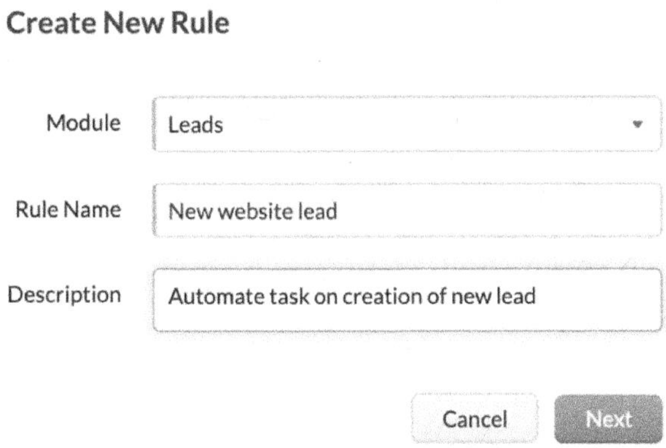

**Create New Rule**

| | |
|---|---|
| Module | Leads ▾ |
| Rule Name | New website lead |
| Description | Automate task on creation of new lead |

Cancel    Next

Figure 6.2 – Defining a new workflow rule

5. In this example, we will select the **On a record action** trigger and then select the **Create** option, as illustrated in the following screenshot:

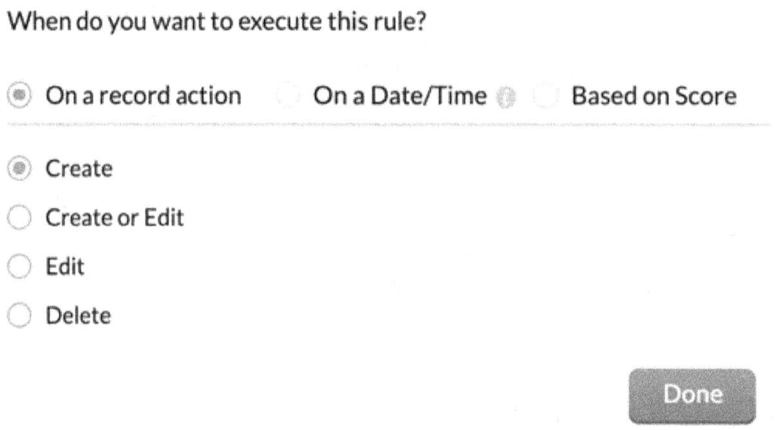

When do you want to execute this rule?

⦿ On a record action      ○ On a Date/Time ⓘ    ○ Based on Score

⦿ Create

○ Create or Edit

○ Edit

○ Delete

Done

Figure 6.3 – Triggering a workflow when a new record is created

Once we have selected *when* to trigger the rule, we must now add a condition to specify *which* records to apply the rule to.

## Adding a single condition

Once we have specified the trigger as shown in *Figure 6.3*, we may add a single condition by selecting the **Leads matching certain conditions** option then **Lead Source is Website**, as follows:

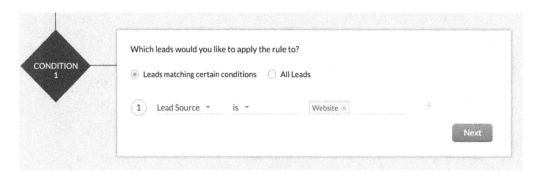

Figure 6.4 – Adding a single condition

Summarizing what we have achieved so far, when a new record is created (*Figure 6.3*) where the lead source is **Website** (*Figure 6.4*), this will trigger this particular workflow rule.

Once we have created our trigger with a condition, we now need to specify what we wish to happen to a record when it triggers our rule.

# Using instant single, multiple, and scheduled actions

Your mind is possibly boggling already at the possibilities the workflows may present us with. It gets even better! We can also perform single and multiple actions immediately or schedule them to happen in the future.

Let's consider initially a single action—creating a follow-up task.

## Instant single action

To automate the creation of a single action, you must firstly click on the **Instant Action** button to reveal the options, as shown in the following screenshot:

Figure 6.5 – List of instant actions

You can create a follow-up task by following these steps:

1. Click on **Task**.

2. Click on the **+ New Task** button in the top-right corner, upon which you will be presented with the following **Assign Task** screen:

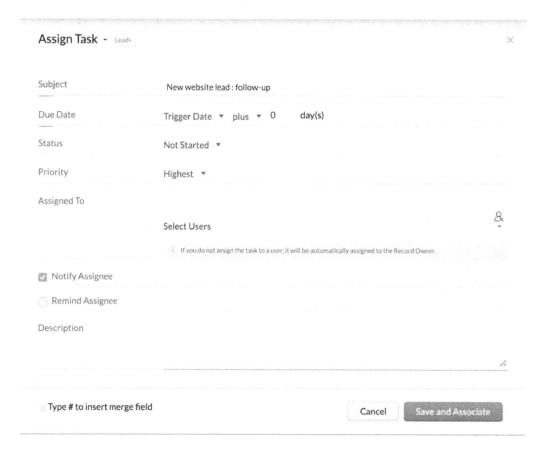

Figure 6.6 – Assigning a task

3. Give your task a concise description of what the user needs to do in the **Subject** field—ideally with some context. In this example, we have used **New website lead: follow-up**.

4. Now, fill in the **Due Date options**, which in this case will be on the same day that the rule was triggered—defined as **Trigger Date plus 0 day(s)**.

5. Set the **Status** dropdown to **Not Started**.

6.  Now, select a user to whom you wish to assign the task by clicking on the icon to the right of **Select Users**. Most of the time, however, it is desirable for the task to be assigned to the owner of the record (in this case, the **Lead**). In such cases, simply do not select a user, and the rule will automatically be assigned to the owner of the record. If you are a single user, then this will always be assigned to you.

7.  Now, select the **Notify Assignee** and/or **Remind Assignee** checkboxes, as required.

    -**Notify Assignee**: This will send an email notification to the assignee as soon as the workflow action is triggered. It is recommended to check this box as it will alert the user that a new lead from the website has just been received.

    -**Remind Assignee**: This will remind the assignee by email or at a time of your choosing. It is recommended to check this box in this scenario too, as it is important that we follow up on new leads as promptly and as quickly as possible.

8.  It is possible to add a description that can also contain merge tags (in other words, include any of the fields within the **Lead**). However, if the subject is succinct and clear, then this may not be necessary. The task will be linked to the **Lead** record, so the user will have visibility of everything they need.

9.  Finally, click on **Save and Associate**.

So, having illustrated how we can assign a single action—a task—let's consider how we could add more than one action to our workflow rule.

## Instant multiple actions

In our example, we may also need to send an instant thank-you message to our prospective customers who submitted their inquiry using the web-form. To assign this, we can follow these steps:

1.  Once we have followed *Steps 1-9* (from the previous section) to add creating a task to our workflow, it is possible to add further actions by clicking on **+ Action**, as shown in the following screenshot:

**Instant Actions**

**Tasks**
New website lead : follow-up

+ ACTION

Figure 6.7 – Adding multiple actions

2.  Now, click on **Email Notification** followed by the blue button on the right, titled **Create Email Notification**.

    You will now be presented with the following **Edit Email Notification** screen:

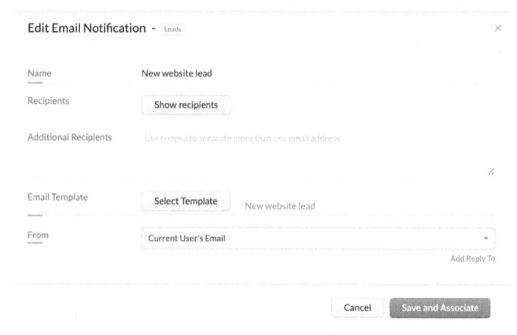

Figure 6.8 – Creating an email notification

3.  Give your notification a name, such as **New website lead**.

4.  Click on the **Choose recipients** button and add the email associated with the lead.

5.  Click on **Select Template**, and then select or create your email template. (See *Chapter 7, Essential Systems Administration* for information on email templates.)

6.  Now, a **From** picklist will appear that will allow you to specify the email address from which the email needs to be sent. Options here include **Record Owner**, **Current User's Email**, **Any User**, or **Any Organization Email** (see *Chapter 7, Essential Systems Administration* for further details).

7.  Click on **Save and Associate**.

Having considered how to add instant actions (single and multiple), let's now take a look at how we can also schedule actions to take place at some point in the future.

# Scheduled actions

Staying with our new website lead example, following on from *step 7* in the *Instant multiple actions* section, in addition to the instant task and email, we may also want to send a couple of lead-nurturing content emails to help keep the prospect warm and engaged. Let's see how to do this, as follows:

1. Firstly, click on the words **Scheduled Actions** to reveal the following pop-up box:

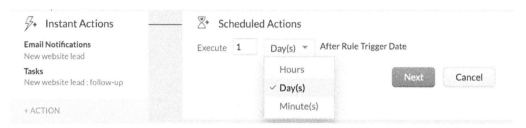

Figure 6.9 – Creating scheduled actions

2. Now, specify a trigger, selecting from **Hours, Day(s)**, or **Minute(s)**. In this example, we will set this at **1 Day After Rule Trigger Date** before clicking **Next**.

3. You will be presented with the same list of actions as earlier, so in this case, select **Email Notification**.

4. Following the same process as in the *Instant multiple actions* section (*Steps 1-7*), you may now create your first scheduled email notification.

5. Once the first email notification is associated, you may now add a second scheduled action by clicking **+ ACTION**, as illustrated in the following screenshot:

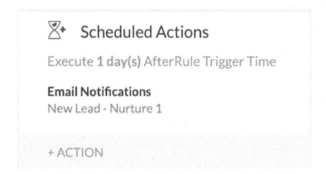

Figure 6.10 – Adding multiple scheduled actions

6.  To add a second email notification after 3 days, click **Add New Scheduled Action**, as illustrated in the following screenshot:

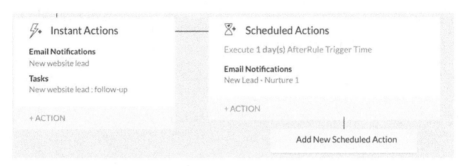

Figure 6.11 – Adding a second scheduled action

7.  Finally, repeat *Steps 5-6* but executing 2 (or 3) days **After Rule Trigger Time** and using a different **Email Template**.

While sometimes a single condition is enough, we often need to specify more than one so that we can define more precise actions for each. Let's consider how to add multiple conditions.

## Multiple conditions

In many cases, we may need to perform a different set of actions based on different conditions being met.

For example, if we also had an additional field on our web-form where our prospect selected from a picklist which product they were interested in (**Training** or **Consultancy**), then we could click on the + to the right of our first criteria before adding **Product Is Training**. This would be like adding an *and* to our criteria, so our amended condition would effectively be this:

```
Apply the rule to Leads where the Lead Source Is Website AND
the Product is Training
```

The benefit of having multiple conditions, in this case, is that we could assign the task to different owners based on the product selected. This would help to ensure that the right person is allocated to the query based on your team's skills and experience. This is automating processes that we would normally require a person to do and thus we are saving time, and also our team is being prompted automatically.

Once we have saved our workflow containing a single condition with actions, a + **Add another condition** link will appear on the left, as shown in the following screenshot. Clicking this link will allow you to select another set of conditions:

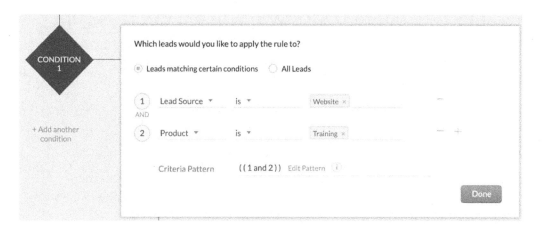

Figure 6.12 – Adding multiple criteria and conditions

Once we have defined which records we wish the workflow to be applied to, it's time to specify *which* action(s) we wish to perform. Refer back to the earlier sections on how to add single instant/multiple and scheduled actions, and repeat the steps as required.

Once you have set up this example on your CRM system and tweaked it for your business, it is useful to reflect on what we have learned in this chapter so far. By creating automated tasks, we are adding value every time the workflow is triggered. The system is prompting the users what needs to be done and when. By sending emails automatically, we are automating what would have been a manual process, one that may have been forgotten about or missed if the user were busy. Finally, by adding scheduled actions, we are automating other manual processes of nurturing the lead, which again would have been vulnerable to a user forgetting to do this or being unable to fulfill the task if they were busy elsewhere.

This is the value added by just one single workflow that will perform these tasks all day, every day. Imagine how much value we could add to our CRM system if we created 10, 20, or 30 workflow rules. This is game-changing!

So, now we are on board with the benefits workflow automation can bring, it's time to consider various additional examples that have all been proven to add significant value to Zoho users.

# Use cases and examples

In this section, we look at some examples for you to try using the skills and techniques achieved from this chapter. Compare these to your processes and relate these examples to those, adjusting them accordingly.

# Example 1 – Update Deal stage when a quote is sent

In the first example, the standard functionality does not update the stage of a Deal when a related Quote is sent, which forces the user to make a manual change. This is inefficient and, if overlooked, will lead to incorrect pipeline reporting.

Detailed next is the name of the module to which the workflow applies, the outcomes you will achieve, and the suitability of the workflow:

**Module: Quotes**.

**Outcomes**: Multiple actions and a task that will help the sales team follow up and facilitate additional workflows later (based on expiry) while also updating the stage of the associated deal.

**Suitability**: Every business that uses the **Quotes** module.

A summary of the trigger, conditions, and actions is illustrated here, as follows:

**Updates when Quote is created**

**Trigger based on** Record Action
**When** Create or Edit

This rule will be executed for all quotes.

INSTANT **ACTION**

**Field Updates**
Update Deal Stage to Quote Sent
Update Valid Until Date

**Tasks**
Follow-Up Quote

Figure 6.13 – Workflow rule with multiple actions when a Quote is created

In summary, this workflow automates two updates that would otherwise have been manual processes (or possibly overlooked) and also creates an automatic follow-up task for the salesperson to try to close the deal.

# Example 2 – Update Quote when Quote expires

In this example, we resolve a common issue of a quote expiring without a final prompt to our client or an alert to the user, which can lead to a missed sales opportunity.

Detailed next is the name of the module to which the workflow applies, the outcomes you will achieve, and the suitability of the workflow:

**Module: Quotes**.

**Outcomes**: Automatically update Quote to **Expired**, send a final reminder email to the client, and add a task for the salesperson to follow up on.

**Suitability**: Every business that uses the **Quotes** module.

A summary of the trigger, conditions, and actions is illustrated here, as follows:

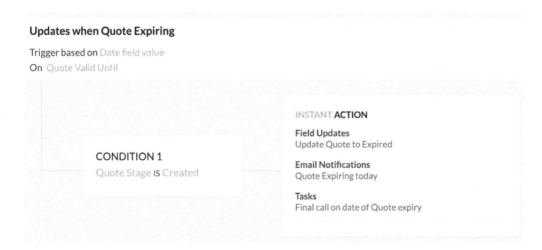

**Updates when Quote Expiring**

Trigger based on Date field value
On  Quote Valid Until

CONDITION 1
Quote Stage IS Created

INSTANT **ACTION**

**Field Updates**
Update Quote to Expired

**Email Notifications**
Quote Expiring today

**Tasks**
Final call on date of Quote expiry

Figure 6.14 – Workflow with multiple actions on date of Quote expiry

This workflow combines a field update, email notification, and task creation all in one, which will help ensure that the sales team is proactively following up quotes and prompting our clients to action.

# Example 3 – Rollover due date of open tasks to today

A common challenge many busy micro-business owners face is not enough time. Some days, despite best efforts, not all the day's tasks get completed, so this workflow was inspired by a Zoho user experiencing this scenario. This workflow literally solved the issue overnight.

Detailed next is the name of the module to which the workflow applies, the outcomes you will achieve, and the suitability of the workflow.

**Module**: Tasks.

**Outcomes**: Automatically updates the due date of the task once it has become overdue. Also marks the task as overdue for reporting, if needed.

**Suitability**: Micro-business owners "spinning a lot of plates".

A summary of the trigger, conditions, and actions is illustrated here, as follows:

**Rolling Task**

Trigger based on Date field value
On  Due Date

CONDITION 1

Due Date IS Till Yesterday
AND Status IS Not Started

INSTANT **ACTION**

**Field Updates**
Update Due Date
Mark as Overdue

Figure 6.15 – Workflow to change due date of open tasks to today

So, this solution is triggered 1 day after the due date, on records that were due yesterday and not completed. Notice that we have added two field updates—one to change the **Due Date** to **Today** and another (optional) to mark as overdue so that we can still report on how many tasks were completed on time or were overdue.

# Example 4 – Various tasks based on the Deal stage being updated

This is an example of workflow with a single trigger—updating the **Stage** field, with multiple conditions, each with its own outcome. This type of workflow will add great value to many stages of the Deal life cycle and help the users become more efficient, and ultimately close more deals.

Detailed next is the name of the module to which the workflow applies, the outcomes you will achieve, and the suitability of the workflow:

**Module**: **Deals**.

**Outcomes**: Multiple actions based on stages being updated by the user.

**Suitability**: All Zoho users.

A summary of the trigger, conditions, and actions is illustrated here, as follows:

**Various tasks based on Stage update**

**Trigger based on** Record Action
**When** Field update

CONDITION 1

Stage IS Discovery

INSTANT **ACTION**

**Tasks**
Schedule Discovery call/meeting

CONDITION 2

Stage IS Quote Sent

INSTANT **ACTION**

**Tasks**
Quote - 2 Day Follow-Up

CONDITION 3

Stage IS Closed Won

INSTANT **ACTION**

**Field Updates**
Update Contact to Client
Update Account Status to Client

**Email Notifications**
New Client Signed Up

**Tasks**
Inform Operations of New Client
Inform Finance of New Client

Figure 6.16 – Multiple conditions and workflows based on Deal stage

In the preceding example, you will notice that there are multiple conditions, each matching a different stage.

As a benchmark, you should be aiming for each stage of your **Deals** module triggering a workflow(s). Use the preceding example directly or tweak it for your business process.

Ask yourself the following questions:

- What needs to happen in order to move this Deal on to the next stage?
- Who needs to action this and when?

Answering these questions will give you the information you need to understand which workflows to create.

While the earlier examples contain instructions to help you get started, there are almost endless possibilities for how a business can benefit from workflow automation. Here are some additional examples of generic workflows that are helping Zoho users around the world gain value from their CRM system every day:

- Sending an email containing a link to a feedback survey—triggered $x$ days after **Closing Date** (or another appropriate date field such as delivery/installation date).
- Creating tasks for the salesperson to give a follow-up courtesy call—triggered $x$ days after **Closing Date**.
- Prompting a user to re-engage with a former prospect—triggered by the **Stage** field being updated to **Lost** with a **Due Date** set to **Closing Date** plus $x$ days.
- Updating the status of a **Lead** record when the **Lead Score** increases beyond a threshold score—triggered based on the score.
- Updating the status of a **Lead** record when the **Lead Score** decreases below a threshold score—triggered based on the score.
- Adding tags to records based on the number of days since the last activity date— used to notify marketing to add to a mailing list (which can also be automated). This will be triggered $x$ days after the **Last Activity Date**.

This list is not exhaustive, and many more examples will be specific to your business. So, it is often beneficial to include other team members in any brainstorming sessions.

> **Tip**
> Aim for around five workflows initially before seeking feedback from users or review yourself how effective these are if you are a single user. Once you have refined these based on feedback and are getting value from them, it's time to brainstorm ideas for the next batch before repeating the *Build > Measure > Evolve* process.

# Summary

In this chapter, you have gained an understanding of the value and importance of workflow automation in Zoho CRM.

You have learned about the different types of triggers and how to add single/multiple conditions. You also have developed your knowledge of the different types of instant and scheduled actions that can be automated.

Most importantly, you realize that the possibilities are endless and probably bound by your imagination only. Successfully adopted workflow automation can in many cases give you a return on your license investment every month, meaning that the software literally pays for itself.

In the next chapter, you will learn about some of the essentials of systems administration.

# 7
# Essential Systems Administration

The setup area of Zoho CRM is the equivalent of the hood of a car. Everything within will help you service and maintain the CRM from the initial build and throughout all the time you and your team use Zoho. Your business will evolve, the software will evolve, and your people will come and go, so your CRM needs to keep up – or better still, be one step ahead!

Using the core elements within the setup correctly will allow you to tweak the system to adapt to such changes, thus protecting your investment and making sure you continue to reap the benefits over time.

In this chapter, we will provide practical scenarios for you to follow or adjust to suit your processes, which will help you to jumpstart your CRM journey with the degrees of security and flexibility that suit your needs.

Topics covered within this chapter include the following:

- General settings
- Users and control
- Channels
- Customization
- Scoring rules

> **Note**
>
> This chapter is *not a complete systems administration guide* – the purpose of this chapter is to highlight the most important areas to help optimize your CRM, keep it tuned, and enable you to take advantage of the features that add the most value.

# General Settings

In this section, you will learn about the best way to get started with **General Settings**.

The instructions in bold provide you with the steps to navigate and, once you're there, you will need to click on the pencil (edit) icon unless otherwise stated. Each of these takes only seconds to complete; however, they go a long way to make sure that parts of the system work properly while ensuring a smoother user experience:

- **Setup | Personal Settings | Locale Information**

  It is essential that you configure all *locale* settings to match the location preferences of each user. The recommended time format is 24 hours as this will simplify date selection in various places – be sure to select the correct time zone and language.

- **Setup | Personal Settings | Signature**

  It is essential that you enter your email signature (or footer) here as it will be added to the bottom of all emails sent from Zoho. This signature may also be added to **Email Notifications**, meaning that it can be dynamically added to automated workflow emails – they will appear to be sent by the record owner or other user as specified.

- **Setup | Company Details | Locale Information**

  You must also make sure that the *locale* is set correctly here to your location. Note also that you do *not* need to set up your home currency (as this will be derived by locale already). Enabling this by setting your **Home Currency** will create two new fields in each module, **Currency** and **Exchange Rate**, which are not needed.

- **Setup | Company Details | Fiscal Year**

  It is desirable to set this up as required as it adds useful filters to some of the reports and the forecasting module.

- **Setup | Company Details | Business Hours**

  It is desirable to set this up as required as it allows workflow automation to consider business days (as well as calendar days).

With this fine-tuning in place, it's time to look at users and access permissions.

# Users and Control

This section will give you an insight into what you need to think about from a security and permissions perspective. The objective should be to provide users access and permissions to the areas they need to effectively perform their role while making sure that overall control and governance of the CRM is maintained by only a small number of **Administrators**.

Let's begin by looking at groups.

## Groups

If you have five or more users then it may be useful to create **groups** of users, such as *Sales* or *Marketing*, as it will speed up the sharing of reports and also provide a shared calendar, both of which may be beneficial.

To create a group, navigate to **Setup | Users and Control | Users | Groups**, then click **New Group**, provide a **Group Name**, and add the users to it.

## Profiles

Unless you are using Zoho as a single user, profiles are among the most important elements to set up before your team starts using the system.

A **profile** controls which modules a user can access and what they can see and do when they are in them. Within Zoho, we have two pre-configured user profiles: **Administrator** and **Standard**. It is important to note that these profiles are not fully customizable, so it is recommended that you clone them and create your own so that you have full control.

Most businesses typically use a three-tier structure, as follows, with a descending order of permissions (most to fewest):

- Administrator (you may use the existing profile for this)
- Manager
- User

In this scenario, it is recommended that you clone the Administrator profile, then remove some permissions to create the Manager profile. The User profile can be cloned from the Standard profile before reviewing and amending the permissions as required.

Let's look at how we might create a *User* profile:

1. Navigate to **Setup | Users and Control | Security Control | Profiles | New Profile**.

2.  Now give your profile a name, such as User, select which profile to clone (**Standard**), and add a description as you wish, as shown in *Figure 7.1*:

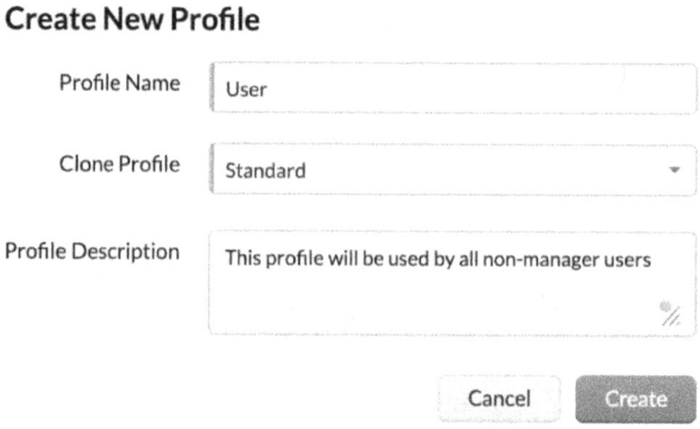

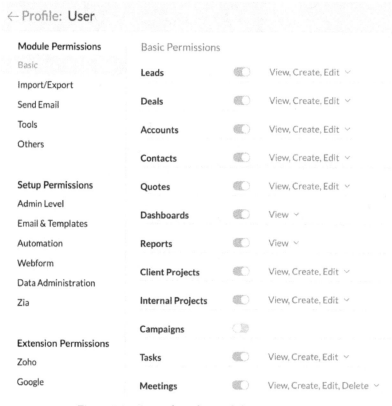

Figure 7.1 – Creating a new profile

3.  Next, you will be presented with the **Module Permissions** screen, as shown in *Figure 7.2*. The layout is in two parts, a menu structure on the left and the editor to the right:

Figure 7.2 – Amending the module permissions

Referring to *Figure 7.2* and using the **Leads** module as an example, we control access to the module by toggling the switch left (off) and right (on). In this example, our user will have access to the **Leads** module. To the right of this, we see the words **View**, **Create**, and **Edit** followed by a drop-down menu. Open this menu to change the permissions; however, for a user, it is recommended that you disable the permission to delete.

The rest of the permissions follow the same process as above using the toggle to enable/disable access to the module (or feature) and the dropdown to further specify from a range of options.

Following the aforementioned process should provide enough information to amend your profiles(s) as required; however, if you require further information on this refer to https://help.zoho.com/portal/en/kb/crm/users-and-control/profile-management/articles/create-profile.

So, now you understand how **Profiles** control which modules and features a user can access and what they can do when they get there. It is time to consider another critical component in setting up permissions – **Roles**.

# Roles

A user's role determines which data (records) they can see in a specific module. The majority of Zoho users wish to share data across teams and users so everybody can see any record at any time, so let's consider that scenario.

In this case, it is recommended that your **Roles** mirror the **Profiles** so that you have consistency and the process of adding/assigning new users is simplified. Therefore, we will have three **Roles**: **Administrator**, **Manager**, and **User**.

Follow these steps to create/amend a **Role**:

1. Navigate to **Setup | Users and Control | Security Control | Roles**.

2. Hover over **Administrator** to reveal the icons:

Figure 7.3 – Add user to a role, add a role, or amend an existing role

3. To create the **Manager** role, click on **+**, enter a **Role Name**, fill in the **Reports To** field, and check the **Share Data with Peers** box, as shown in the following screenshot:

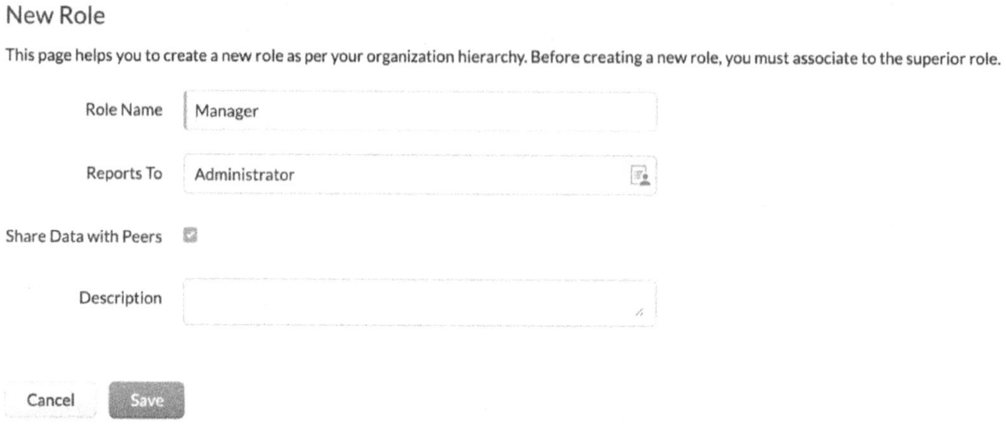

New Role

This page helps you to create a new role as per your organization hierarchy. Before creating a new role, you must associate to the superior role.

| | |
|---|---|
| Role Name | Manager |
| Reports To | Administrator |
| Share Data with Peers | ☑ |
| Description | |

Cancel    Save

Figure 7.4 – Creating a new role

Next, hover over the new **Manager** role, click the **+**, then create a new subordinate role named User.

For further information on creating roles, see https://help.zoho.com/portal/ en/kb/crm/users-and-control/role-management/articles/role- management-introduction#Creating_Roles.

Now that you have created the roles, it is time to align these roles with how we wish data to be shared within **Data Sharing Settings**.

# Data Sharing Settings

In a scenario where we need all users to see all records, then we also need to make the following change:

1. Navigate to **Setup | Users, and Control | Security Control | Data Sharing Settings**.

2. Next, click on the **Edit All Default Permissions** button:

Profiles    Roles    Data Sharing Settings    Zoho Mail Add-on Users

Data Sharing Settings                                                    ? Help

This page helps you to manage the sharing rules for all the modules and also for default Organization share settings. From these rules Zoho CRM will define the level of access to each others data.

**Default Organization Permissions**                    Edit All Default Permissions

Figure 7.5 – Edit all default permissions

3. Once you access this area, you will see three options for each of your modules:

   - **Private**

   - **Public Read Only**

   - **Public Read/Write/Delete**

4. To share access to all records with everyone, select **Public Read/Write/Delete**, as shown in the following screenshot. Note that this option *does not* take precedence over the **Roles**, so if we have disabled the right to delete in the **Role** that will not be overridden here. Think of this as allowing users to view the data for all records:

Profiles    Roles    Data Sharing Settings    Zoho Mail Add-on Users

## Edit Default Organization Permissions

| **Leads:** | ○ Private | ○ Public Read Only | ◉ Public Read/Write/Delete |
|---|---|---|---|
| **Accounts:** | ○ Private | ○ Public Read Only | ◉ Public Read/Write/Delete |
| **Contacts:** | ○ Private | ○ Public Read Only | ◉ Public Read/Write/Delete |
| **Deals:** | ○ Private | ○ Public Read Only | ◉ Public Read/Write/Delete |
| **Campaigns:** | ○ Private | ○ Public Read Only | ◉ Public Read/Write/Delete |
| **Activities:** | ○ Private | ○ Public Read Only | ◉ Public Read/Write/Delete |
| **Products:** | ○ Private | ○ Public Read Only | ◉ Public Read/Write/Delete |

Figure 7.6 – Setting all default organization permissions

Following the steps described will put you in line with how most Zoho users will want to use this. If you have any specific scenarios where records cannot be shared with other users then you should set the module as **Private** and also edit the **Role** to uncheck the **Share Data with Peers** option. For further details on this and other scenarios, refer to https://help.zoho.com/portal/en/kb/crm/users-and-control/role-management/articles/role-management-introduction#Creating_Roles.

Now that we have optimized some of the key internal settings, it's time to look at some of the channels of communication we can integrate our CRM with.

# Channels

In this section, you will gain an overview of the different channels you may wish to integrate your CRM with. Then we focus on the most important channel, **email**, and explain how to integrate the CRM with your emails. This integration will add huge value and improve the CRM user experience significantly.

The key communication channels that we can integrate with Zoho CRM within the setup are as follows:

- Email: You may send emails from Zoho CRM to your **Leads/Contacts**. Once you have enabled the configuration, inbound emails and replies from your customers will also appear in the CRM against the respective record. Refer to the next section for further details on this.

- Telephony: It is becoming increasingly popular to have a **Voice Over Internet Protocol** (**VOIP**) integration with Zoho. This enables inbound and outbound calls to be automatically logged against the contact or lead record. A simple click to dial feature also improves the user experience. Speak to your telephony provider or visit the Zoho Marketplace to peruse the options.

- Social: Useful native integration exists here with Facebook and Twitter. If your brand uses either of these platforms then this integration will help bring all the interaction and engagement inside the CRM. Visit `https://help.zoho.com/portal/en/kb/crm/connect-with-customers/social/articles/social-profiles` for further details on this.

- Chat: This is a great integration with SalesIQ that notifies your CRM users when someone visits your website and provides an easy way to chat with them live – refer to *Chapter 12, SalesIQ*, for information on this extremely powerful tool.

- Signals: This is a useful way of receiving real-time notifications when customers engage with you using one or more methods (Email, Campaign, Survey, Desk, Sign, Call, Social Media, or SalesIQ).

- Portals: This is probably the least used channel. However, it may be useful if you wish to grant restricted access to your CRM to customers, partners, or vendors. For further information, visit `https://help.zoho.com/portal/en/kb/crm/connect-with-customers/portals/articles/setting-up-portal`.

# Email integration

By some distance, the most valuable channel to integrate with, which is seen as mandatory for most CRM users today, is email. Synchronizing your email account with the CRM will allow you to send emails from CRM, and see any responses back into the CRM record. We will also have visibility of which emails were opened, clicked, or bounced. This insight will be invaluable to marketing, sales, and operations teams.

You can access email integration settings here:

**Setup | Channels | Email | Email Configuration**

Now follow the step-by-step instructions here for the service that you use for emails:
`https://help.zoho.com/portal/en/kb/crm/integrations/zoho/zoho-mail/articles/configure-imap-account#Set_up_IMAP_Account`.

Once you have completed this, there is one more essential configuration to complete that will help enable your email deliverability. This will reduce the volume of your emails that will potentially end up in your recipient's junk folder. We can complete this in two steps as follows.

Firstly, we must *validate the domain*. Navigate to **Setup | Channels | Email | Email Deliverability | Email Authentication | Add Domain**.

Now enter your email address and click **Add Domain**. Within a minute or so you will receive a code via email to that address. Click **Enter code** and input the code received.

Once this step is completed, you must proceed to the second step, which is to *validate records*.

When you send emails, the recipient's email client will check what is known as the email header to check, among other things, that the email has been sent from a valid domain. Typically, in the past, this meant many emails sent from a CRM mail server such as Zoho were held in junk folders. However, Zoho has provided a neat solution for this.

Navigate to **Setup | Channels | Email | Email Deliverability | Email Authentication | Validate Records**.

Upon accessing this screen, you will be provided with what is known as **Sender Policy Framework (SPF)** and **Domain Keys Identified Mail (DKIM)** values, which need to be added to your website domain. Normally, this is something that can be completed for you by your IT provider (if outsourced) or your webmaster (the person who looks after the hosting/certification of your website), so simply send the details for them to complete. Once they have completed these changes, then return to this section and click **Validate records** and you will see a success/confirmation message appear.

Next, we will look at another useful feature that many users overlook – adding organization emails.

## Organization emails

Many organizations use a shared inbox within their business, such as `info@` or `enquiries@`. In Zoho, we can set up and validate these email addresses and allow certain profiles to send emails from that mailbox from within the CRM. We may also configure our workflows for automated emails to be sent from these mailboxes. This can be of great benefit; however, please note that email addresses added this way (and not as a user) will not be synchronized within the CRM. To learn more about setting up organization emails, please refer to `https://help.zoho.com/portal/en/kb/crm/connect-with-customers/email/articles/organization-email`.

Having considered the most important channel to integrate with, let's now take a look at some of the key elements within the customization that will potentially provide you the most value, and quickly.

# Customization

While most of the basics have been covered within *Chapter 2, Leads – Getting It Right the First Time*, to *Chapter 4, Accounts and Contacts – The Beating Heart of Your CRM*, to customize modules and fields, there are a few tips and additional areas that are helpful, which will improve your overall experience and success with Zoho CRM.

Firstly, let's look at how we can organize our modules.

## Organizing modules

It is possible to arrange our modules, meaning that we can easily enable or disable and also change the order in which they appear on the main menu. This improves the user experience as we are not being presented with unnecessary modules and can remain focused on what is needed with the menu structured logically. This can be achieved as follows:

1.  Navigate to **Setup > Customization > Modules and Fields**.
2.  Click on the **Organize Module** button located toward the top right, upon which you will be presented with the following popup:

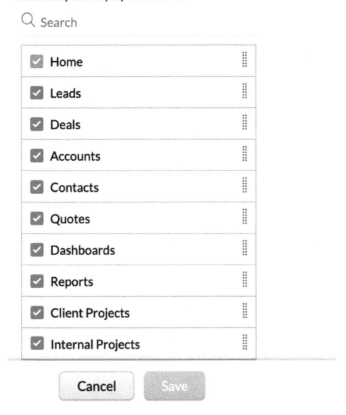

## Organize Modules

You can choose to show or hide modules, or change the order in which they are displayed in the tab.

Figure 7.7 – Enable/disable or reposition modules using this screen

This popup works as follows:

- To enable a module, check the box.

- To disable a module, uncheck the box.

- To reposition where a module appears on the main module, drag, and drop.

# Renaming modules

It is possible to rename all of the non-activity-related modules in Zoho with something that fits your business. Typical examples of this include renaming **Leads** to **Enquires**, **Deals** to **Opportunities**, and **Accounts** to **Organizations**. There are no right or wrong names to give each module; it is simply what matches best to your business process and the terminology you use. Let's go through the process of renaming a module.

Navigate to **Setup** | **Customization** | **Modules** and **Fields**. Hover over the module you wish to rename, then select **Rename** from the menu that appears as shown in the following screenshot:

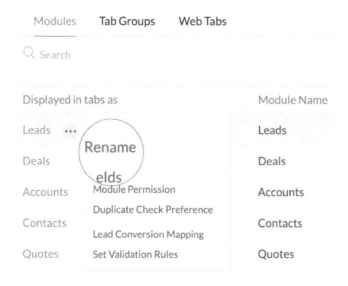

Figure 7.8 – Renaming a module

Note that while this process renames how the modules are displayed to the user, the actual module name within the database does not change. This is important as it ensures that any integration to other applications and services is not disrupted by any cosmetic user changes.

## Pipelines

Another really useful feature for some users is pipelines. This allows us to have multiple sales processes for different products or services. Generally, most businesses do not require this as their main sales process (defined as **Stages** within the **Deals** module) covers everything they provide.

However, where a business does have a second or third sales process to follow, the pipelines feature allows us to accommodate this with minimal effort and minimal disruption to the rest of the setup. Let's illustrate this with an example.

A lighting manufacturer provides bespoke lighting design, manufacturing, and installation services to the private commercial sector. It processes all sales inquiries using Leads, Deals, and Quotes. However, it also submits tenders for local government or public sector contracts. This tender process is different from their commercial sales process and thus the stages previously defined in **Deals** are not valid for this type of deal. The solution is to use pipelines:

1.  Navigate to **Setup | Customization | Pipelines | Create New Pipeline**.

2.  Give your pipeline a name – for example, `Tenders`.

3.  Click on **Stages**, and while you may use any of the existing ones, it is most likely you will need to click on **Create New Stage**:

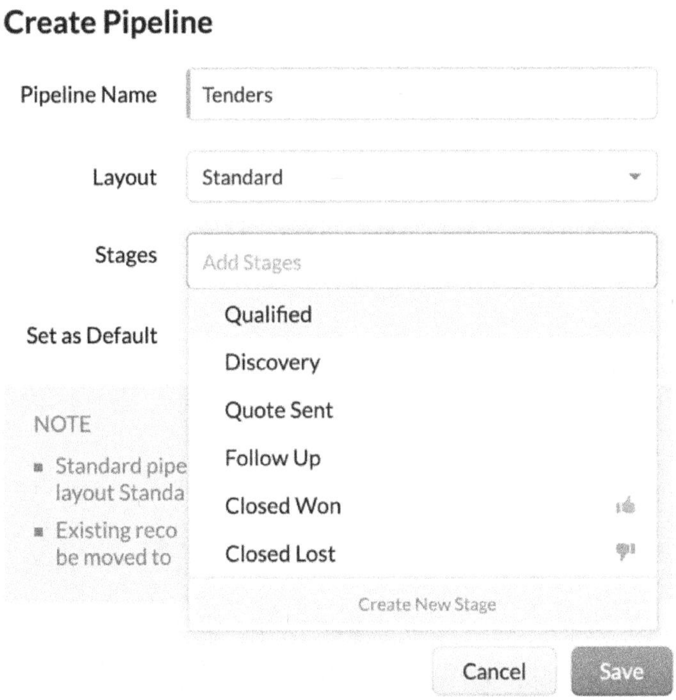

## Create Pipeline

| | |
|---|---|
| Pipeline Name | Tenders |
| Layout | Standard ▾ |
| Stages | Add Stages |

Set as Default

Qualified

Discovery

Quote Sent

Follow Up

Closed Won    👍

Closed Lost    👎

NOTE

■ Standard pipe
layout Standa

■ Existing reco
be moved to

Create New Stage

Cancel    Save

Figure 7.9 – Creating a new pipeline

4.  On the following screen, add a new stage name – for example, **Pre-Qualification Questionnaire (PQQ)**.

5.  Add **Probability**, **Forecast Type**, and **Forecast Category** as required, as shown in the following screenshot:

Figure 7.10 – Adding a new stage to the pipeline

6.  Now repeat *steps 5–7* until all stages have been added, as shown in the following screenshot, then click **Save**:

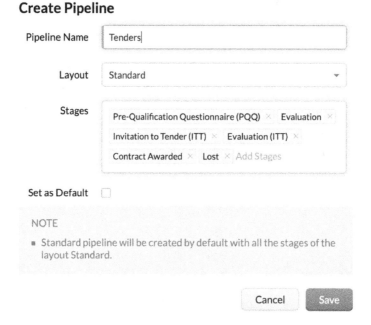

Figure 7.11 – Adding all stages to your new pipeline

7.  On the next screen, you will note that all the new stages have been added to your already existing stages (pipeline) so you will need to hover over each one and click **X** to delete.

8. Once removed, your pipelines will look similar to the following:

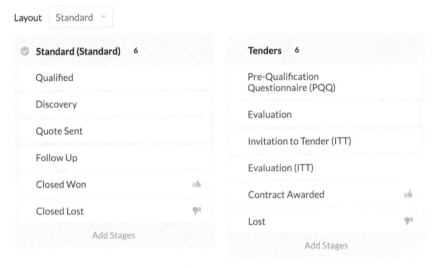

Figure 7.12 – Completed pipelines

Having considered how and when pipelines may add value to your CRM, we shall now look at one of the most important and valuable features to use, templates.

# Templates

Your use of Zoho will never reach its potential unless you are using a few templates within your process(es). There are three types of templates, which we cover in the subsequent sections. You can access these templates by navigating to **Setup | Customization | Templates**.

Let's start by looking at the most widely used type – email templates.

## Email templates

By using email templates, we are saving time and improving the consistency of the content and style of our email communication. It is possible to create email templates in one of three ways:

- Using a blank template (good for messages consisting mostly of text)
- Using a pre-designed template (good if you need a design-based message)
- Using an HTML template (you get the best results, but you do require HTML design skills)

Creating email templates is intuitive. However, the guide provided by Zoho is very easy to follow if you need more information. This may be found at `https://help.zoho.com/portal/en/kb/crm/customize-crm-account/customizing-templates/articles/email-templates#Create_an_Email_Template`.

## Inventory templates

If you are using any of the inventory modules, then you will also need to use an Inventory template. These templates provide a professional-looking document that may be shared via email or PDF with prospects, customers, or suppliers. Using these templates will save a huge amount of time and provide a professional and consistent image for your business. In *Chapter 5, Working with Other System and Custom Modules*, we looked at when and how to create a **Quote** template. The process is identical to the other modules, so refer to the details contained within that chapter.

> **Tip**
> While the existing Inventory templates look good, you cannot fully customize the product table, so if you do need the product table amending in the template then you should create your own, starting from a blank template.

## Mail-merge templates

If you are sending letters, contracts, forms, or producing envelope labels, then using mail-merge templates will also save you time. Any of the data held in the CRM, for example, customer, contact, and transactional information, can be merged into the document template. There are two ways we can produce a mail-merge template, which we will see in the following sections.

## Creating a template from scratch

The following steps will help you to create a template:

1. Go to **Setup | Customization | Templates**.
2. Click on **+ New Template**.

3.   Next, select the **Module**, input a **Template Name**, then click **Create**, as shown in the following example:

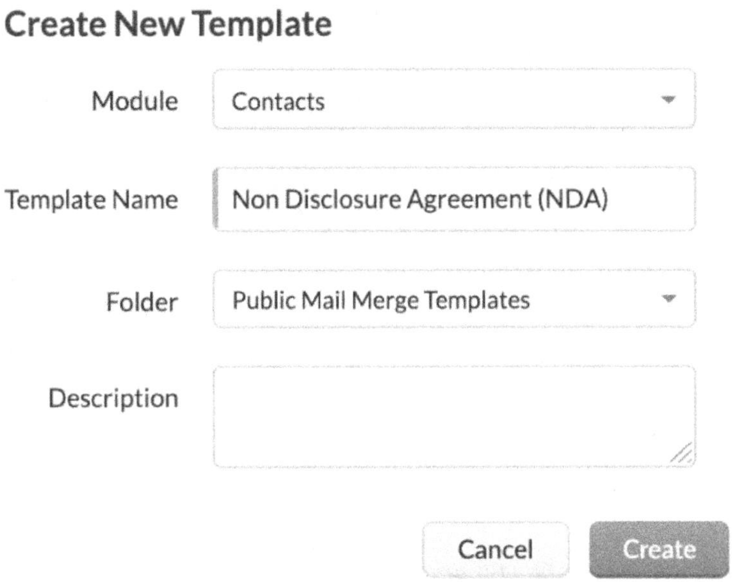

## Create New Template

| | |
|---|---|
| Module | Contacts ▾ |
| Template Name | Non Disclosure Agreement (NDA) |
| Folder | Public Mail Merge Templates ▾ |
| Description | |

Cancel    Create

Figure 7.13 – Creating a mail-merge template from scratch

Now you will have the mail-merge editor open, which is intuitive but may require some reference to the user documentation at some point (`https://help.zoho.com/portal/en/kb/crm/customize-crm-account/customizing-templates/articles/mail-merge-templates#I_Create_Mail_Merge_Template_From_Scratch`).

While creating from scratch is the most effective method when you do not have an existing template, many times you will already have a template document available, usually in Microsoft Word format. If this is the case, then you can use the second method: importing your existing document into Zoho.

## Importing from an existing Microsoft Word document

This is often the quickest method, and it is recommended that you try this first, providing you already have a template to hand:

1.  Go to **Setup | Customization | Templates**.

2.  Click on the **Import Template** icon next to the **New Template** button, as shown in the following screenshot:

Figure 7.14 – Importing an existing Microsoft Word template

3.  Next, select the **Module**, input a **Template Name**, then click **Create**, as shown in the following screenshot:

### Import Template

| | |
|---|---|
| Module | Contacts ▼ |
| Template Name | Non Disclosure Agreement (NDA) |
| Select File | Choose file |

Supported Formats : .zdoc , .doc , .docx    MaxSize : 5MB

| | |
|---|---|
| Folder | Public Mail Merge Templates ▼ |
| Description | |

Cancel    Import

Figure 7.15 – Setting up the import

The document editor will now open, and you should see the document imported ready for you to merge the data fields.

> **Tip**
> While importing templates may sound quick and often is, if the Word document you currently use has complex formatting, including multiple images and tables, then it may not import well and as a result, you may have to resort to creating from scratch.

Creating templates using either method may be a time-consuming task and can sometimes be frustrating; however, do persevere because once you have completed this, you and the team will save much more time in the long run, so it is worth the effort. Now, having considered the key customization that can add the most value, it is time to conclude this chapter by exploring arguably the most valuable yet most overlooked tools available within Zoho CRM, scoring rules.

# Scoring rules

**Scoring rules** help you prioritize leads, contacts, accounts, and deals based on the data you have recorded within the module and the customer touchpoints, such as email, calls, and social media. You can assign both positive and negative scores to each element when defining the rules, and all these points dynamically add up to a score when adding or creating a record. It is highly recommended you try this, especially in **Leads** or **Contacts** if your team will be processing a medium/high volume of leads on a weekly basis.

To understand how this works, let's consider a simple example whereby the Zoho user, a software development company, wants to use scoring rules to help the sales team prioritize which leads are more engaged than others:

1. Navigate to **Setup | Automation | Scoring Rules**.
2. Staying on the **Leads** module, click on **+Add** within the **Lead Field** section.
3. In the following popup, select one or more fields, the score of which we wish to increase/decrease. In this example, our Lead has visited our website more than once:

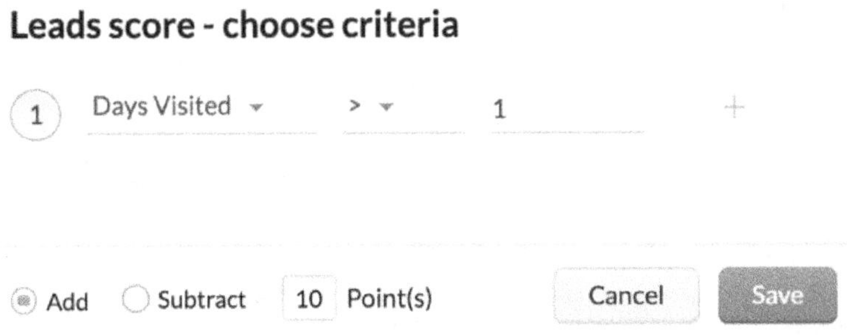

## Leads score - choose criteria

Figure 7.16 – Adding 10 points to the Lead score if the lead has visited the website more than once

4. Use the + if you wish to insert an **AND** or an **OR** condition and choose the number of points you wish to add/remove (with a value between 1–10), then click **Save**.

5. Once you have added this rule, you will see it displayed as follows, and you are ready to add the next one by clicking on +. Each rule name (for example, **Days Visited**) is a link, so if you need to amend it, simply click on the given rule name to amend:

| Lead Fields | Lead Fields | Score |
| --- | --- | --- |
| 1. Days Visited > 1 | 1. Days Visited > 1 | Add 10 Points |
| + Add | + Add | |

Figure 7.17 – View/amend this rule or create another from this screen

6. Repeat *steps 2–4* for any other fields within **Leads** that you desire the values (or lack of) to increase or decrease the lead score. Examples to consider include **Turnover**, **Number of Employees**, **Lead Source**, and **Budget**.

While this is a very handy tool considering the **Leads fields** alone (providing we have the respective integrations enabled), we can also consider the following examples as contributing factors affecting the score:

- Email: Add 5 points for every incoming email received.

- Email Insights: Add 5 points for an email that's opened or clicked on, and subtract 10 if an email to our prospect bounces.

- Survey: Add 5 points for a survey being completed or subtract 5 for a survey being visited and not responded to.

- Email Campaigns: Add 5 points for an open, add 10 for a click, and subtract 10 for a bounce.

- Facebook: It is possible to add between 1–10 points for a Like and/or a Comment.

- Zoho Sign: Add 10 points for a document being signed or deduct 10 points for a document being declined.

Once you have added the rules, your screen will resemble the following:

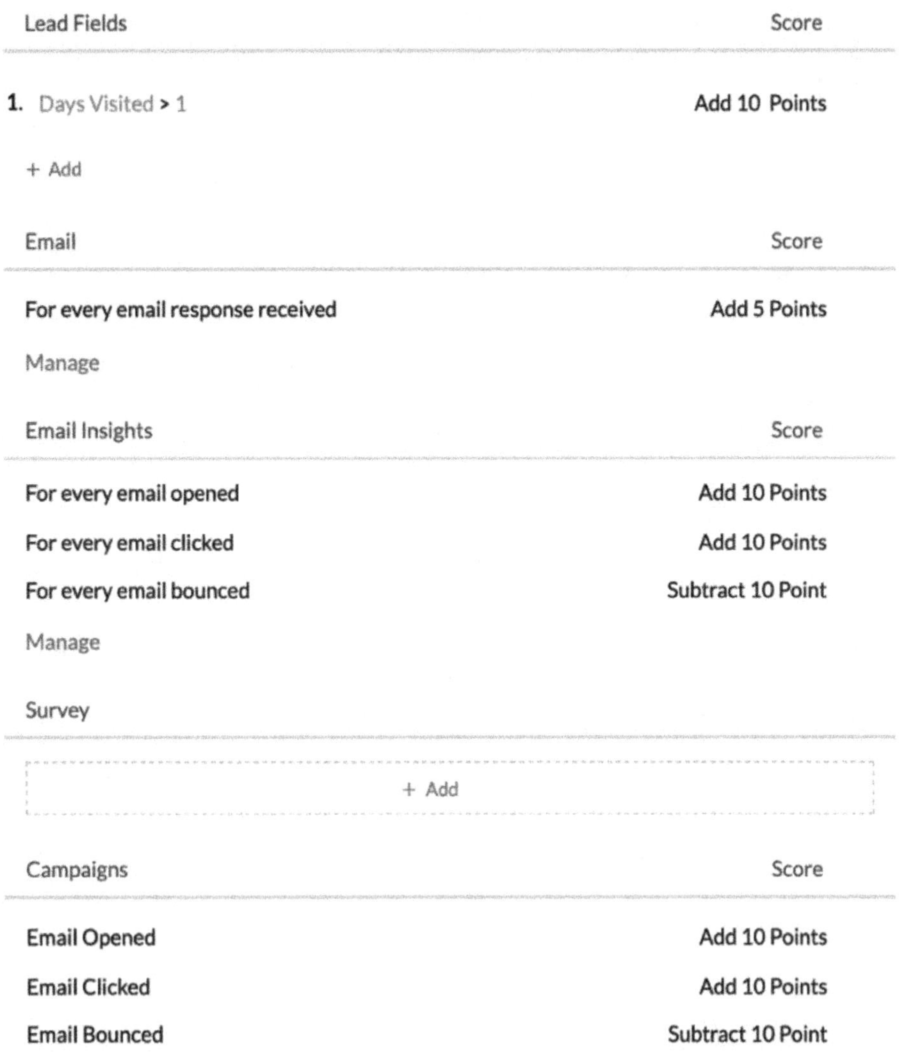

| Lead Fields | Score |
| --- | --- |
| **1.**  Days Visited > 1 | Add 10  Points |

+ Add

| Email | Score |
| --- | --- |
| For every email response received | Add 5 Points |

Manage

| Email Insights | Score |
| --- | --- |
| For every email opened | Add 10 Points |
| For every email clicked | Add 10 Points |
| For every email bounced | Subtract 10 Point |

Manage

Survey

| + Add |
| --- |

| Campaigns | Score |
| --- | --- |
| Email Opened | Add 10 Points |
| Email Clicked | Add 10 Points |
| Email Bounced | Subtract 10 Point |

Figure 7.18 – An example of multiple rules contributing to a Lead Score

Finally, when you are ready to calculate the scores, click on **Run Scoring Rules for All Records** (located at the top of the screen).

The scores will be generated for each lead record when it is created or edited and also, as a bonus, will be calculated for all existing leads created/modified in the last 6 months. The individual lead score will be visible inside each record, and it is a searchable field within **List View** that can be used as filters and/or within a custom view. It can also be used to trigger a workflow that can create a task and/or email notification to Sales.

It is recommended that you experiment with this functionality – there is nothing to lose, and if you wish to amend the rules it will overwrite the scores, so there is nothing that cannot be undone. This functionality can and does help sales teams all over the world prioritize which records to focus on.

This concludes the chapter. So, let's have a quick recap.

# Summary

In this chapter, you have learned how to prepare, optimize, and fine-tune your user profiles and roles so that your users have the right level of access while retaining control and governance of the system. You will appreciate the benefits of integrating email and using organization emails where applicable and know how to improve email deliverability.

You have also learned and gained insight into some of the most valuable features of Zoho CRM, including the customization of modules, pipelines, and templates. You should feel encouraged to try out the scoring rules, especially within **Leads** and **Contacts**.

The skills you have gained in this chapter enable you to be a mechanic for your Zoho CRM. Should any of the key components need tweaking or optimizing, you will know where to go and what to do. This will mean that not only will your CRM help your business today, but you will also able to continue to evolve the solution as your business evolves too.

In the next chapter, we will help you supercharge your CRM even further with custom functions and marketplace extensions.

# 8
# Supercharge CRM with Marketplace Extensions, Custom Functions, and Integrations

Now that you have designed and configured the necessary modules of your CRM, the opportunities to further extend the reach and value of your CRM do not and should not end there. We have countless opportunities to enrich the data, extend the functionality or automate other business processes by integrating with other systems.

In this chapter, we will explore the main ways to achieve this while opening our eyes to what is available. We will learn where and how to access yet more ways to enhance your experience of Zoho and how to increase the benefits it can deliver for our business.

You will learn about the Zoho Marketplace and the multitude of extensions that are available, along with some hand-picked favorites. You will gain insights into the ability to create your own custom functions, with some examples to get you started. Finally, in this chapter, we will discuss other types of third-party integrations you can and should think about and how you may approach them.

Topics covered within this chapter include the following:

- Introducing Zoho Marketplace

- Highlights and valuable extensions from the Marketplace

- Introducing *Deluge* and custom functions

- Custom function examples

- Integrating Zoho with other third-party software

## Introducing Zoho Marketplace

In July 2016, Zoho launched an online store, a place for users to purchase extensions and custom-built applications. Their launch partners included software companies such as DocuSign, Eventbrite, Mailchimp, SurveyMonkey, and Zendesk, among many others. Five years on, there are now over 1,000 applications (or extensions as they are commonly known), most of which are free.

Zoho has developed several extensions that enhance the CRM experience by providing a seamless link between Zoho CRM and some of its other business applications. Extensions provide feature enhancements, integrations with third-party software, and many other solutions for common business needs.

There are two ways to access the Marketplace, either by visiting `https://marketplace.zoho.com/home` or, more conveniently, directly from within your CRM by navigating to **Setup** | **Marketplace** | **All**.

When accessed from within Zoho CRM, you can search by category (from the drop-down list) or by entering some keywords into the **Search apps** bar in the top-right corner. You will have a tab listing the extensions you currently have installed and another tab containing a list of those extensions that have an update available. This page looks like this:

Figure 8.1 – Marketplace home page accessed from within Zoho CRM

Each extension has its own listing page, the layout of which is consistent across all extensions. Upon landing on a page, you will be presented with an overview, which may include a video, screenshots, ratings and reviews, and some information about the vendor. Most of the extensions provide a button in the top right to install the extension; in some cases, there is a link to the vendor's website. An example listing page is as follows:

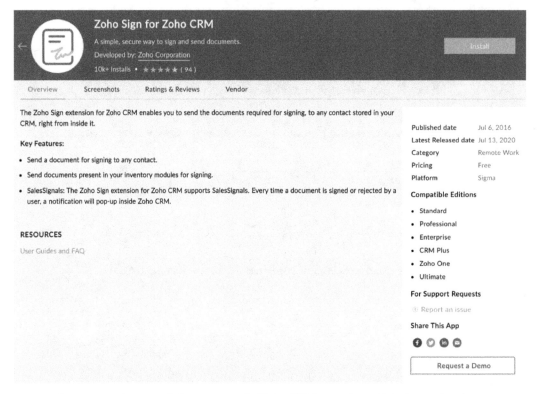

Figure 8.2 – An example listing page of a Zoho CRM extension within the marketplace

Now you understand more about what the Zoho Marketplace is, and why it was created. Use this knowledge of how to navigate to help you understand the extensions, including how to assess what each one does and how it may add value to your CRM. Let's now take a look at some of the popular extensions that will add value to your CRM.

# Highlights and valuable extensions from the marketplace

As mentioned earlier, there are over 1,000 extensions to choose from. In this section, you will find some hand-picked extensions selected for their broad appeal, along with some details of what each one does and how it will benefit you.

# Zoho Sign for Zoho CRM

This extension integrates the Zoho Sign application with your CRM. It allows a user to use any mail-merge or inventory template and send it for an electronic signature from within a CRM record. It also alerts the user within the CRM when a document has been signed/rejected and conveniently attaches the signed document to the CRM record.

This is a great extension that improves the user experience through automating what previously might have been manual tasks while improving the experience of your buyer. How much easier is it for them to sign a document electronically than having to print, sign, scan, and return the signed document by email or post? It saves time and helps close more deals.

# Google Drive

This extension integrates Google Drive with your CRM. The way this works is great – every time you create a **Lead**, **Deal**, **Contact**, or **Account**, the tool creates a folder with a corresponding name in Google Drive with a link to the folder inside the actual CRM record. This saves time by automating what would have been a manual process. The folders and contained documents are accessible from the CRM application, so it means that your team can upload and view any related documents from any device or location.

# Global Email Finder for Zoho CRM

This extension is a great tool for finding and validating lead and contact emails from within your CRM. Having a valid email address is valuable for your marketing, sales, and customer service teams, and it's a really good example of how a marketplace extension can help enrich the data within your CRM.

# Global Address Finder for Zoho CRM

One of the most common issues found in many CRM databases is missing or incorrect address information. This can cause varying degrees of frustration or missed opportunities for marketing, sales, and operational teams. Global Address Finder helps to solve this problem by connecting your CRM to a worldwide database of addresses for over 200 countries. From within a CRM record, the user may start typing the address (or postcode/zip code) and select the desired address from a list, push a button, and have all the address fields in the record updated automatically. This extension is a great time-saver that reduces data entry and validates vital customer data.

## SMS Magic

In addition to telephone and email, many businesses communicate with prospects and clients via SMS (text messages). If these messages are not managed or tracked within the CRM then it may cause issues, as not everybody in the team will be able to see this communication. Bringing this within the CRM solves the issue and also allows the users to trigger SMS messages automatically with workflow automation. This is one of the most popular and widely installed extensions, so if SMS is used by your business it is certainly worth checking this one out.

Each of these example extensions improves user experience by reducing manual processes, reducing data entry, enhancing data, helping to eliminate data entry issues, and making documents easier to store and locate, all of which make it a better CRM for users to work with, with less effort.

If you think any of the aforementioned extensions will be useful, by all means have a look yourself.

However, make sure to also browse the various categories and set a reminder to check every month or so, because many new extensions are added each month.

Now we have considered perhaps the easiest way of adding features to Zoho CRM, it is time now to introduce you to another method of extending the functionality of your system – custom functions using Zoho's very own scripting language, Deluge.

# Introducing Deluge and custom functions

**Data Enriched Language for the Universal Grid Environment** (**Deluge**) is Zoho's scripting language for customizing Zoho CRM and other Zoho software. Deluge lets developers add functionality to the CRM, yet the syntax is easy to read and may be recreated or modified by non-developers. Within Zoho CRM we can utilize Deluge by creating custom functions.

Custom functions are user-built functions that can help us to add new features to Zoho CRM as per our requirements. These are written in Deluge and are easy to construct. The syntax and logic are simple to formulate and aid in the continuous development of the code.

Let's consider some challenges we may face that can be resolved using a custom function:

- Pushing data from parent record to child records

  For example, when a user adds a new contact to an existing account, ABC Foods, we need the **Sector** from the **Account (Food Manufacturing)** to map to the sector of our new contact.

Another common example is needing to pull through the **Payment terms** from the **Account** to the **Quote** and/or **Sales order**.

- Updating the value of a field in a module with the same value as a field in a related module

  For example, when a user creates a **Quote**, we need the **Total amount** of the quote to also update the value of the **Amount** in the related **Deal** record.

- Updating the **Deal name** with the value(s) of another field(s) in the **Deal** record

  This is useful when the structure of a **Deal** record is logical but could be forgotten or mistyped by users. An example is merging (concatenating) the **Account name**, **Site name**, and **Site city** fields to provide a deal name of `Slate Gravel – Deansgate, Manchester`.

- Aggregating the sum of related records from multiple child records to a single account record

  An example of this is rolling up the total amount of all deals won for the account record – sometimes called **Total revenue** or **Lifetime value**.

Once you have considered these challenges, you may notice a pattern. One or more of the fields we need to update is a custom field and, often, the content of this field will need to be passed from a related module. Once you see the actual Deluge script you will see how these patterns are visible within there too. In the *Custom function examples* section, you will find some code that you may copy and paste within your CRM that will help you solve some of these scenarios.

However, while some users may have the aptitude and time to learn how to write in Deluge, it may not suit everyone. So, here is a brief summary of the options available to create custom functions:

- **Learn**: A fantastic interactive resource with a chance to practice is available at `https://deluge.zoho.com/learndeluge#Welcome!`. Zoho also hosts a number of (mostly paid) regular online training courses, which can be found at `https://www.zoho.com/creator/training/online.html`.

  There is also a **Business User Certification program** for those who prefer and value a more formal training path. The details are available here: `https://www.zoho.com/creator/certification.html`.

- **Gallery**: There are about 12 custom functions available within Zoho CRM, which can be accessed and installed by navigating to **Setup | Developer Space | Functions | Gallery.**

- **Community Forum**: Another fantastic resource containing answers to common questions is the Zoho CRM forum. In fact, searching for `Custom Function` returns over 10,000 results. Be sure to only use code added after January 2019 due to a major update to the Deluge language as a result of Zoho updating the API from 1.0 to 2.0.

  The CRM forum can be accessed at `https://help.zoho.com/portal/en/community/zoho-crm/`.

- **Online resource**: Provided by Zoho, a list of 15 functions including code can be accessed at `https://www.zoho.com/crm/help/automation/custom-function-examples.html`.

- **Hire a Partner or Certified Developer**: As great as the aforementioned resources are, many Zoho users are simply too busy to take time out to learn. So, they will hire a partner or developer to write and deploy the functions. A list of certified developers can be viewed at `https://www.zoho.com/creator/developers/find-a-developer.html`.

We have now considered some of the scenarios where a custom function may help solve the challenge and the various ways to approach writing the function. This knowledge will be of benefit because now you know that if the functionality you require does not exist there are ways and means of solving this. It opens up avenues for further customization of Zoho to meet more of your business needs. This will improve the user experience and effectiveness of the CRM even further.

Let's now take a look at a couple of examples that you may try for yourself.

# Custom function examples

In this section, we will work through examples for you to try that will add value to your CRM and also help you understand some of the practical uses of functions. This will help you realize what is possible.

## Example 1 – updating the amount deal record

This is an extremely useful example that updates the amount deal record with the total of the related quote whenever a quote is created or edited. Here are the details that you need to consider:

- **Function Type**: Function

- **Function Description**: Updates the deal amount with the total of any related quote. This will work only when a user has associated a Deal record to a quote (by updating the Deal lookup field in the Quote record).

Now, let's see how to get it to work:

1.  Click **Setup | Automations | Actions | Functions | Configure Function**.

2.  Select **Write your own**, then complete the pop-up box that appears as follows:

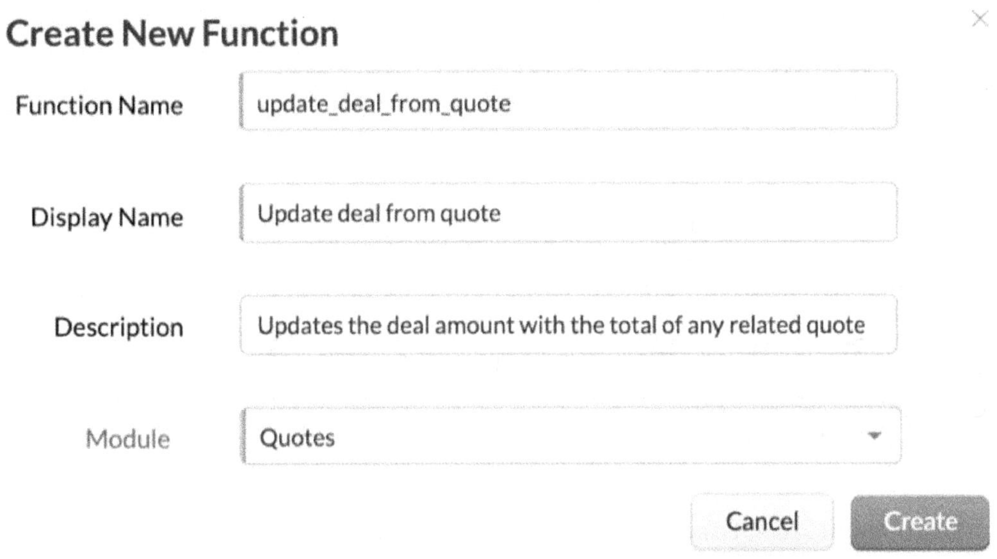

## Create New Function    ×

| Function Name | update_deal_from_quote |
|---|---|
| Display Name | Update deal from quote |
| Description | Updates the deal amount with the total of any related quote |
| Module | Quotes ▾ |

Cancel    Create

Figure 8.3 – Creating a custom function

3.  Copy and paste this code into the white space on the screen that appears upon completing the previous step:

```
DealsIDString = DealsID.toString();
DealsMap = Map:String();
DealsMap.put("Amount",QuoteAmount);
updateResp = zoho.crm.
updateRecord("Deals",DealsIDString,DealsMap);
info updateResp;
```

4. Click **Edit arguments** and input `QuoteAmount` into the first box, followed by # in the next box, to bring up the **Add Merge Field** popup, as shown here:

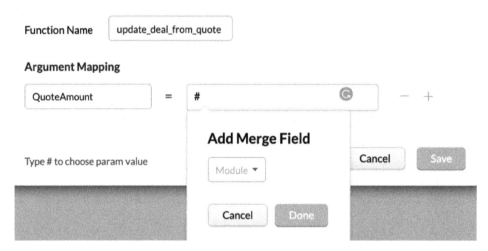

Figure 8.4 – Adding the first key (variable) to the argument

5. Select **Quotes** then **Grand Total** from the next screen that appears, as shown next:

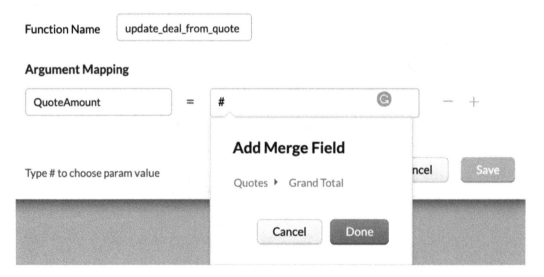

Figure 8.5 – Assigning the value we wish to assign to the first variable

6.  Click on + to add the second key named `DealsID`, then #, followed by **Deals |
    Deal Id** as follows:

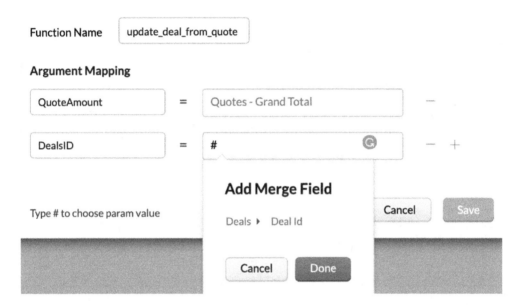

Figure 8.6 – Assigning the second key and value to our function

7.  Click **Save** followed by **Save** on the screen containing the code when it appears.

8.  Now we need to trigger our function either in an existing workflow or create a new
    one. So, navigate to **Setup | Automation | Workflow Rules | Create Rule**.

9.  Complete the pop-up window as follows:

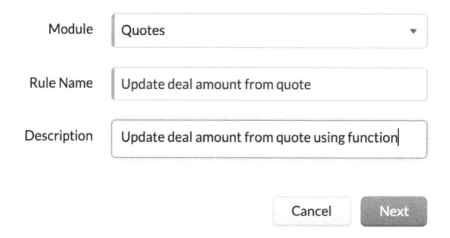

## Create New Rule

Module — Quotes

Rule Name — Update deal amount from quote

Description — Update deal amount from quote using function

Cancel    Next

Figure 8.7 – Creating a new rule to trigger the function

10. Define the trigger as follows, then click **Next**:

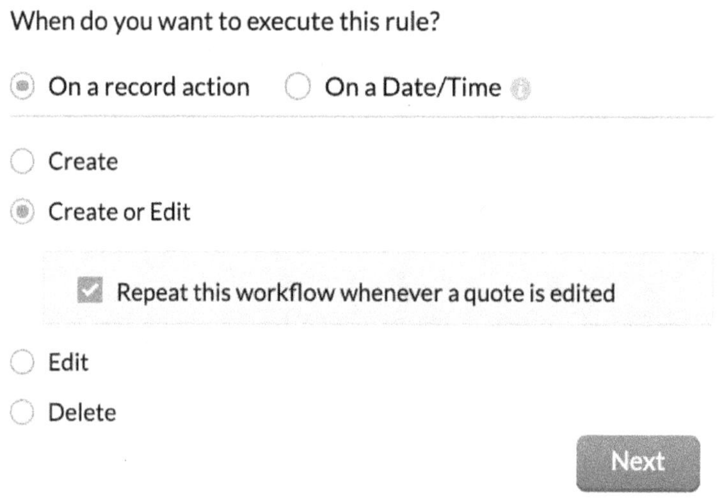

When do you want to execute this rule?

◉ On a record action     ○ On a Date/Time

○ Create

◉ Create or Edit

   ☑ Repeat this workflow whenever a quote is edited

○ Edit

○ Delete

Next

Figure 8.8 – Setting the trigger for the function

11. Select **All Quotes**, then **Next**.

12. Click **Instant Actions | Function**.

13. Select your function, click **Associate**, then click **Save**.

Congratulations, you have successfully created a custom function – well done! Your pipeline reports will be more accurate, or you have saved a user what would have been a manual update – either way, we've improved the user experience and effectiveness of this part of the CRM.

> **Tip**
> If at first the function does not update the deal amount as expected, then double-check all the code and parameter names, as they are all case and space sensitive.

Next, let's consider another common and valuable example.

## Example 2 – automating field values of a new contact

The scenario is that when a user adds an additional contact onto the CRM related to an existing account, we need the new contact to inherit one or more values of the account in the contact record. For example, the sector of the account is manufacturing, so we also need the sector of any related contacts to inherit this sector. This is important for two reasons. Firstly, we need to be able to segment and market to the contacts based on the sector – for example, a marketing communication to prospects in one sector may be different to a communication we send to prospects in another sector. The other reason this function is important is because it automates a manual process and eliminates the chance of human error.

Here are the details that you need to consider:

- **Function Type**: Function
- **Function Description**: Passes the value(s) of a field in the parent (account) record to any child (contact)

Let's try this function now and see how to get it to work:

1. Click **Setup | Automations | Actions | Functions | Configure Function**.

2.   Select **Write your own**, then complete the pop-up box that appears, as follows:

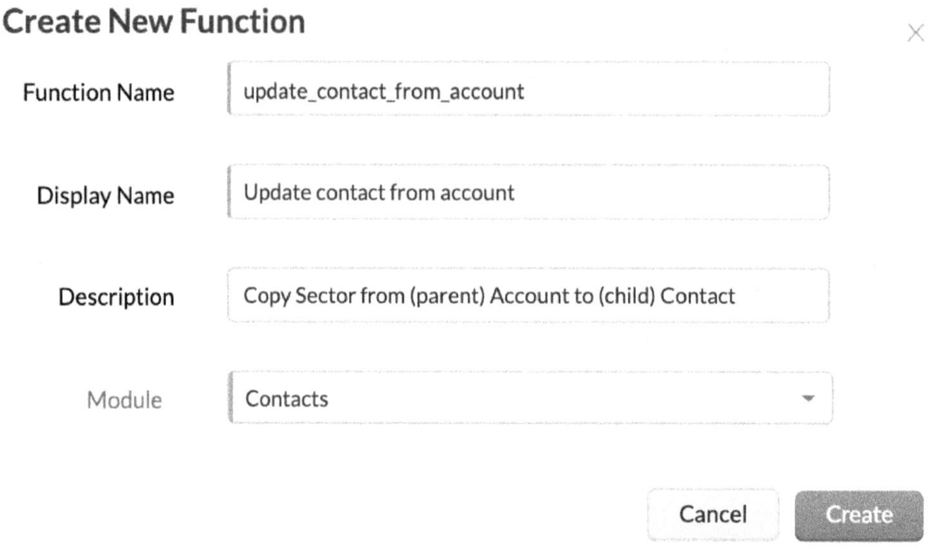

## Create New Function                                              ✕

Function Name
> update_contact_from_account

Display Name
> Update contact from account

Description
> Copy Sector from (parent) Account to (child) Contact

Module
> Contacts                                               ▾

Cancel      Create

Figure 8.9 – Create New Function

3.   Copy and paste this code into the white space on the screen that appears upon completion of the previous step:

```
Resp = zoho.crm.getRecordById("Contacts",ID.toString());
AccountMap = Resp.get("Account_Name");
if(AccountMap is not null)
{
    AccountID = AccountMap.get("id");
    AccountResp = zoho.crm.
getRecordById("Accounts",AccountID);
    ContactsMap = Map();
    ContactsMap.put("Sector",AccountResp.get("Sector"));
    info ContactsMap;
    UpdateResp = zoho.crm.updateRecord("Contacts",ID.
toString(),ContactsMap);
    info UpdateResp;
}
```

4.  Click **Edit arguments** and then add the argument, as follows:

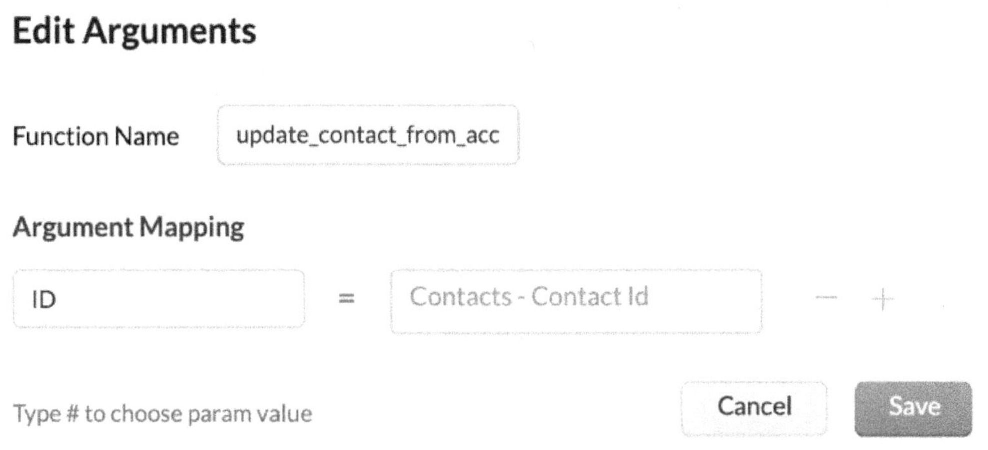

## Edit Arguments

Function Name        update_contact_from_acc

### Argument Mapping

ID        =        Contacts - Contact Id        —    +

Type # to choose param value                    Cancel        Save

Figure 8.10 – Adding the Contact Id argument

5.  Click **Save**, followed by **Save** on the screen containing the code when it appears, as follows:

Figure 8.11 – The completed function, including arguments

6.  Now we need to trigger our function either in an existing workflow or create a new one, so navigate to **Setup | Automation | Workflow Rules | Create Rule**.

7.  You will see a pop-up window. Complete it as follows:

**Create New Rule**

| | |
|---|---|
| Module | Contacts ▾ |
| Rule Name | Update sector from Account |
| Description | Copy sector from Account to Child |

Cancel    Next

Figure 8.12 – Creating a new rule in the Contacts module to trigger the function

8.  Set up the workflow with the following details:

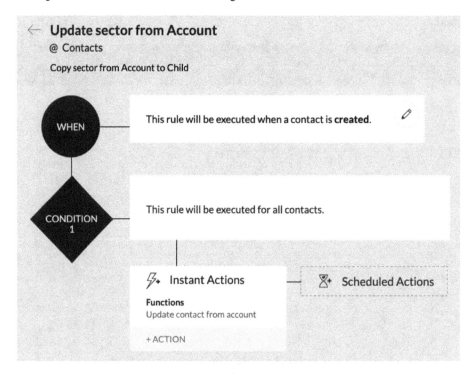

Figure 8.13 – Complete workflow rule to trigger this function

9.  Click **Save**.

Congratulations, you have now completed another function. With this script, we are pulling data from a parent record (**Account**) and pushing it into a child record (**Contact**) when it is created. You are taking the customization of Zoho to the next level.

The code used in this example may be amended by adding additional fields in *step 3* if needed, or you may also adapt this code to work on different modules by amending the arguments (in *step 4*) and field names (in *step 3*) as required.

By completing this function, you should now understand that as long as a relationship exists between two modules (one is a look-up of another), we may pass any value from one record in a related module to another. This is really useful for customer segmentation, reporting, and workflow automation. It also means that when creating records in related modules (including custom modules) and passing values this way, we are reducing data entry and eliminating the chance of errors. Overall, by adding this type of function we are improving the user experience and increasing the quality and integrity of our database.

Having considered the value of custom functions and the different ways to acquire them, let's now look at another way of supercharging your CRM – integrating with other third-party software.

# Integrating Zoho CRM with other third-party software

In this section, we will consider some of the types of software we can integrate with and get you started on how you can achieve this.

Before we begin integrating the software, it is necessary to understand why we should consider integrating Zoho with other business applications.

## Reasons to integrate with a third-party application

The most common reason(s) for integrating with third-party software is to further automate business processes, thus avoiding duplicate data entry and reducing human error. In an ideal world, we may have all of our processes managed within a single application, and in certain industries, industry-specific software can and does manage this. However, historically these systems were expensive and not cost-effective as a small business may have needed only 20% of the capability but would have to pay 100% of the price.

While Zoho has a peerless ecosystem that does allow businesses to manage the entire business from a single platform, the reality is that many Zoho users still have another business application in place.

Let's consider some examples of departments within your business that may benefit from integrating software with Zoho CRM:

- **Marketing**: Many Zoho users have to integrate a third-party email campaign application to push leads into Zoho CRM.

- **Operations**: This department may benefit from being notified when a new deal has been closed and/or a new job or project is initiated in another application so that they can start planning and scheduling the delivery of the goods or services purchased.

- **Finance**: This department will benefit from an invoice being automatically created in the accountancy software application when a deal has been closed.

- **Sales /Account Managers**: This department will benefit from having visibility in the CRM if there are invoices outstanding.

In each of these examples, we have a customer at a particular point in a customer journey and a business process to complete. The aim is to effectively manage these processes from end to end with everyone having visibility of where each customer is up to. If it's not possible to achieve all in one system, by using integration we automate the process of moving on to the next stage and eliminate the need for data entry in both systems.

> **Tip**
> List the other business applications (software) in use within your organization and identify which ones may add value by being integrated with the CRM, along with the reasons why.

In addition to automating business processes, the other reason you may need to integrate with a third-party application is to extend the functionality of your CRM. Some of the most common features that are not available within Zoho CRM can be easily integrated, including the following:

- **SMS**: Mostly for appointment confirmation/reminder

- **Telephony**: Used to make and log calls easily from within Zoho CRM

- **Electronic signature**: Used to capture customer signatures electronically

- **Document Templates**: Used to present information and/or obtain signatures

This is by no means an exhaustive list. The best way to consider the possibilities is to ascertain if your third-party application has been developed or updated within the last 5-10 years. If so, and if the application is fully accessible from any device anywhere, then it is likely that integration is achievable in one of the ways discussed in the next section.

# How we can achieve integration

There are four main ways by which we may integrate our CRM with third-party software. Here, they are prioritized by ease of implementation and cost. The easiest and cheapest method is at the top and the most difficult and more expensive is at the bottom:

- **Zoho CRM Marketplace**

  As described earlier in this chapter, the Marketplace is a treasure trove of readily available integration. Check this option before any of the others. In some cases, integration can be achieved within minutes.

- **Third-party software vendor integration**

  If there is nothing within the Marketplace, then check your vendor's website for details of Zoho CRM integration. Even if it is not listed, it is worth checking with their sales or support teams because this is often the best option available to you.

- **Configuring a plugin or connector**

  If there is nothing readily available, quite often the vendor will refer you to a plugin or connector. This is where another third-party software company (or integration specialist) has created an integration between the two systems already, which is available for you to use – normally for a monthly or annual fee. Sometimes such an integration can meet your needs, but you should check the features meet your requirements. If you are unsure that all your needs are met, ask the vendor if customization is available and at what cost. For a small business that wants to keep the costs as low as possible, this is often quite a good option.

  Popular worldwide connector tools include Zoho Flow, Zapier, and Kloud Connectors. Search the internet to find vendors that provide the integration you are seeking. An example search could be something like `Integrate Zoho CRM with <insert name of third-party application>`. Often, you will find multiple links, so be sure to read the reviews.

- **Develop your own (using the Zoho API)**

  If the other options don't provide a solution or you have a bespoke requirement, then this option should provide the flexibility you need. As this option requires a developer resource, it may often be the costliest solution, but not always, so do check if possible.

By now, you should be able to understand the reasons why we should integrate Zoho with third-party applications and also what options we have available to achieve this. This is important for you and your team. Not having to enter the same data into two systems is an achievable objective, and having data from one system update the value or status of another improves the user experience and effectiveness of the systems.

It's now time for a chapter recap!

## Summary

In this chapter, you have learned some of the key ways to enhance, extend, and improve your CRM through the integration of third-party applications or by bespoke customization.

You have gained insights into how the Marketplace can be used and why this dynamic online store is somewhere you should visit regularly to identify new ways of adding value to your CRM and your business. You have gained an understanding of the alternative integration options if the Marketplace does not have what you are looking for. You have also been introduced to Deluge and learned some of the practical ways that custom functions can be used to tailor the CRM to meet your requirements.

With all this knowledge, you should understand that your Zoho CRM is not just a CRM system that will support your business today; it is a platform from which you can evolve, develop, and grow your future business.

In the next chapter, we commence *Section 3*, *Six of the Best Zoho Apps to Integrate with Your CRM*, of the book by taking a look at Zoho Campaigns. It is one of six great Zoho applications you need to integrate with.

# Section 3: Six of the Best Zoho Apps to Integrate with Your CRM

In this section, you will gain an insight into the many benefits of integrating your Zoho CRM with some of the other great business applications developed by Zoho.

Done well, these integrations will further streamline and automate your business processes. Learn from real-life use cases that will inspire you and your team to extend your Zoho adoption into areas of the business you had never considered nor thought possible:

This section comprises the following chapters:

- *Chapter 9, Zoho Campaigns*
- *Chapter 10, Zoho Forms*
- *Chapter 11, Zoho Survey*
- *Chapter 12, SalesIQ*
- *Chapter 13, Zoho Analytics*
- *Chapter 14, Zoho Creator*

# 9
# Zoho Campaigns

**Zoho Campaigns** is an enterprise-level email marketing platform, comparable in functionality to most other software in this sector. If you have Zoho CRM and do not use this application, you could be missing a trick due to its powerful two-way integration with Zoho CRM.

In this chapter, you will gain an understanding of the key functionality of Zoho Campaigns. You will learn about one of the fundamentals missed by a lot of users – how to automatically connect Zoho CRM to Campaigns and keep your mailing lists constantly up to date. You will get an understanding of how to create a basic email campaign before finishing off with many a marketeer's dream – how to create email workflows and automate your marketing.

The topics covered in this chapter include the following:

- Getting an overview of Zoho Campaigns
- How to synchronize mailing lists with Zoho CRM
- Getting started with one-off campaigns
- Using workflows to automate your email marketing

By the end of this chapter, you will have discovered the key steps required to make sure you are effectively getting the right messages to the right people at the right time.

# Getting an overview of Zoho Campaigns

Zoho Campaigns is an email marketing platform that has similar functionality to other software in this category. However, the ability to have two-way synchronization with your CRM gives you a level of flexibility and control that would be practically impossible to replicate with another email platform.

It is important to note that Zoho Campaigns has more to offer than just email marketing and includes other valuable features, which can be summarized as follows:

- **Sign-Up Forms**

  There are many pre-designed and responsive email sign-up templates to choose from. The form editor allows you to change colors and background images easily. You may also easily edit the call to action, fields, and text to customize the forms to meet your needs. Further information is available at `https://www.zoho.com/campaigns/help/user-manual/signup-forms.html`.

- **Pop-Up Forms**

  If you need a pop-up form on your website, then there are templates that are almost ready to go that you can tweak and then deploy quickly and easily as you attempt to convert website visitors into leads.

- **Social Media Forms**

  You can create and embed sign-up forms directly in your **Facebook** page. It is also possible to share sign-up forms as links on other social media channels. Further information on this can be found at `https://www.zoho.com/campaigns/help/user-manual/social-campaigns.html`.

- **Mailing List Management**

  Within Campaigns, you can create unlimited mailing lists that can be populated from numerous sources, including sign-up forms, pop-up forms, social media links, data import, and of course the CRM itself.

However, it is the ability to create professional, mobile-responsive mail and automated workflows that is most valuable, and we will explore all that in detail later in this chapter.

Before we start creating campaigns, we must first consider how to synchronize our mailing lists with Zoho CRM.

# How to synchronize mailing lists with Zoho CRM

Setting up a two-way synchronization between Zoho CRM and Campaigns is such a critical and valuable step that you must complete this before you do anything else. Arguably, it is the best feature we have within Campaigns and the main reason we must try Campaigns ahead of any third-party email marketing software.

Let's consider a scenario whereby we have had an inquiry from Bob Brown at ABC Foods, which is a manufacturing business that has been added as a lead in Zoho CRM. Our user (a member of the sales team) will follow up this lead, but we also want to add the prospect to a mailing list specifically for leads within the manufacturing sector so that we can send them an email or potentially a series of nurturing emails.

The steps to synchronize this lead between Zoho CRM and Campaigns is as follows:

1.  Create a custom view in Zoho CRM with a suitable name – such as `Nurture – Manufacturing`.

    For information on custom views, visit this page: `https://help.zoho.com/portal/en/kb/crm/customize-crm-account/managing-module-views/articles/list-view`.

2.  Open Campaigns at `campaigns.zoho.com`. Then, from the menu on the left side of the screen, navigate to **Contacts | Manage Lists** as shown here:

Figure 9.1 – Accessing your mailing lists in Campaigns

3.  Click on the red **Create List** button, which is toward the top right-hand corner.

4.  Now complete the pop-up box that appears as shown in the following figure:

Figure 9.2 – Creating a new mailing list

5.  You will now be asked how you wish to get contacts into your list – select **Sync Contacts** from **Zoho CRM** as shown in the following screenshot:

Figure 9.3 – Creating a new sync with Zoho CRM

> **Note**
>
> Note that depending on which edition of Zoho you subscribe to, you may need to associate your CRM account at this step – simply follow the onscreen prompts

6. You will now have a choice between **Periodic sync** and **Immediate sync**. Most of the time, **Periodic sync** (daily or weekly) will suffice. However, it is recommended to select **Immediate sync** as it gives you the option at a later date to send the first email in a series immediately (within 5-10 minutes of the record being created in Zoho CRM).

> **Note**
>
> Note that **Immediate Sync** is not available if you are using the **Free** edition of Campaigns.

7. Once you have selected the type of sync (**Period/Immediate**), you must select which module of Zoho CRM you wish to sync with, from a choice of **Leads**, **Contacts**, and **Custom Module**, as shown next:

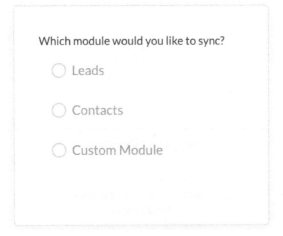

Figure 9.4 – Selecting which CRM module to sync with

8. In this example, we will select **Leads**, upon which we are presented with a further screen, which should be completed as shown in *Figure 9.5* – using the following guidance notes:

   - It is good practice to name the sync the same as your custom view as it will be easier to associate in the future.

- In our example, we have selected an individual custom view. However, it is possible to create a mailing list for **All Leads** (or **Contacts**). If you are likely to segment your **Leads** or **Contacts** and send different messages to different segments, then a custom view is going to be the most effective route.

- Following on from the aforementioned points, it is still possible to send campaign emails to more than one mailing list at a time (for example, a newsletter).

- **Consent status**, **Exclude email otp-out**, and **Exclude converted leads** all have a tooltip (a small *i*) that will explain what is meant by each. The defaults selected for you (as shown here) are generally what most users will keep, but do read the tooltips if you are unsure:

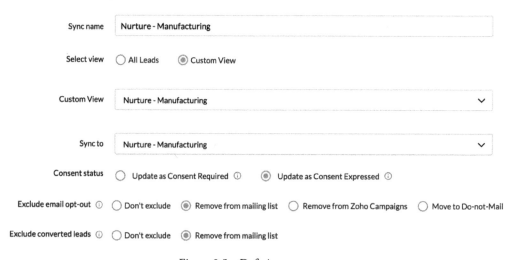

Figure 9.5 – Defining your sync

9.  Click **Next** and then **Go Ahead**.

10. You will now be presented with a mapping screen, on which you will probably wish to fill in **First Name** so that you can address the email recipient by their first name in the email. If so, click **Map more fields**.

11. Select **First Name** from each of the dropdowns provided, then click **Add**, and then **Initiate**, as shown here:

Figure 9.6 – Mapping your fields between Zoho CRM and Campaigns

12. The sync will start and may take several minutes, at the end of which you should receive an email notification. You may also refresh your browser to indicate the status after a couple of minutes, and once completed, you will see the following section within the screen:

Figure 9.7 – The sync contact status summary

The following guidance notes may prove useful to help understand some of the terminology:

- You will see the status of the sync become **Completed** once it has run successfully.

- In **Campaigns**, all email addresses are defined as **Contacts**.

- Note the different statuses of the records that you have attempted to sync.

- It is possible to have up to 50 syncs per month – or in other words, up to 50 different mailing lists, which should be more than enough for most business needs.

Once you have completed the first sync between Zoho CRM and Campaigns, you have made a key step toward an efficient marketing platform that will always have up-to-date mailing lists. Consider the following example scenarios to understand how we may create and use different mailing lists:

- As new leads are added to Zoho CRM, they will be added to Campaigns.

- As leads are converted in Zoho CRM, they may be added to a different mailing list by creating a new custom view in Zoho CRM.

- As prospects purchase from us, we can add them to a different mailing list (customers) automatically.

- Customers who have not purchased from us in the last *x* days can be added to a mailing list.

The possibilities are numerous. It is important to know that by using a combination of automated *workflows + custom views + Campaign Sync,* all of these updates to mailing lists can and should be automated. This will have a significant positive impact on your marketing team and efforts.

With the mailing list and sync now set up, you are ready to create your first campaign.

# Getting started with one-off campaigns

In this section, you will learn how to create what Zoho refers to as a **Regular Campaign**. At the end of this section, you will know the basic controls and functions well enough to send an email to one of your mailing lists.

We may begin this process as follows:

1. From the main menu in **Campaigns**, click **Campaigns |Regular Campaign | Create Campaign**.

2. You will now be presented with the following screen that contains a sequence of steps that need to be carried out to create your campaign email:

Untitled Campaign

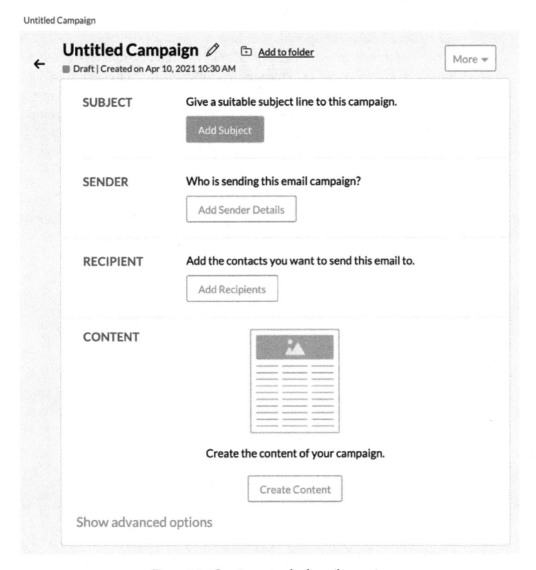

Figure 9.8 – Creating a standard email campaign

3.  Click on the edit icon (the pencil) next to **Untitled Campaign** at the top of this screen.

4.  Now give your campaign a suitable name – which is for internal use only and will not be seen by our contacts (prospects). If we have a simple yet structured and logical way of naming our campaigns, mailing lists, syncs, and custom views (in Zoho CRM), then it is much easier to manage. So, following on from the earlier example in the chapter, we will create an email that will be sent to our contacts in our **Nurture – Manufacturing** mailing list, which in turn was pulling newly created leads from the manufacturing sector. So, therefore, `Nurture - Manufacturing` would be an appropriate name for our campaign, as it both describes the purpose of our email and also contains information about our recipients (manufacturing).

5.  Next, click on **Add Subject** to reveal the following pop-up screen:

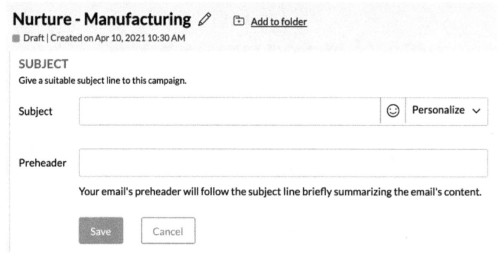

Figure 9.9 – Adding a subject and pre-header

6.  **Subject** and **Preheader** are what your recipient will see when they receive your email. There is lots of content online about how to create these; it is fair to say that whatever you enter here will have a huge bearing on your open rates, so it is worthwhile reading up on this. As with anything, a lot will be down to trial and error – experiment with different options. If email campaigns are an important part of your customer acquisition and retention strategies, then it is recommended to use a copywriter as they should have the skills and experience already.

7.  Once you have set **Subject** and **Preheader**, click **Save.**

8.  Click on the **Add Sender** details, where you are presented with a choice of using the same sender for all or using a CRM owner address. There is no right or wrong selection here; it is all about what is best within the context of the message you are sending and where the customer is in the life cycle.

If you choose the same sender for all, you can pick any of the campaign user emails or any other email account you own – again, whatever feels right for that specific email.

You also have the choice to specify a different reply-to address, which is not a widely used option. These options are as follows:

**SENDER**

Who is sending this email campaign?

Personalize Sender Details    ◉ Same sender for all    ○ CRM owner address

Sender address will be same for all the recipients.

Sender Details    | Sender Name |    | hello@cloud-sauce.com  ∨ |  ↻

**Show reply-to address details**

[ Save ]    [ Cancel ]

Figure 9.10 – Specifying who the sender of the email is

9.  Next, click **Add Recipients,** then select the mailing list(s) you wish to send the email to. In this case, we will select the **Nurture – Manufacturing** mailing list.

10. Now click on the **Create Content** button.

11. You will now be presented with the following templates to choose from:

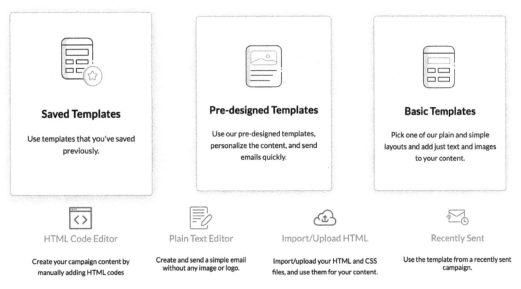

**Saved Templates**

Use templates that you've saved previously.

**Pre-designed Templates**

Use our pre-designed templates, personalize the content, and send emails quickly.

**Basic Templates**

Pick one of our plain and simple layouts and add just text and images to your content.

HTML Code Editor

Create your campaign content by manually adding HTML codes

Plain Text Editor

Create and send a simple email without any image or logo.

Import/Upload HTML

Import/upload your HTML and CSS files, and use them for your content.

Recently Sent

Use the template from a recently sent campaign.

Figure 9.11 – Selecting an email template

To start with, most new users will use **Pre-designed** or **Basic Templates**. In this example, we will look at **Basic Templates | Blank Template**, which, when opened, will provide a screen split into two sections, as shown here:

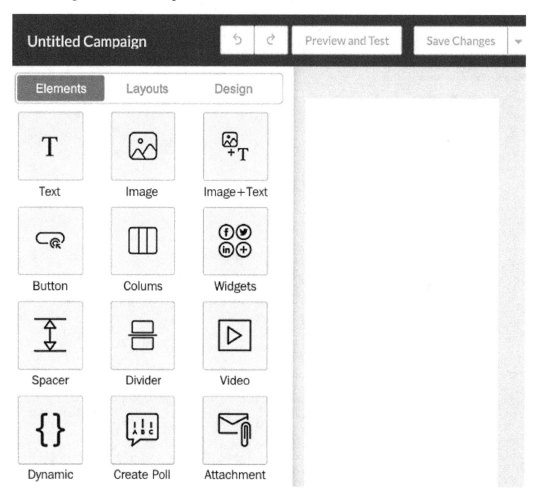

Figure 9.12 – A blank email template

12. To create your email, simply drag and drop your component(s) from left to right. The most commonly used components are text, image, and button (for any call to action). An example of a draft email using this template can be seen here:

**7 Energy saving tips every manufacturer needs to know in 2021**

1. Tip number one
2. Tip number two
3. Tip number three
4. Tip number four
5. Tip number five
6. Tip number six
7. Tip number seven

Find out more

Figure 9.13 – Example email content with three basic components – image, text, and button

13. Once you have saved your template, you will be returned to the **Campaign setup** screen as shown in the following figure. This screen summarizes everything you have set up so far. Upon review, if you wish to make any changes, you can use the edit buttons on the right-hand side for each element:

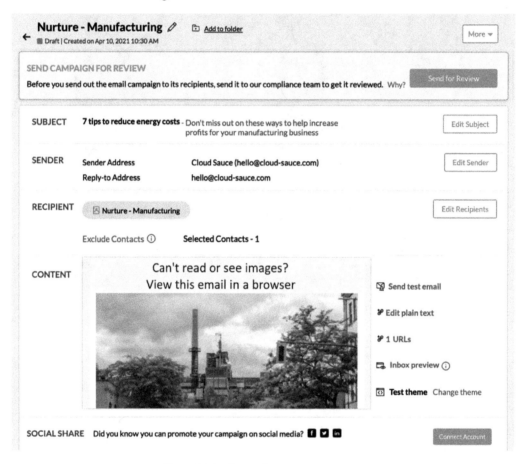

Figure 9.14 – Campaign summary screen

14. It is important to send test messages to yourself and possibly a colleague for peer review – which can be done within the content edit screen by clicking on **Send test email**. Open the messages on a mobile, desktop, and in different browsers just to check whether the appearance is how you expect it to be. This is a very important step, as otherwise you run the risk of your message not being received properly, which will reduce the impact.

15. Once you are happy with everything, you must click on **Send for Review** (located toward the top of the screen as seen in *Figure 9.14*) for the Zoho Compliance team to review before sending. Click on **Why?** to read Zoho's explanation for this. This check usually takes no more than 5 minutes.

Once approved, your email you will have three options for delivery, as shown in the following figure, each of which is self-explanatory.

If your email is not approved, the email from Zoho will explain the reason for this and detail any corrective action needed:

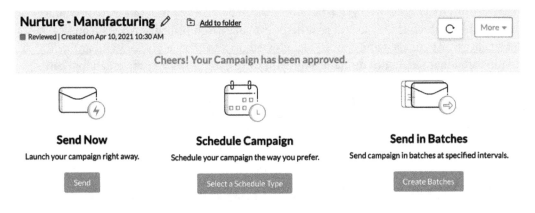

Figure 9.15 – Once the campaign is approved, select when you wish to send the email(s)

Once the email has been sent, the campaign preview page will display a summary report, including figures for **Delivered**, **Opened**, **Clicked**, and **Unsubscribes**; a detailed report can be accessed by clicking **View Report**:

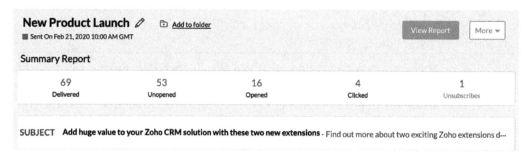

Figure 9.16 – A summary report visible in Campaigns and Zoho CRM

Provided that you have enabled the **Campaigns** module in Zoho CRM, the same report will be visible within Zoho CRM (Campaigns) and the member status (**Open**, **Click**, or **Bounce**) of each lead or contact will be visible inside the record. As mentioned earlier in *Chapter 7, Essential Systems Administration*, this can be factored into our lead or contact scoring rules – which is very useful as it helps the sales team prioritize which leads/contacts are most engaged and should be followed up first. This is so powerful and will provide value that would not be achieved if you were using a third-party email marketing platform.

Now that you have sent your first campaign and seen the benefits of how Campaigns links to Zoho CRM, it is time to understand how we can now increase the value even further and learn how to start automating our email marketing.

# Using workflows to automate your email marketing

If you search the internet and/or read books about marketing, you will read consistently that it takes an average of 6-8 instances of contact before a qualified prospect will purchase from you. This is much more about building a *know, like, and trust* relationship than a box-ticking exercise and it is by no means guaranteed that all customers will actually purchase at all. There are lots of variables, such as brand, product, sector, and customer, at play here, but it is fair to say that automated email marketing has an important role to play in all this.

Lots of marketing experts will also report that this email communication must be personalized, relevant, and timely for it to truly resonate with the reader. This is where the CRM linked to Campaigns comes in. The CRM will hold all the details of our prospects and customers, including personal details, how they heard about you, where they are up to in the customer life cycle, and previous purchase history. So, you should realize now that if we are able to build this insight into our mailing lists, then we can really make an automated campaign that sends the right message to the right person at the right time. The key to this is to *sync* a custom view in Zoho CRM with a mailing list in Campaigns as described earlier in this chapter. A custom view is a filtered list of contacts/leads taking into consideration any of the data points (fields) and/or any tags that have been assigned. When you start to appreciate the value of this by building these automated workflows, it is natural that you will review your CRM to make sure that you maximize the potential – by adding fields, tags, and workflows. This is a natural progression.

So, now that we understand why automated workflows can help our business and how the sync from our CRM can help create and update our mailing lists, it is time to look at how we achieve this in Campaigns:

1.  From the main menu in **Campaigns**, navigate to **Automation | Workflows**.
2.  Click on the **Create Workflow** button (top right).
3.  You will be presented with a number of templates, which are great for ideas and inspiration. However, you will master this tool quicker if you create your own from scratch, by clicking on the **Custom Workflow** button (top right).

4.  In this example, we will show how we can create a series of three nurturing emails that will be sent within the first 3 days of a lead being entered in Zoho CRM. Our sales team will already be following up, but we want to take this opportunity to supplement what they are doing with some content that will hopefully engage the prospect and demonstrate some of the value we have to offer – again building the *know, like, and trust* relationship. With this in mind, we need the new leads that are added to our **Nurture – Manufacturing** mailing list to enter this workflow. We tell the system this by defining a trigger by selecting an option from the left:

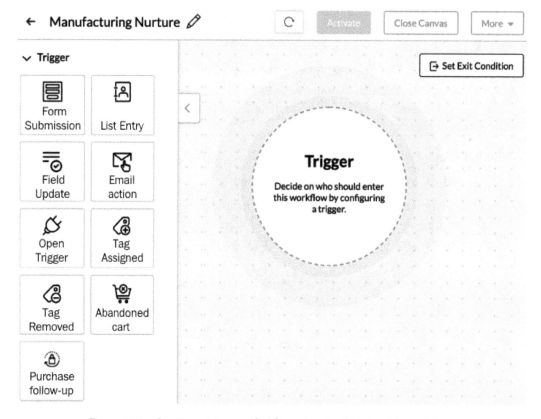

Figure 9.17 – Creating a trigger – deciding who should enter this workflow

5.  Drag the **List Entry** component from the left and drop it on top of the trigger. Note that the on-list icon now replaces the trigger.

6.  Click on **Select List** within this icon:

Figure 9.18 – Select the mailing list

7.  Now complete the following popup by naming your trigger and specifying the two options (as shown in the following screenshot) before clicking **Save**:

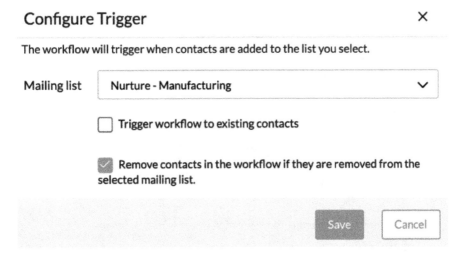

Figure 9.19 – Configuring the trigger

8.  Click on **Process** in the left-hand column to reveal the different options. In this example, we will keep it simple and send an email. This can be achieved by dragging the **Send Mail** element on the left into the main window and dropping it beneath the trigger we just configured (as shown here):

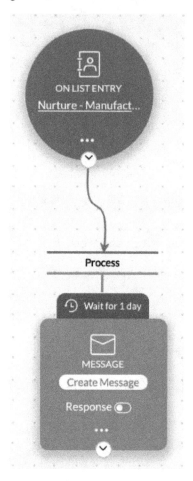

Figure 9.20 – Creating the first action in our workflow process

9.  Hover over **Wait for 1 Day**, then click on the pencil that appears as shown here:

Figure 9.21 – Amending the trigger to specify when to send

10. Within the next popup, select when you wish the message to be sent – the options include **Immediately**, **Wait x Days**, and **Wait x Days** (only on certain days).

11. Next, click on **Create Message**, which is the exact same process as described in *steps 3-13* in the *Getting started with one-off campaigns* section.

12. Now repeat *steps 8-11* until you have added all three messages and specified the waiting periods as required. Your workflow now should resemble the following:

Figure 9.22 – A sequence of three automated emails sent daily, upon a lead being added to the CRM

Note in *Figure 9.22* that there are a couple of exclamation marks next to the first two messages. This is because the messages have yet to be sent for review. Look out for other similar symbols, which will be an intuitive prompt that something needs to be actioned.

Click on **Activate** (top right) once finished, where you will be prompted if there are any outstanding actions that you need to complete.

Congratulations, you have created your first automated workflow in Campaigns. The possibilities of this are endless and you are on your way to creating a marketing platform that will be the envy of your peers (and clients).

The example detailed in this section is a really simple one, just to help you walk before you can run, so do check out the other workflow templates for ideas and examples of other, more complex ones.

The other really valuable feature within a workflow is the ability to create multiple paths based on the recipients opening, clicking, or not opening one of the emails. One of the outcomes that can be specified is actually creating a task in Zoho CRM for the lead/contact assigned to the record owner – so we can really help our sales team know when to contact someone who is interested. Try this by clicking on **Response** within one of your message setup boxes.

A lot more examples and information on this powerful feature can be found at `https://www.zoho.com/campaigns/help/handbook/workflow-automation.html`.

So, now that we have created our first automated workflow, it is time for a recap!

# Summary

In this chapter, you have learned how to integrate Zoho CRM with Campaigns and, most importantly, how to create your mailing lists and synchronize them with CRM. You have learned the basic skills needed to create a standalone email campaign. You have also learned how to set up automated workflows – this will enable you to build an automated marketing platform.

Used alongside other marketing tools and in conjunction with the sales process, email marketing has a very important role to play. Integrating the email function with a CRM like we can do in Zoho gives us the best possible chance of being effective and successful. Remember also that success mostly does not happen overnight with this medium, so be patient, measure the results, evolve your campaigns, and iterate.

In the next chapter, we will look at Zoho Forms, another highly useful application with real value to be added by integration with Zoho CRM.

# 10
# Zoho Forms

**Zoho Forms** is a powerful yet intuitive web-form builder application that requires no development or website builder plugins. Zoho Forms can be used to replace emails and spreadsheets for collecting data and, once integrated with Zoho CRM, can trigger workflows, thus unlocking the potential for more automation and saving your team a huge amount of time and effort.

In this chapter, you will learn how to create a form and integrate it with your CRM. You will also gain insight from fantastic, real, working examples from a networking business and a training company.

We will cover the following topics in this chapter:

- Getting started with Zoho Forms
- Integrating your form with Zoho CRM
- Transforming the feedback gathered from members of a business networking (membership) company
- Transforming the feedback and certification processes of a training company

By the end of this chapter, you will have knowledge and experience of what Zoho Forms does and gain inspiration as to ways it can potentially add value to your CRM and business.

# Getting started with Zoho Forms

If we had to summarize what Zoho Forms does in a few words, it would be **electronic data capture**. Throughout the customer journey within our business process, there is a lot of data that we must capture. Let's consider several examples of ways in which we can utilize Zoho Forms within our businesses:

- **Lead capture**: We can replace our **Contact** forms on the website with a Zoho form to easily capture inbound inquiries/leads.

- **Lead generation**: We can use Forms as a sign-up process. For example, a prospect wanting to download a report or receive some exclusive content can complete a short web form, which will add them as a lead in Zoho CRM and automatically provide them with an email with an attachment or redirect them to a hidden page on your website.

- **Discovery/needs analysis meeting**: Our internal sales team can use a form to ask all the questions needed to fully understand the customer's needs. Very useful for professional services, consultants, software development agencies, and medical services.

- **Onsite survey**: Often in many businesses, a surveyor or engineer needs to attend a site to complete a survey before any work is agreed and/or estimated.

- **Application forms**: We can use forms for prospective or existing members or students to complete.

- **Fact finding**: Especially for financial services, claims, and insurance – completed by or on behalf of the client/claimant/insuree.

- **Customer signup**: We can use this to help onboard new clients, capturing additional information that is needed by other departments including operations and finance.

- **Customer feedback**: As an alternative to Zoho Survey, we can use Forms to capture feedback if we need to share those results in PDF format with any party/parties.

- **Engineer report**: We may need our onsite engineers to capture information, photos, and client signatures upon completion of the job.

This is by no means an exhaustive list, so please use this as a starting point for your own brainstorming.

Many of the web forms may save your business material costs, including paper, ink, and postage, while also reducing labor costs, not only in the sending of the forms but also in the data entry once completed.

Better still, we can send a link to a form automatically based on where we are up to in the customer journey (linked to Zoho CRM workflows) and also capture some/all of the data within our CRM. This saves even more labor costs and speeds up the process at the same time. Finally, once a form has been completed by a prospect, customer, partner, engineer, or salesperson, we can use the form data to trigger workflows within our CRM. This makes us more efficient and allows us to respond faster, which will improve the service to our customers.

So, now that we understand the when and why, let's consider how to create a Zoho form.

## Creating a Zoho form

Zoho Forms linked to Zoho CRM will save your business time and money while increasing efficiency and improving customer service. When we think in these terms, it really should be a compelling reason to use and integrate Zoho Forms. To use Zoho Forms, we first need to create a form. Let's see how to do it:

1. Open Forms by navigating to `forms.zoho.com`.

2. Click on **New Form** (located in the top-right corner).

3. Choose whether to create a blank form or use a form template. In this example, we shall use a blank form and complete the fields as shown in *Figure 10.1*, and then click on **Create**:

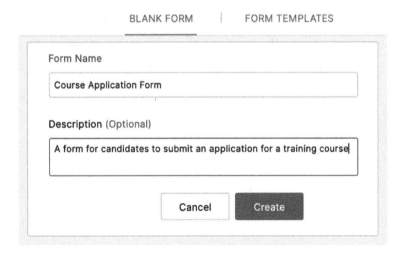

Figure 10.1 – Creating a new form from a blank template

Now you are presented with a drag and drop form builder with a selection of **Basic** and **Advanced** fields. A glossary of these field types can be found at `https://www.zoho.com/forms/help/tools/field-types.html`.

4. Starting with the basics, we will need to capture the candidate's first name, so drag and drop a **Single Line** field into our form area from the left to the right of the screen:

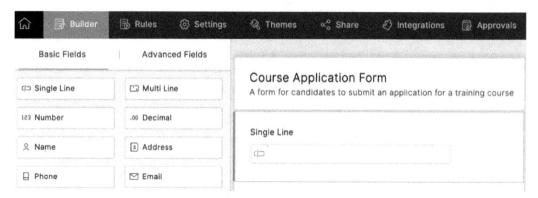

Figure 10.2 – Adding a single line field onto the form

5. Now click on this **Single Line** field on your form to display the **Properties** popup and complete it as shown in *Figure 10.3*. Note that once you have clicked **Save**, it is necessary to click on **X** (top right) to return to the form:

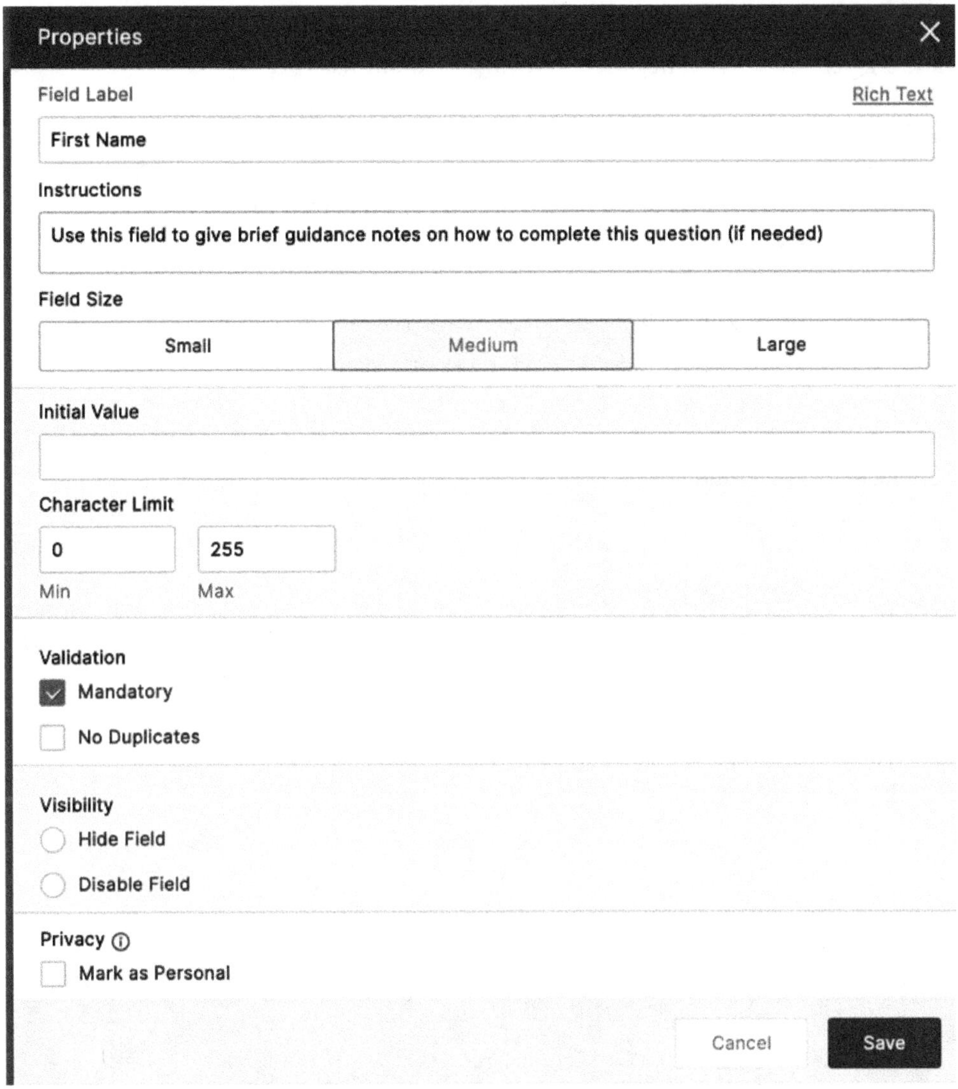

Figure 10.3 – Completing the properties of your field

In this case, we have added an example instruction and made the field mandatory.

The main ways we can validate the fields include the following:

**Mandatory**: When checked, this will force the user to complete the field.

**No Duplicates**: When checked, this will not allow the same value to be entered by more than one person completing a form, for example, an email address.

**Allow Negative Value** (numerical/currency datatypes): When checked, this will allow a person to add a negative value to a field of this type.

> **Tip**
>
> The properties available will change depending on the type of data, and the other options presented here will be very useful as/when we are integrating the form with the CRM.

6.  Now let's add a second **Single Line** field to capture the last name.

7.  Next, we shall add a **Dropdown** field type to our form to enable us to capture the actual course the prospective candidate is interested in. The drop-down form is preferred here over the **Radio** or **Checkbox** datatype in case we need to integrate the form at a later date:

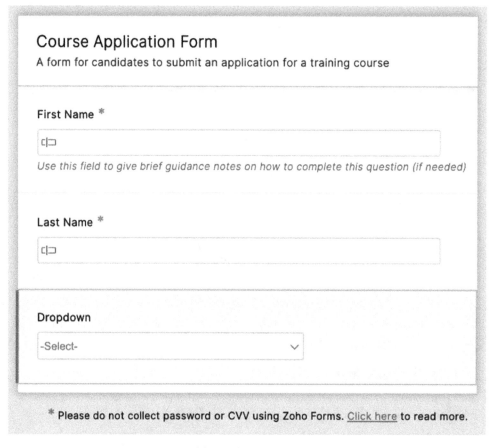

Figure 10.4 – Adding a drop-down field to our form

8.  When selecting the properties of the drop-down field, the main difference compared to the single line is the process of defining the dropdown (picklist values). This can be achieved in one of two ways:

a) Adding the values manually by replacing the **First Choice**, **Second Choice**, and **Third Choice** values with your own and clicking on + to add more as shown here:

Figure 10.5 – Adding drop-down values manually

b) Alternatively, if we have multiple options to add, we can import them from another source – such as an Excel sheet. You even have some pre-configured, commonly used list values that Zoho has included by clicking on the **Advanced** label seen in the top-right corner of *Figure 10.4*. To use this shortcut, navigate to **Advanced | Import**, then add your values using one of the options provided on the left of the screen:

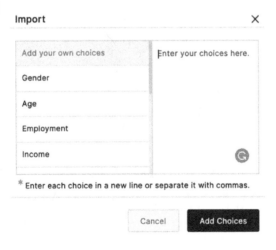

Figure 10.6 – Importing drop-down values

Now add the remaining fields to your form by using the same drag and drop method and setting the properties for each one. In this example, we have added a few more fields for personal and contact details, so our completed form is now as follows:

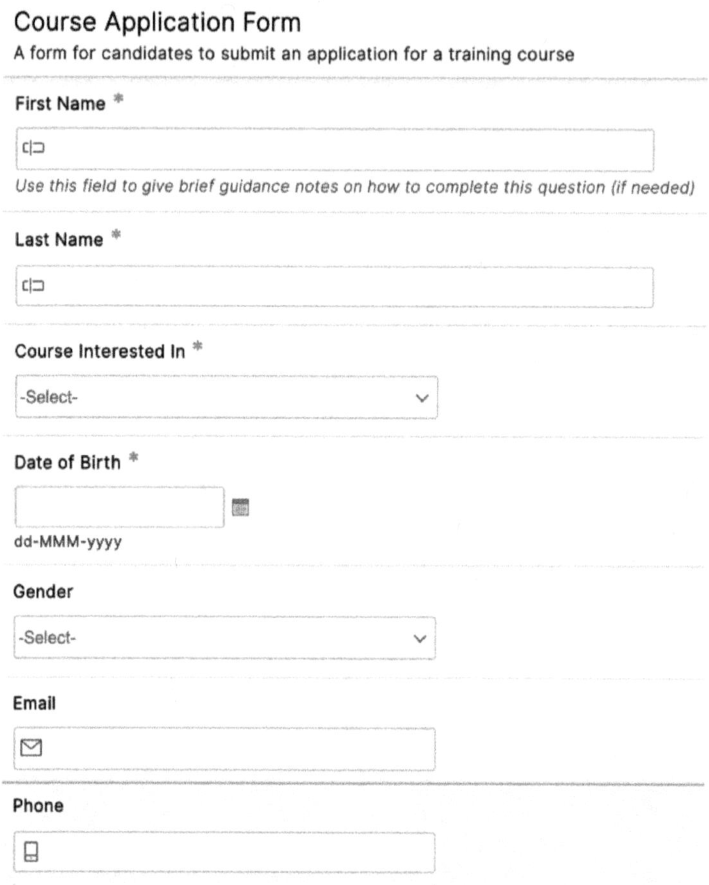

## Course Application Form
A form for candidates to submit an application for a training course

**First Name** *

> *Use this field to give brief guidance notes on how to complete this question (if needed)*

**Last Name** *

**Course Interested In** *

-Select-

**Date of Birth** *

dd-MMM-yyyy

**Gender**

-Select-

**Email**

**Phone**

Figure 10.7 – A sample form designed and ready for sharing

Once you have finished building your form, the next step is to share the form so that it can be completed.

# Sharing your form

There are two main ways we can share our form so that it can be completed by our prospects, partners, clients, or employees (our network) as required by our business process:

1. To share your form, navigate to the main menu across the top of the screen and click on **Share** as shown here:

Figure 10.8 – Accessing the Share feature from the main menu

2. You will be presented with one of the main ways of sharing access to your form using a link. This link can be used in the body of an email so if the lead/contact already exists in Zoho CRM, we can send them a link to our form to complete the application form within an email template in Zoho CRM. (See *Chapter 7, Essential Systems Administration*, for information on email templates.) This link can be seen in the following figure:

**Form Permalink (URL)**

https://forms.zohopublic.com/dominicharrington/form/CourseApplicationForm/formperma/1TrcTlEtVhgdkqXVDbCCLBEZHxC34_K7VvXFkOgM-hY

Figure 10.9 – Sharing access to the form using a link

3. Another typical scenario would be where the applicant did not already exist in Zoho CRM, in which case you can embed the form within your website. To select this option, click on **Embed** on the left-hand menu as shown here:

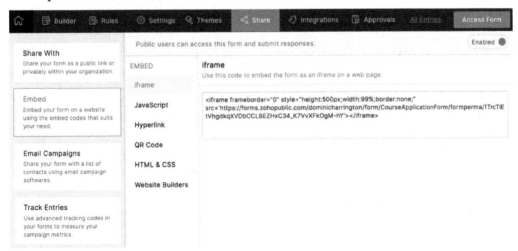

Figure 10.10 – Embedding the form within your website

4.   There are five different ways to embed a form within your website. Speak to your website developer and ask them which one will work the best within your current website:

- iframe

- JavaScript

- A hyperlink

- A QR code

- HTML and CSS

- Website builders (plugin)

Congratulations, you have just built your first form and shared it; this is such a key milestone when it comes to capturing data. You will be improving the customer and CRM user experience as well as becoming more efficient with each form that you implement.

So, now that we understand how to create a form and share/embed it within our network, this will allow us to capture data in real time in a variety of ways. Let's look at how we integrate the form with Zoho CRM.

# Integrating your form with Zoho CRM

The ability to integrate our form with Zoho CRM is one of the best ways to gain value from Zoho Forms. We are automating what would have been a manual process and also speeding up the process by allowing our team to view and act upon new information immediately.

There are three ways we may integrate a form with Zoho CRM:

- **Adding a CRM lookup field**: This is a method of pushing data from the CRM to a form where the form is being completed by a Zoho user.

- **Pre-populate fields using a field alias**: This is an alternative way to push data from the CRM to a form, where the form is completed by a contact or lead that exists in Zoho.

- **By pushing the values of a completed form back into Zoho CRM upon completion.**

Let's take a look at each of these in turn.

# Adding a CRM lookup field

Adding a CRM lookup field will allow you to pre-populate fields when a form is being completed by one of your Zoho users. The following steps guide you to create a lookup field:

1. Within Forms, locate your form and click **Edit** – this will open the **Builder** menu.

2. Click on **Advanced Fields**.

3. Drag and drop the **Zoho CRM** field to the top of your form.

4. Now complete the **Properties** pop-up window that appears. Set the module, layout, and the field you wish to use as the lookup reference as shown here:

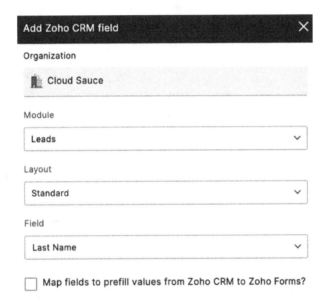

Figure10.11 – Adding a Zoho CRM lookup field mapping the Last Name field in the lead record

5. Check the box next to **Map fields to prefill values from Zoho CRM to Zoho Forms?**.

6. Complete the field mapping table by selecting the fields you want to pre-populate in Forms from Zoho CRM. This will improve the user experience and save time. It is important to note that the data types need to match across both systems:

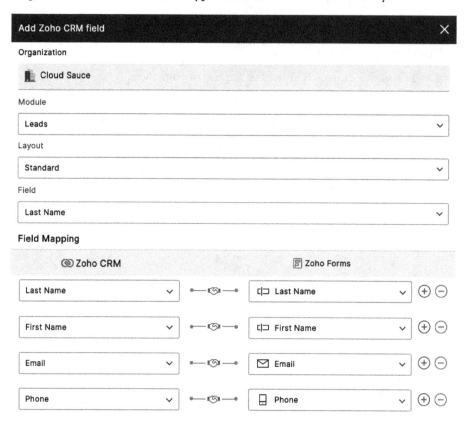

Figure 10.12 – Mapping fields that we wish to pre-populate in a form

7. Click **Save**.

8. Next, you will need to obtain the internal link for the form by navigating to **Access Form**.

9.  Copy the URL from your internet browser window as shown here:

Figure 10.13 – Copying the forms URL to use in a link

10. Open Zoho CRM and navigate to **Setup | Customization | Modules and Fields | Leads** (or the module you are linking the form to) | **Links and Buttons**.

11. Click on the **New Link** button (top-right corner).

12. Give your link a label, paste the link copied in *step 9*, and select the profile(s) you wish to access the link as shown here, then click on **Save**:

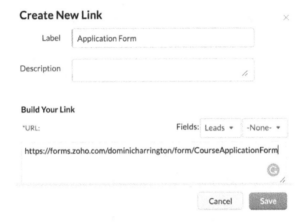

Figure 10.14 – Creating a new link to our form for a CRM user to complete

13. When you open a lead record, you will now see a link with the label name provided in *Step 12* beneath **Related List** under the **Links** sub-heading as shown here:

## Links

🗋 Application Form

Figure 10.15 – Accessing your form from within the CRM record

14. When the user accesses the form, they must first complete the Zoho CRM lookup and that will pre-populate the fields that you mapped earlier.

Note that if your users are onsite/without the use of the Zoho CRM desktop application, they must access the form directly from within the **Zoho Forms** mobile application.

This approach works well, provided that the form is being completed by one of your Zoho users. However, there are many occasions where the form will be completed by external network contacts such as prospects, customers, or partners. In this case, we can use an alternative method to pre-populate fields, as we will see in the next section.

## Using a field alias to populate forms

This method is extremely useful when we wish to pre-fill fields in a form that will be completed by a lead or contact. We must share an email containing a link to a form that will be sent from within Zoho CRM.

This method is a two-stage process. First, we must add the field alias within **Forms** and then we reference this alias within **CRM Workflow Email Alert**:

1. Open **Forms**, find the form you wish to integrate with, and select **Settings**.

2. Select **Field Alias** from the menu on the left and then click **Set Alias**.

3. Now select the field you wish to map, which in this example is **First Name**, and then input `first` in the **Field Alias** textbox.

4. Click on + and then select **Last Name** for **Field Label**, then input `last` for **Field Alias**.

5. Click on + and then select **Email** for **Field Label**, then input `email` for **Field Alias**.

6. Click on + and then select **Phone** for **Field Label**, then input `phone` for **Field Alias**.

7. Click **Save**.

An example of the field alias mapping screen is shown in the following screenshot:

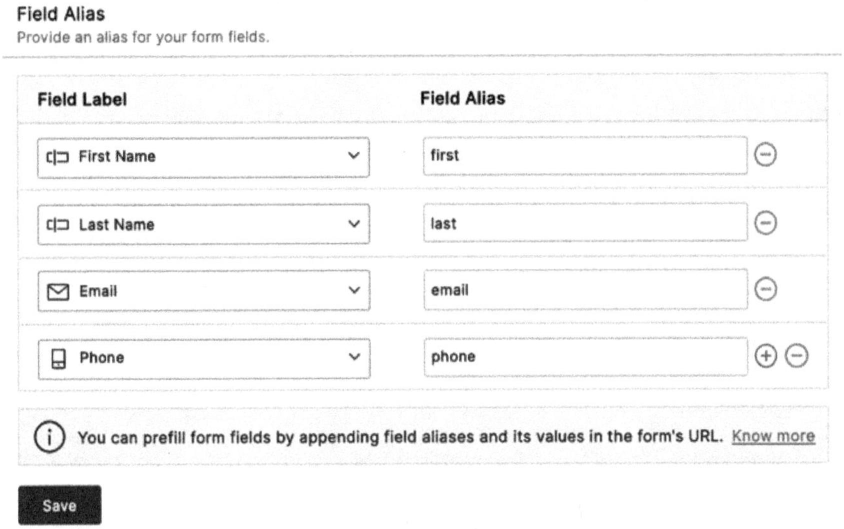

Figure 10.16 – Setting the field alias values

8. Next, we need to insert the link into **CRM Workflow Email Template** by navigating to **Setup | Customization | Templates | New Template**.

9. Select the module using which you wish to pre-populate the form, in this example, **Leads**.

10. Within the body of an email, you need to insert a link following this syntax:

```
https://forms.zohopublic.
com/.../?<fieldalias1>=<fieldvalue>&<fieldalias2>=
<fieldvalue>
```

In this example, ours would be as follows:

```
https://zfrmz.com/rzvKvFisLKn0cwVJZx2L/?email=${Leads.
Email}&first=${Leads.First Name}&last=${Leads.Last
Name}&phone=${Leads.Phone}
```

This link can be constructed by completing the following steps:

a) Add the public link to the form, `https://zfrmz.com/
rzvKvFisLKn0cwVJZx2L/?`.

b) Input ?email= followed by #, then select the **Email** field to add ${Leads. Email} (which is the CRM field name inserted as a merge tag).

c) Input &first= followed by #, then select the **First Name** field to add ${Leads.First Name}.

d) Input &last= followed by #, then select the **Last Name** field to add ${Leads.Last Name}.

e) Input &phone= followed by #, then select the **Phone** field to add ${Leads.Phone}.

The preceding steps will result in a similar mail being sent:

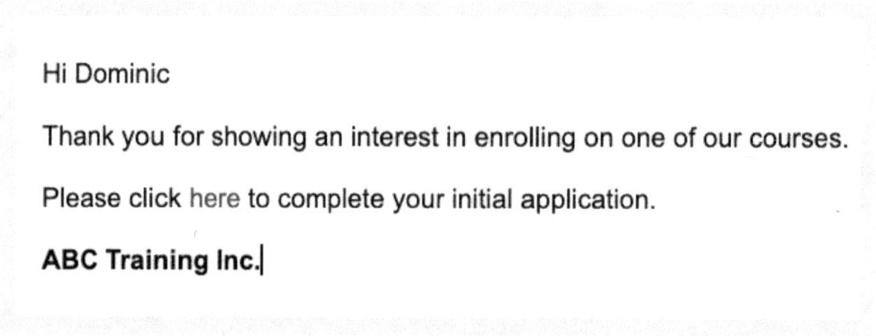

Hi Dominic

Thank you for showing an interest in enrolling on one of our courses.

Please click here to complete your initial application.

**ABC Training Inc.**

Figure 10.17 – The email that will be sent containing a link that includes all our components to pre-fill fields

Upon the recipient clicking on the link within the email, they will be taken to the form, and the first name, last name, email, and phone fields will be pre-filled with the values in the associated CRM record. This is an extremely valuable integration and will reduce the time it takes to complete a form and improve the user experience.

Additional information on this can be found at https://www.zoho.com/forms/help/settings/field-alias.html.

So, now that we have looked at the two ways to pre-fill fields in a Zoho form, we shall now look at how we push the values of a completed form back into Zoho CRM.

# Pushing the values of a form into Zoho CRM

One of the most frequently used and most beneficial ways of integrating a form with Zoho CRM is to push the values from a completed form into a new or existing record within a CRM module. This can be achieved as follow:

1. Build your form, ensuring that your form contains all the mandatory fields that you have within Zoho CRM. Most probably, you will need to add a hidden field for **Lead Source** and pre-select the drop-down value of this for it to identify where the lead (or record) came from.

2. Add your hidden field(s) as required using the values shown here:

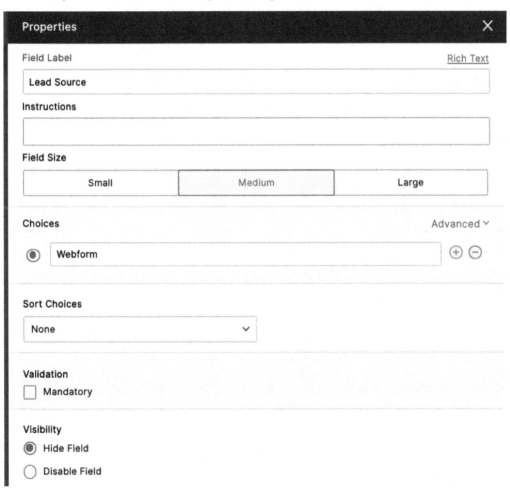

Figure 10.18 – Adding a hidden field for Lead Source, pre-selecting Webform as the option

3. Navigate to **Integrations | Zoho CRM | Integrate**.

4. Set **Module** and **Layout**, complete the field mapping, and check the box for **Automation and Process Management**.

5. Click **Integrate**.

Once you have completed these steps, when the form has been completed it will either create a new record in your CRM module or it may update (upsert) an existing record with the values from the form. Either way, the time and resource savings here just for one form are great, and when multiplied by the number of times the form is completed, this is one of the most time-saving tools that you can utilize in the whole Zoho ecosystem.

To gain further insight and inspiration as to how you can utilize this within your business, it is instructive to consider our first use case.

# Transforming the feedback gathered from members of a business networking (membership) company

In this section, we will look at how a well-established business networking (membership) company utilized Zoho CRM and Forms to fully automate business processes that would have needed at least one full-time resource to administer manually.

This example could be adapted by any business that wishes to obtain customer feedback on a regular basis and share the results instantly with a group of people.

The requirements comprise the following two elements: **seven-month check-in** and **rate your experience**.

## Seven-month check-in

The objectives seven months into the membership were as follows:

- To notify the team that it's time to contact a specific member and conduct a seven-month check-in (questionnaire/interview).

- The results of this interview need to be shared instantly with a committee consisting of a few other members.

- One of the questions asked respondents to rate on a scale from 1-10 how likely they were to renew if asked today, and the management team needed to be alerted if the answer fell within certain thresholds.

# Rate your experience

There was a requirement to automate the capturing of feedback from each member, as follows:

- An email needed to be sent automatically to each member every two months asking them to rate their experience with the business networking organization (on a scale of one to five stars).

- While the capture of the results was to remain anonymous, the business networking management team needed to be able to report on the percentage of respondents, average score per networking group, and average score overall, and then to monitor trend changes over time.

# Solution

It was identified that the solution would entail the use of Zoho CRM and Zoho Forms.

## Seven-month check-in

- The Zoho CRM **Contacts** module was renamed to **Members**.

- Each member record held contact and renewal date details.

- A workflow rule would be triggered 152 days before the annual renewal date (7 months in) to send an automated email to a member contact containing a link to the Zoho form. This form would have the member contact fields pre-filled using a field alias (as per the *Using a field alias to pre-populate forms* section earlier in this chapter).

- Upon completion of the form (using the unique member link), a workflow rule inside Zoho Forms was set up to send a PDF document to a small group of members so they could instantly view the results of the completed questionnaire. See `https://www.zoho.com/forms/help/create-pdfs.html` for details on how to complete this step.

- This form was also integrated with Zoho CRM by pushing completed forms into a custom module named `7 Month Review`, which was created as a related list of contacts (members). This provided the management team with visibility of reviews completed, along with information on by whom, with whom, and when. The renewal rating question was also mapped in addition to a CRM workflow to create a task if the results fell within certain thresholds.

## Rate your experience

- A Zoho form named `Ratings` was set up that held the question as a picklist (one to five stars) and a multiline text field to capture any feedback.

- A date field in Zoho CRM was added to the **Member** (contact) record named `Ratings Start Date`, which was bulk updated across all member records on a specific date of choosing.

- This triggered a Zoho CRM workflow to send an email as an instant action to all members on that date containing a link to the Zoho form.

- This form was integrated with Zoho CRM so that completed entries would create a record in a custom module named **Ratings**.

- The name of the group the member belonged to was pre-populated using a field alias and then integrated back to Zoho CRM.

- Reports/dashboards were created in Zoho CRM that displayed and summarized the results.

- The workflow also contained five more scheduled actions 60 days apart, which made sure that, overall, there would be six forms sent to each member during the year.

- A second workflow was created that would update the rating's start date for all members by pushing it forward 12 months once it had cycled through the six cycles. This workflow will continue running indefinitely, gathering feedback from members and collating results with zero human input.

# Results

The project continues to be a success. 2 years since adoption, the business is gaining more, better-quality, and more regular feedback from members than it ever received previously. It can identify the likelihood of renewals much earlier and is gaining insight into any potential issues while having the time to take action to remedy adverse situations. The renewal rate of first-year members has increased, and generally, the feedback from all parties involved – management, the committee, and members – has been positive.

There are several steps involved in this example that can be adapted for many different types of businesses, so hopefully, you will be inspired to try something similar for your business in the near future.

Let's have a look at a second use case now.

# Transforming the feedback and certification processes of a training company

In this example, we will look at how a global training provider in a niche sector took advantage of Zoho CRM and Forms to automate the process of gaining feedback and issuing certificates to all delegates who attended its courses.

The requirement was to specifically resolve the following two key challenges or issues: **delegate feedback** and **certificates**.

## Delegate feedback

Firstly, the feedback forms were printed out and provided by the trainer at the end of each session. Some would be completed on the day at the end of the session, but not everybody completed them and left them with the trainer. It was then a manual process to collate and report this information, which could take hours to complete manually. In many cases, this would not be completed until several days later – which may be too slow for the trainer to react if there was anything that needed to be dealt with quickly.

## Certificates

Secondly, the training certificates were being printed and posted manually. This was expensive as sometimes there could be 20-40 delegates on a single course. The cost of ink, paper, postage, and labor was an overhead that the business owners wanted to eliminate.

## Solution

Zoho CRM and Forms were identified as the solution, and how they were set up and implemented can be summarized as follows:

- Zoho CRM was used to support the process of responding to inquiries, sending quotes, and managing bookings – all using the standard modules tailored for the business.

- A custom module named `Delegates` was created to capture the contact details of the attending delegates, details that were unknown to the training company until the day of the training.

- This module was used to drive both the feedback and certificate-issuing processes.

- On the day of a course, each trainer had a Zoho form named `Registration` to complete. As part of their setup routine, they simply had to pre-populate the name of the course, the location, and the booking reference within the form builder.

- Upon the arrival of delegates at the start of a session, a tablet computer was passed around for each of them to enter their full name and email address into the registration form.

- The form was integrated with Zoho CRM and as such pushed all the completed entries and completed a delegate record for each delegate – which included all the course details entered by the trainer (at the start of the day) and the contact details of each delegate. This was also linked back to the **Bookings** module within Zoho CRM.

- A workflow was triggered within the **Delegates** module upon record creation that sent an email to each delegate containing a link to complete the feedback form (after the course). This email could have been timed to be sent any number of hours after record creation, but the business chose to send it immediately.

- As mobile phone internet or Wi-Fi could not be guaranteed at each location, the ability to use Forms offline enabled 100% data capture with or without an internet connection.

- When the delegate completed the **Feedback** form, this triggered a workflow in Zoho Forms, which sent a PDF certificate automatically to each delegate as well as updating the **Delegate CRM** record status to **Feedback received, Certificate issued**.

- The answers to key questions were also mapped from Forms to Zoho CRM, triggering a workflow to notify the trainer of any adverse responses to one or more key questions.

## Results

The project was a resounding success. Due to the nature of the setup and timings, several changes needed to be made during testing and the soft launch, but once these were identified and resolved, these business processes were completely transformed; the key results are summarized as follows:

- Feedback was received from 100% of the delegates.

- Certificates were automatically produced and sent by email as PDFs.

- The business saved time and money previously spent on producing and collating feedback forms.

- The business saved time on collating feedback.

- The business was able to report upon and react to feedback from delegates much more quickly and efficiently.

- The business saved time and money on the production and postage of the certificates.

- Delegates were also opting in to receive marketing communications, so the business started building a quality mailing list to help promote refresher and other courses in the future.

So, in both of these examples, the Zoho user saved time, saved money, and provided a better service, using a scalable solution that will support future sustainable growth. Let's now have a quick recap of the chapter!

# Summary

In this chapter, you have learned how to create and share forms with both internal and external users. You have gained an understanding of the three different ways of achieving a two-way integration between Zoho CRM and Forms. You have gained insights from how globally successful businesses have significantly transformed business processes by using Zoho Forms and Zoho CRM together.

The knowledge and insights gained from this chapter should either inspire you to transform existing processes or allow you to create new value-adding processes that would have been previously unattainable due to a lack of resources.

In the next chapter, you will learn about Zoho Survey, how it works, and the value it can add to your business process by integrating it with Zoho CRM.

# 11
# Zoho Survey

**Zoho Survey** is an intuitive survey tool that makes capturing feedback fun and insightful. Gaining regular, good-quality feedback is often a challenge for many businesses. However, with Zoho Survey we have an amazingly simple solution that will transform the way that your business collects feedback from customers, suppliers, partners, and employees.

As with other Zoho apps, the value gained is increased exponentially by integrating with Zoho CRM. In this chapter, you will learn the basics of survey creation and integration, looking at real-life examples that may inspire your own thoughts and ideas on how to implement Survey yourself.

The topics covered in this chapter include the following:

- Getting started with Zoho Survey
- Integrating surveys with Zoho CRM
- Use case – customer feedback at the end of delivery/project

So, let's start at the beginning.

# Getting started with Zoho Survey

In this section, you will learn the basics of survey creation, which is best illustrated by a working example. The survey we shall create is a simple training course evaluation to be completed by delegates upon the completion of a training course.

Let's start by creating the survey and adding questions.

## Creating your survey and adding questions

The process of creating a survey is simple and involves using an intuitive drag and drop interface. This can be achieved by completing the following step:

1.  Open Survey by navigating to `https://survey.zoho.com/`.

2.  Click on **Create Survey**.

3.  Note that there are numerous templates available to browse and use; however, we will focus on creating one from scratch as shown here:

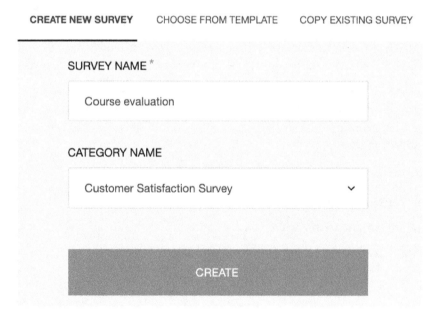

Figure 11.1 – Creating a new survey

4.  Click on **Create**.

5.  To add questions to our survey, select a question type and then drag and drop from left to right. If you think that you will wish to push the data into Zoho CRM later, then use a question type that exists in Zoho CRM such as text fields and picklists. Note that if integrating with Zoho CRM (to update/create a record), you will see the complete survey response within a related list in Zoho CRM, so mapping is only required if you wish to trigger workflows or generate reports. A full list and description of available question types can be found at `https://help.zoho.com/portal/en/kb/survey/survey-builder/question-types`.

6.  So, assuming we are going to integrate this survey with CRM later, let's begin with the delegate's first name by adding a short-answer question and making it mandatory as shown here:

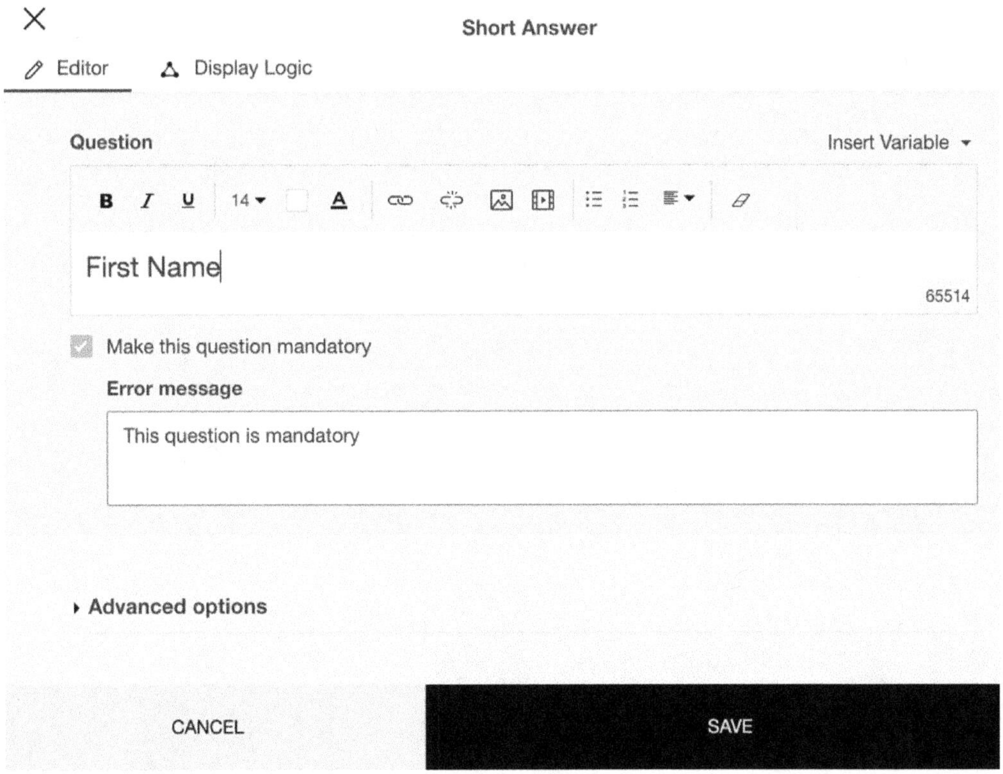

Figure 11.2 – Adding a short-answer question to capture the first name

7.  Repeat *step 6* to add further questions to capture last name, course, and trainer details as well. Later, in the *Integrating surveys with CRM* section, we will explore how we can pre-populate these fields if we already know this information:

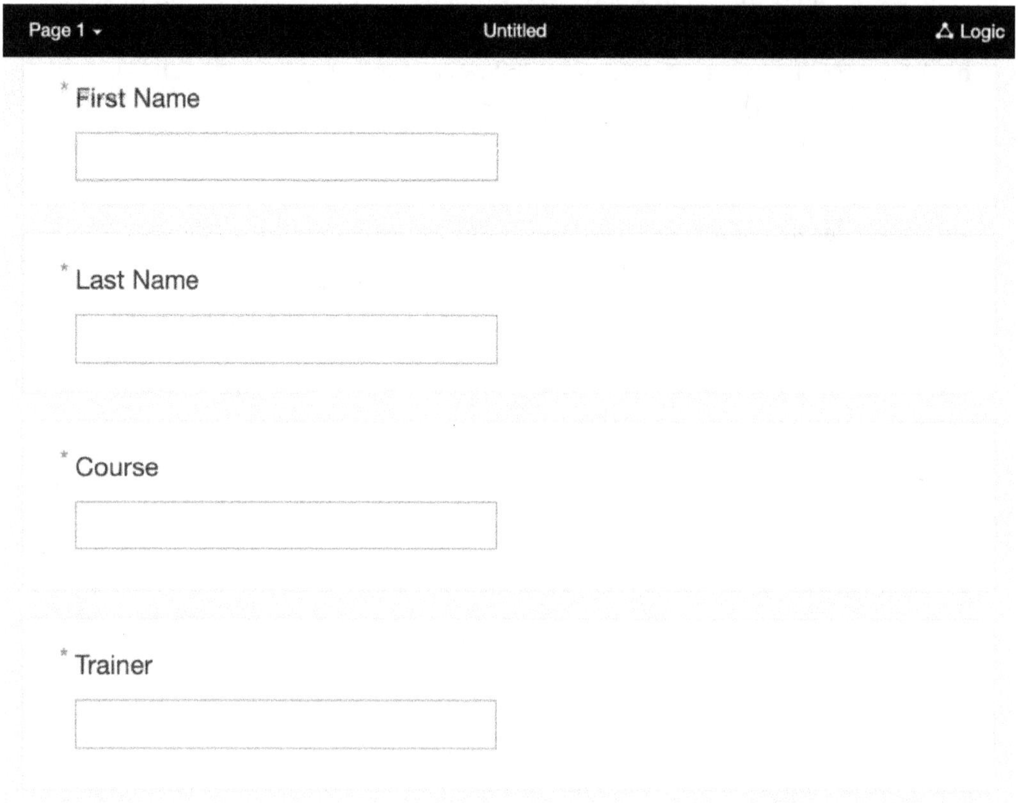

Figure 11.3 – Our survey with the delegate name, course, and trainer questions added

8.  Now we are going to use a **Matrix Rating Scale** question type that will allow us to capture feedback on multiple aspects of the course in a way that will keep the time it will take the respondent to give the feedback to a minimum. Add each aspect to the **Choices** section as shown here:

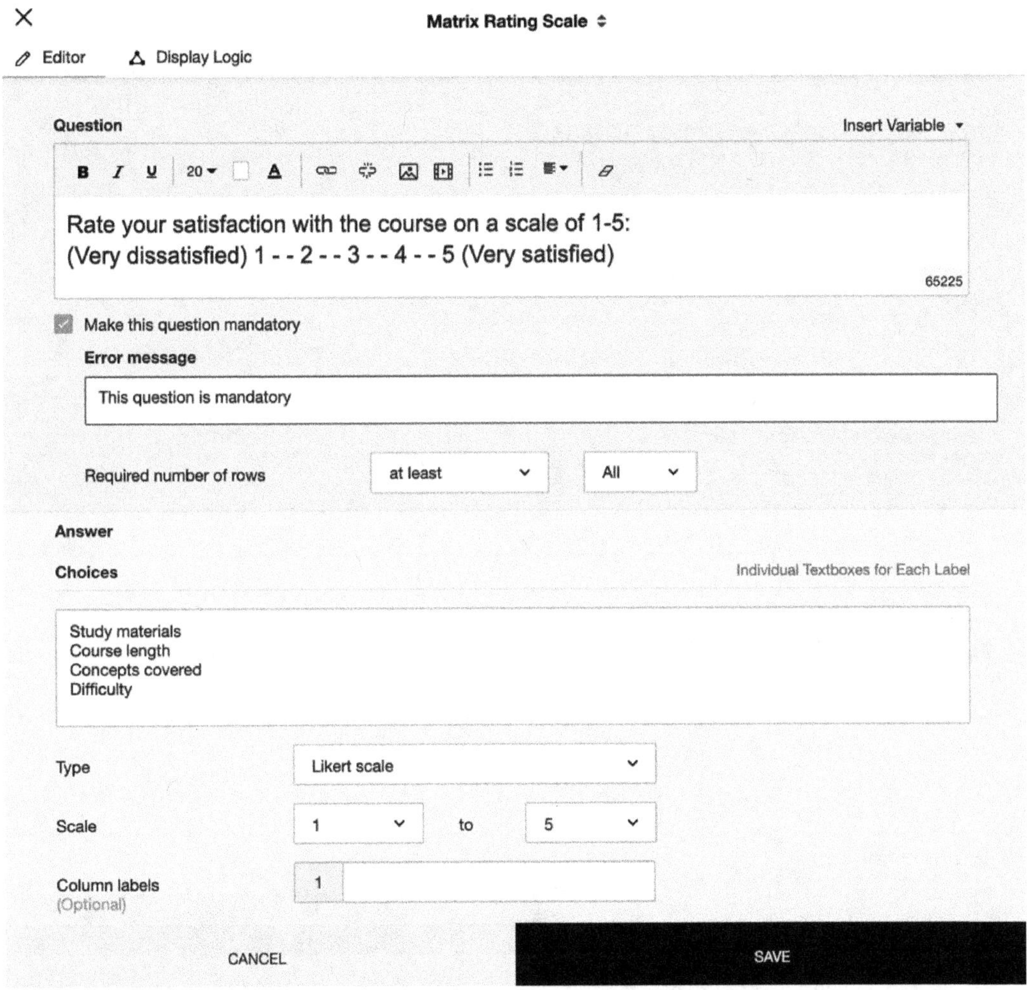

✕                                               **Matrix Rating Scale** ⇕

✎ Editor      △ Display Logic

Question                                                                           Insert Variable ▾

**B**  *I*  U   20 ▾   ☐   **A**   ∞   ✂   🖾   🔢   ≔   ≡   ▮▾   ⬭

Rate your satisfaction with the course on a scale of 1-5:
(Very dissatisfied) 1 - - 2 - - 3 - - 4 - - 5 (Very satisfied)

65225

☑  Make this question mandatory

   **Error message**

   This question is mandatory

   Required number of rows         at least        ⌄        All      ⌄

Answer

Choices                                                          Individual Textboxes for Each Label

   Study materials
   Course length
   Concepts covered
   Difficulty

Type                    Likert scale                      ⌄

Scale                   1          ⌄     to     5      ⌄

Column labels           1
(Optional)

         CANCEL                                      SAVE

Figure 11.4 – Creating a matrix question with ratings

9.   Now you may wish to add another similar matrix to obtain feedback on the trainer
     by completing the fields as follows:

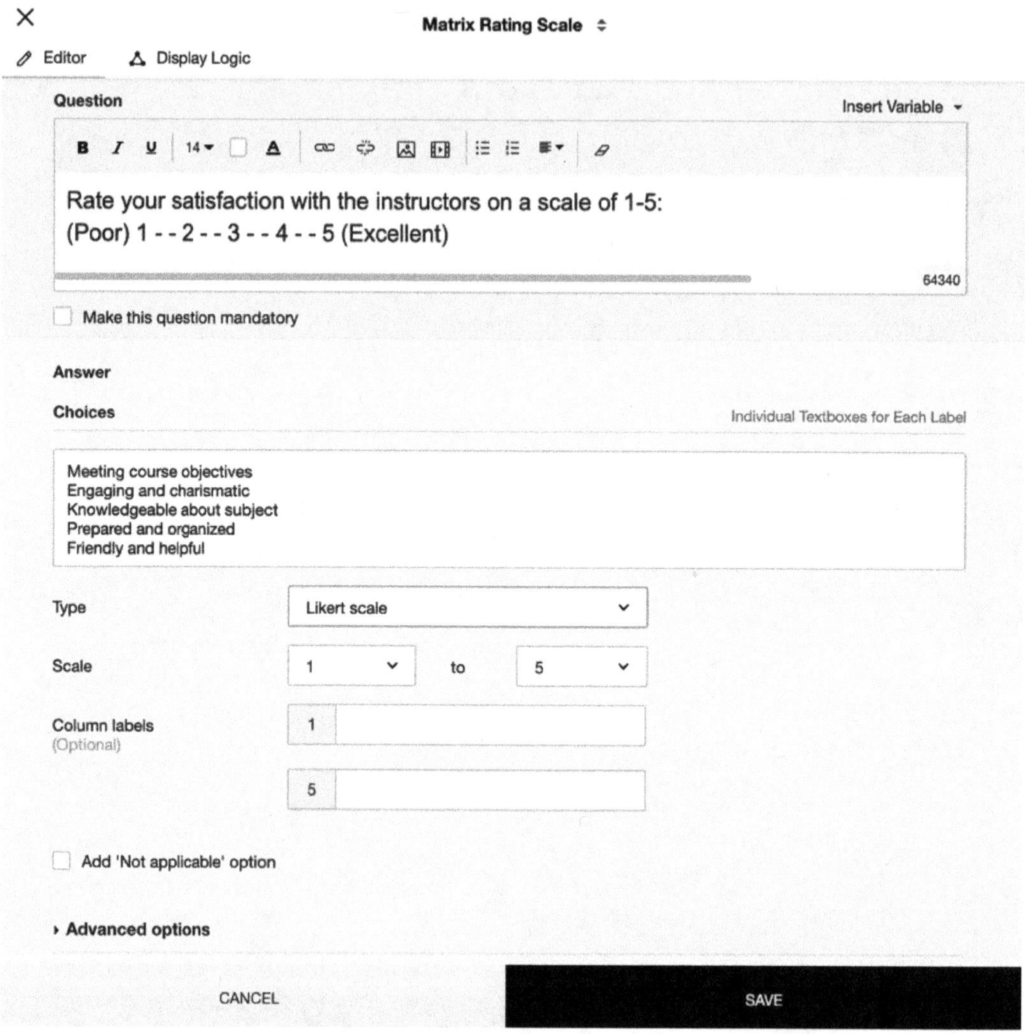

✕                                    **Matrix Rating Scale** ⬍

🖉 Editor      △ Display Logic

---

**Question**                                                          Insert Variable ▾

| **B** *I* <u>U</u>   14 ▾   ☐   **A**   ∞   ⇴   🖾 🖽   ☰ ☷ ☷▾   ✐ |

Rate your satisfaction with the instructors on a scale of 1-5:
(Poor) 1 - - 2 - - 3 - - 4 - - 5 (Excellent)

                                                                              64340

☐  Make this question mandatory

**Answer**

**Choices**                                              Individual Textboxes for Each Label

Meeting course objectives
Engaging and charismatic
Knowledgeable about subject
Prepared and organized
Friendly and helpful

Type                    | Likert scale                        ⌄ |

Scale                   | 1      ⌄ |   to   | 5      ⌄ |

Column labels           | 1 |
(Optional)

                        | 5 |

☐  Add 'Not applicable' option

▸ Advanced options

                CANCEL                                   SAVE

Figure 11.5 – A matrix question to capture feedback on the trainer

10. Now drag and drop a long-answer question onto the survey, which we will use to gather some comments on how we can improve the course:

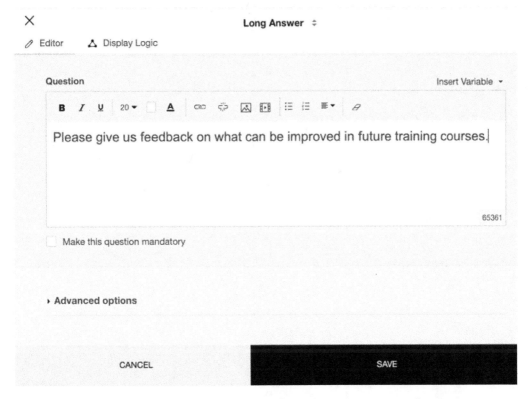

Figure 11.6 – Adding a long-answer question to obtain some qualitative feedback

11. Finally, let's get an overall rating. There are a few ways you can ask this question, for example, matrix, dropdown, or slider; however, we've chosen a number **Datatype** field for this example. This will allow us to compare scores, average scores, and break scores down by course and/or trainer later when we integrate with Zoho CRM. Add this question by completing the fields as illustrated here:

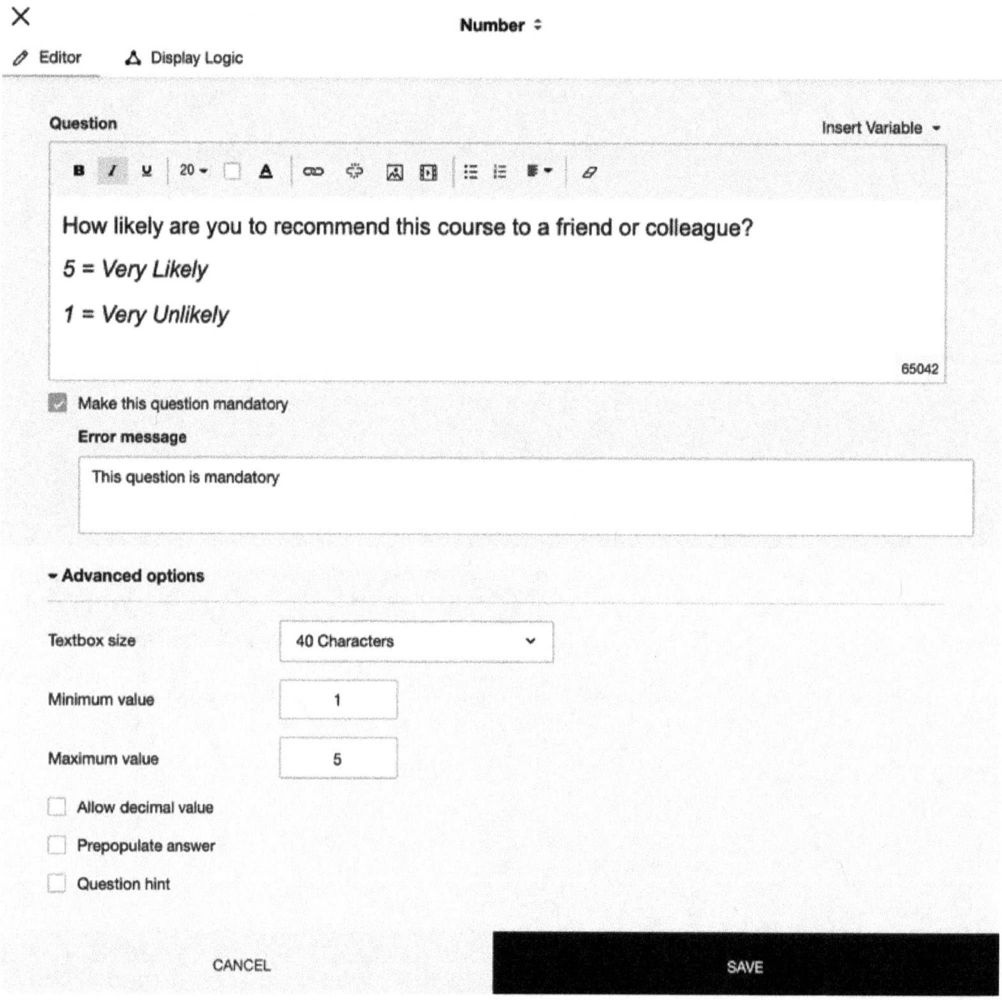

Figure 11.7 – Adding a number question with validation, allowing only values between 1 and 5

Once you have added your questions, you may wish to preview the survey by clicking **Preview** in the top-right corner. Here, you will see how the survey will appear on multiple device types, including desktop, mobile, and tablet:

\* First Name

\[                    \]

- - - - - - - - - - - - - - - - - - - - - - - - - - - - - - - - - - - - - - - - - - - - -

\* Last Name

\[                    \]

- - - - - - - - - - - - - - - - - - - - - - - - - - - - - - - - - - - - - - - - - - - - -

\* Course

\[                    \]

- - - - - - - - - - - - - - - - - - - - - - - - - - - - - - - - - - - - - - - - - - - - -

\* Trainer

\[                    \]

- - - - - - - - - - - - - - - - - - - - - - - - - - - - - - - - - - - - - - - - - - - - -

\* Rate your satisfaction with the course on a scale of 1-5:
(Very dissatisfied) 1 - - 2 - - 3 - - 4 - - 5 (Very satisfied)

| | | | | | |
|---|---|---|---|---|---|
| Study materials | (1) | (2) | (3) | (4) | (5) |
| Course length | (1) | (2) | (3) | (4) | (5) |
| Concepts covered | (1) | (2) | (3) | (4) | (5) |
| Difficulty | (1) | (2) | (3) | (4) | (5) |

Rate your satisfaction with the instructors on a scale of 1-5:
(Poor) 1 - - 2 - - 3 - - 4 - - 5 (Excellent)

| | | | | | |
|---|---|---|---|---|---|
| Meeting course objectives | (1) | (2) | (3) | (4) | (5) |
| Engaging and charismatic | (1) | (2) | (3) | (4) | (5) |
| Knowledgeable about subject | (1) | (2) | (3) | (4) | (5) |
| Prepared and organized | (1) | (2) | (3) | (4) | (5) |
| Friendly and helpful | (1) | (2) | (3) | (4) | (5) |

Please give us feedback on what can be improved in future training courses.

\[              \]

Figure 11.8 – A preview of the survey on a desktop device

Once you have added all the questions you need, you may wish to add some branding and personalize some of the other settings and the appearance of the survey.

### Settings and themes

The **SETTINGS** and **THEMES** options can be accessed from the main menu under **SETTINGS** and **THEMES**. Further information about this can be found here:

```
https://help.zoho.com/portal/en/kb/survey/design/settings/
articles/survey-settings
```

```
https://help.zoho.com/portal/en/kb/survey/design/themes/
articles/survey-themes
```

Figure 11.9 – Personalizing your survey using SETTINGS and THEMES

Once you have made your changes to the appearance, you are ready to launch the survey.

# Publishing and sharing your survey

You may publish your survey by clicking **Launch** from the same menu as in *Figure 11.9*. Before clicking **Publish**, it is worth checking the **Restrictions** tab on the sub-menu on the left in case you wish to add an end date and prevent multiple responses.

Once the survey is published, you will see a number of options available to share the survey; however, the two most common ones are sharing by email or sharing on your website (as a button or popup). So, now that we have looked at creating and sharing our survey, it's time to look at how to increase the value of our survey exponentially by integrating with Zoho CRM.

# Integrating surveys with CRM

There are two key benefits gained from integrating surveys with Zoho CRM.

Firstly, we can automate the sending of a survey to a contact using a workflow that will send the survey to the right person at the right time. The second key benefit is that by pushing all or some of the results back to Zoho CRM, we are able to provide access to this information to our wider team and use this data to trigger workflows and follow-up actions. The feedback we gain will be helpful to the marketing, product, delivery, and customer service functions and help your business to build stronger relationships with current customers, which will help retention and repeat purchase opportunities.

We can integrate the survey as follows:

1.  Open the Survey editor/builder and then click on the **Hub** tab.

2.  Click on **INTEGRATE** next to **Zoho CRM**:

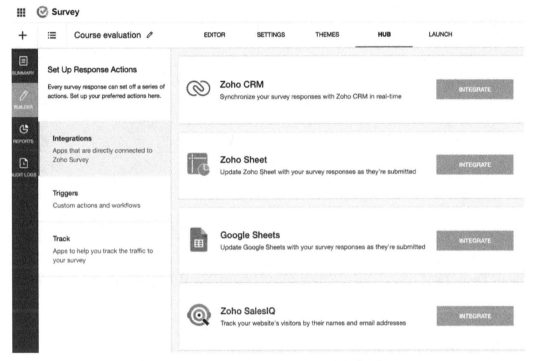

Figure 11.10 – Integrate your survey with Zoho CRM

3.  Select the module with which you wish to integrate (this will usually be a module relating to a contact, so leads, contacts, or a custom module):

Figure 11.11 – Select the CRM module to integrate with – in this example, Delegates

4.  Next select one of the following **Sync** types:

    - **Add record**: Add a new record even if there are duplicates.

    - **Update record**: Update an existing record in Zoho CRM. If you send your survey through Zoho CRM and wish to pre-populate answers (for example, name and email), then also check the **Prepopulate survey answers with information from Zoho CRM** box.

    - **Add/update record**: Create a new record or update an existing record (it does not have the option to pre-populate).

5.  Now let's map our **Course Evaluation** survey to a custom module in Zoho CRM where the following fields will be pre-populated from Zoho CRM to the survey:

    - **First Name**

    - **Last Name**

    - **Course**

    - **Trainer**

The remaining fields shown in the following mapping table will be pushed into Zoho CRM when the respondent completes the survey. You will need to set **Sync Type** as **Update Record** and check the **Prepopulate survey answers with information from Zoho CRM** box:

Integrations → CRM Module → Delegates

# Zoho CRM Integration

Map Zoho CRM fields to questions, custom variables, scores, response URLs, or distinct values

SYNC TYPE

○ Add record          ◉ Update record          ○ Add/Update record

Uses Zoho CRM's unique record IDs to update existing records. Distribute your survey using Zoho CRM for the best results.

☑ Prepopulate survey answers with information from Zoho CRM

| ZOHO CRM | | ZOHO SURVEY | |
|---|---|---|---|
| First Name ⌄ | ⇄ | First Name ⌄ | ✕ |
| Last Name ⌄ | ⇄ | Last Name ⌄ | ✕ |
| Course ⌄ | ⇄ | Course ⌄ | ✕ |
| Trainer ⌄ | ⇄ | Trainer ⌄ | ✕ |
| Likely to recommen... ⌄ | ⇄ | How likely are you t... ⌄ | ✕ |
| Pleased suggest ho... ⌄ | ⇄ | Please give us feed... ⌄ | ✕ |
| Evaluation Complet... ⌄ | ⇄ | Response end time ⌄ | + ✕ |

INDIVIDUAL RESPONSE AS PDF

☑ Include each individual response as a PDF in the Zoho CRM record while syncing

ATTACHMENTS

You can add uploads from File Upload and Signature questions to your Zoho CRM records. Your survey currently has neither.

Figure 11.12 – Integrating some of the survey questions with a custom module in Zoho CRM

6.    Once you have set up the mapping as shown in *Figure 11.12*, click **Save**.

Now that we have integrated the survey, we need to set up an email template within Zoho CRM so that we can share a link with each delegate to ensure that the completed survey is matched back to each respective delegate record.

## Sharing the survey from Zoho CRM

We create this email template including the survey link within Zoho CRM as follows:

1. Navigate to **Setup | Customization | Templates| Email | New Template**.

2. Create the name, subject, and body of your email as you wish, then click on the survey icon on the far right of the toolbar as shown here:

Figure 11.13 – Inserting your survey link in Zoho CRM

3. Now complete the pop-up box, selecting the survey from a list, and then add the text to display as shown here (note that the survey link is added for you automatically). Click **Insert**:

Figure 11.14 – Inserting a survey link into your email

4. Now test your integration by creating a new delegate record in Zoho CRM and then from within the record, click **Send Email | Select Template**.

5. Select your email template and then click **Send**.

6. Open the email when you receive it, then complete the survey.

7.  Now open the CRM record and check that all fields have been pushed back as expected and that you can view the full survey response as a related item:

**Delegate Information**

| | | | |
|---|---|---|---|
| First Name | Dominic | Last Name | Harrington |
| Email | dominic@cloud-sauce.com | Course | Zoho Systems Admin |
| Trainer | Peter Jones | Date | 10/05/2021 |

**Evaluation**

| | | | |
|---|---|---|---|
| Evaluation Completed On | 08/05/2021 11:27 | Pleased suggest how we can improve the course | Enjoyable course but would have been better with some more hands-on exercises to complete |
| Likely to recommend (5 High) | 4 | | |

Figure 11.15 – A delegate record in Zoho CRM, the fields within the Evaluation section having been completed within the survey and integrated with the record

Finally, once you are happy with everything, you will need to create a workflow to automate the sending of your email. Please refer to *Chapter 6, Game-Changing Workflows and Automations*, for information on how to do this using the course date field as your trigger.

Congratulations, you have now grasped the basics of Zoho Survey and learned how to achieve an effective two-way integration with CRM. You should realize also that the scope and possibilities for this within your business are significant. However, to further illustrate the value and simplicity of this, we shall consider one additional use case.

# Use case – automate your customer feedback and build a constant source of quotes and testimonials

One of the best ways we can use surveys with Zoho CRM is to gain customer feedback when or shortly after we have delivered our products and/or services. It is a great way to measure how the customer feels about dealing with our business as well as building a pool of quotes that can be used by marketing in future to help attract more customers.

To achieve this, we will need the following components:

- A survey
- An email template associated to a workflow to trigger sending the email

Let's start with the survey, which is created in the same way as described earlier in this chapter. This survey starts with a **Net Promotor Score (NPS)** question followed by a couple of questions to give the respondent opportunities to provide a testimonial and also suggest how the service could be improved.

Finally, the checkbox will obtain permission to use the quote in subsequent marketing material. So, you get lots of value from just four questions that will only take the respondent up to a minute to complete – meaning you should get a high response rate. This customer feedback survey, including an NPS question, is shown here:

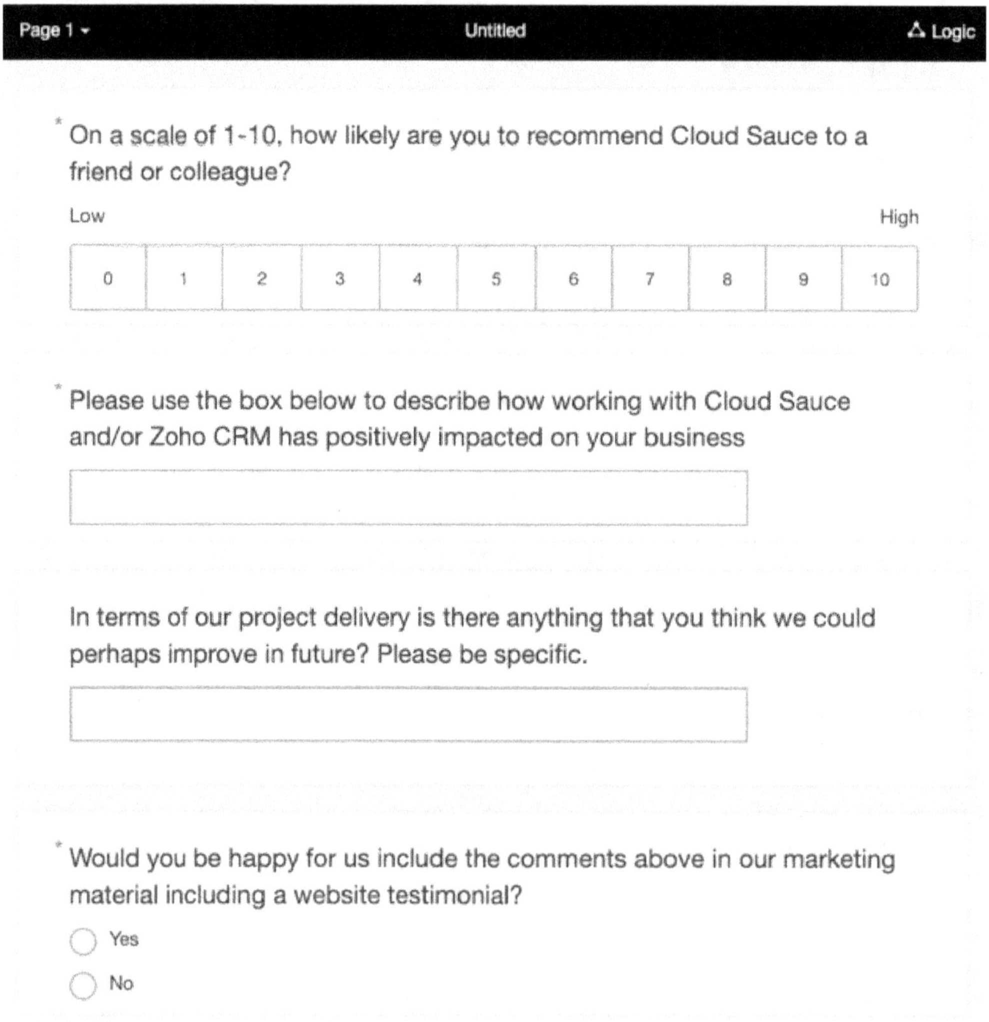

| Page 1 ▾ | Untitled | ⚠ Logic |
|---|---|---|

*On a scale of 1-10, how likely are you to recommend Cloud Sauce to a friend or colleague?

Low                                                                                            High

| 0 | 1 | 2 | 3 | 4 | 5 | 6 | 7 | 8 | 9 | 10 |
|---|---|---|---|---|---|---|---|---|---|---|

*Please use the box below to describe how working with Cloud Sauce and/or Zoho CRM has positively impacted on your business

In terms of our project delivery is there anything that you think we could perhaps improve in future? Please be specific.

*Would you be happy for us include the comments above in our marketing material including a website testimonial?

○ Yes

○ No

Figure 11.16 – Example survey that should deliver a high response rate and lots of value

Once you have created the survey, you need to create an email template in Zoho CRM. As we typically do not need to integrate the results back to CRM for this one, we can simply use the survey link within the **Launch** tab in **Surveys**.

Finally, create a workflow in CRM that will be triggered based on a user updating the stage of an opportunity or by a **Date** field (**Delivery Date** or similar). An example of this is displayed here:

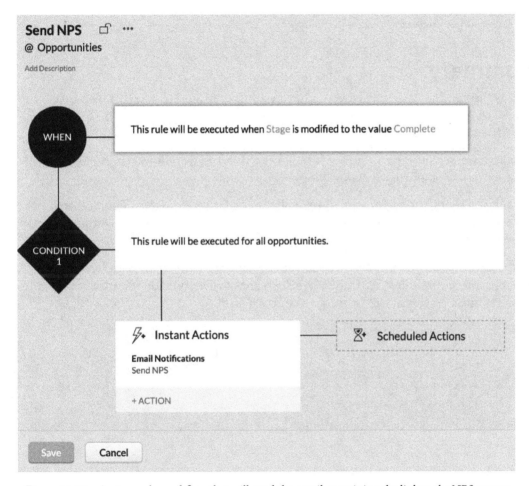

Figure 11.17 – An example workflow that will send the email containing the link to the NPS survey automatically when the stage is updated to Complete

Further information on the NPS survey question in Zoho Survey can be found here:

```
https://www.zoho.com/blog/survey/track-customer-loyalty-with-
the-net-promoter-score.html
```

Once you have created a couple of surveys with/without integration with Zoho CRM, you should start to feel comfortable with the process and, in time, should be able to create many other surveys that will help your business to gain feedback.

So, let's end the chapter with a brief recap!

## Summary

In this chapter, you have learned how to create a survey using Zoho Survey. You have gained an understanding of the benefits of integrating a survey with Zoho CRM and the different ways in which this can be achieved.

You have worked through a couple of example surveys and workflows that can be adopted by your business immediately or adapted slightly for future use.

Finally, you should now appreciate the simplicity and far-reaching possibilities that Zoho Survey (with Zoho CRM) offers and should now realize that gathering insightful feedback from clients and other network partners should be a pleasure and not a chore.

In the next chapter, you will learn about Sales IQ, another great application from Zoho that integrates with Zoho CRM and other Zoho apps to help provide you with real-life business intelligence that will help your marketing team.

# 12
# SalesIQ

**SalesIQ** is a powerful and insightful tool that will allow you to engage with prospects and clients using a live chat facility. This tool, when enabled, will also track website visitors so that you can better tailor communication to them and trigger alerts for your team.

In this chapter, you will learn the basics of live chat that will help you convert leads and personalize some of the marketing content once you know which pages have been visited, by whom, and when. As the saying goes – *knowledge is power*!

The following topics are covered within this chapter:

- The importance of connecting SalesIQ to your website
- How can you connect SalesIQ to your website?
- Integrating SalesIQ with CRM
- Getting to know your website visitors
- Live chat, visitor tracking, and workflow automation

By the end of this chapter, you will have gained an understanding of the unique value proposition of SalesIQ and how to connect this tool. You will have learned about the key features, including live chat, visitor tracking, and workflow automation.

However, as is often the best place to begin, let's start with why.

# The importance of connecting SalesIQ to your website

In the digital world we live in today, most of the research our prospects will conduct, other than asking their peers, colleagues, and friends, will be online. So, it's fair to say that most (if not all) of our prospects will visit our website at some point at least once during their buying process.

It's also fair to say that not all website visitors will convert or become a customer during their first visit. A popular opinion, in fact, is that on average it will take as many as seven touches before a prospect becomes a customer. So, with this in mind, consider the value of each of the following points:

- Imagine if you knew who visited your website at any given time.
- Imagine if you knew how many times they had visited, what pages they looked at, and what activities they performed when they were on them.
- Imagine also if you could trigger alerts to our sales team based on this insight and send personalized emails to your prospects that were relevant to their visitor activity.

*Does these sound like valuable and actionable insights?* Yes, of course they do. This is why we should connect SalesIQ to our website and integrate it with our CRM.

*Unconvinced? What have you got to lose?* You won't know unless you try. *Convinced?* Good, so now let's look at how you can do this.

# How can you connect SalesIQ to your website?

You can create a SalesIQ account and link it to **Zoho CRM** in a few steps, as follows:

1. Navigate to `https://www.zoho.com/salesiq/signup.html` (if you subscribe to **Zoho One/CRM Plus**, you can just add SalesIQ from the Admin Portal).

2. When you have created/added your SalesIQ account, the SalesIQ code will appear on the SalesIQ welcome page. You (or your webmaster) have to copy the code from the welcome page, which will appear as follows:

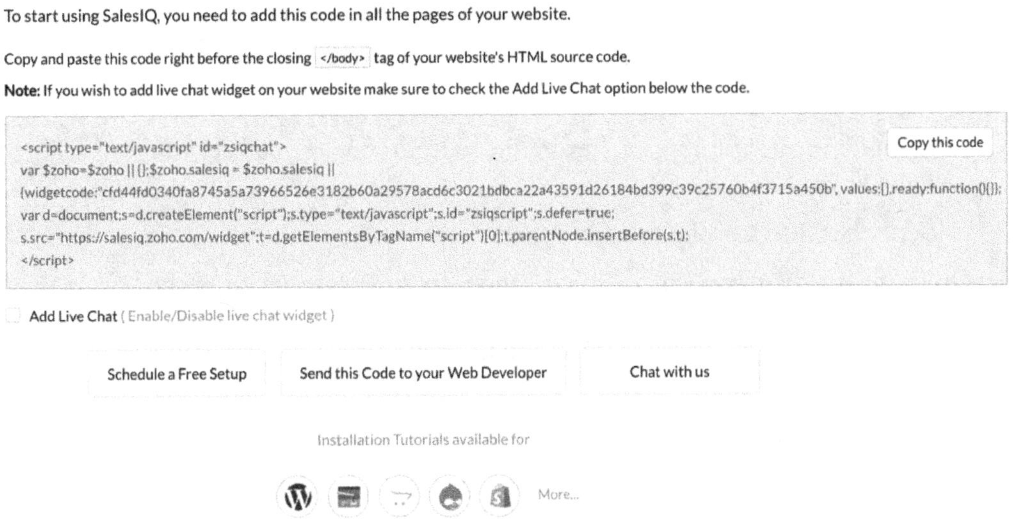

To start using SalesIQ, you need to add this code in all the pages of your website.

Copy and paste this code right before the closing `</body>` tag of your website's HTML source code.

**Note:** If you wish to add live chat widget on your website make sure to check the Add Live Chat option below the code.

```
<script type="text/javascript" id="zsiqchat">
var $zoho=$zoho || {};$zoho.salesiq = $zoho.salesiq ||
{widgetcode:"cfd44fd0340fa8745a5a73966526e3182b60a29578acd6c3021bdbca22a43591d26184bd399c39c25760b4f3715a450b", values:{},ready:function(){});
var d=document;s=d.createElement("script");s.type="text/javascript";s.id="zsiqscript";s.defer=true;
s.src="https://salesiq.zoho.com/widget";t=d.getElementsByTagName("script")[0];t.parentNode.insertBefore(s,t);
</script>
```

Copy this code

Add Live Chat ( Enable/Disable live chat widget )

Schedule a Free Setup          Send this Code to your Web Developer          Chat with us

Installation Tutorials available for

More...

Figure 12.1 – The code that needs to be copied to your website

3. If you wish just to track your website visitors and do not wish to enable live chat on your website, then remember to uncheck the **Add Live Chat** box below the code snippet. By default, this option will be enabled/checked.

4. In your website's source file, paste the code into your existing code anywhere before the `</body>` tag. Then, save and publish the changes made to your website.

If for any reason you do not see the code as described in the preceding steps upon accessing SalesIQ, you can obtain this code by navigating to **Settings | Brands | Your Brand Name | Installation | Website**. Once you've copied the code onto your website, it's time to integrate SalesIQ with your CRM, which will bring add a lot of value and enable your marketing and sales team to take action based on these insights.

# Integrating SalesIQ with your CRM

Integrating SalesIQ with CRM will bring all this website visitor data into one place. It will allow you to better understand your buyer's journey and interact with them using live chat, or send relevant emails based on their recent activity.

We can achieve this integration by executing the following steps:

1. Navigate to `salesiq.zoho.com` and then sign in.

2. Click on the settings icon (the cog) in the top-right corner.

3. Then, select the **Integrations | Zoho CRM** options.

4.   Select the **Connect with your Zoho CRM account** option.

5.   After that, click on **Enable Integration** and select the matching CRM account that is shown on the screen.

6.   Click on the arrow pointing left next to the settings (taking you back to the previous screen).

7.   Click on the **CRM Configurations** option.

8.   On the next screen, you will see some options for how data will be pushed to CRM. Mostly, you won't know your preferences until you have used this tool for a few weeks. So, if unsure, keep the standard configuration as shown in the following screenshot:

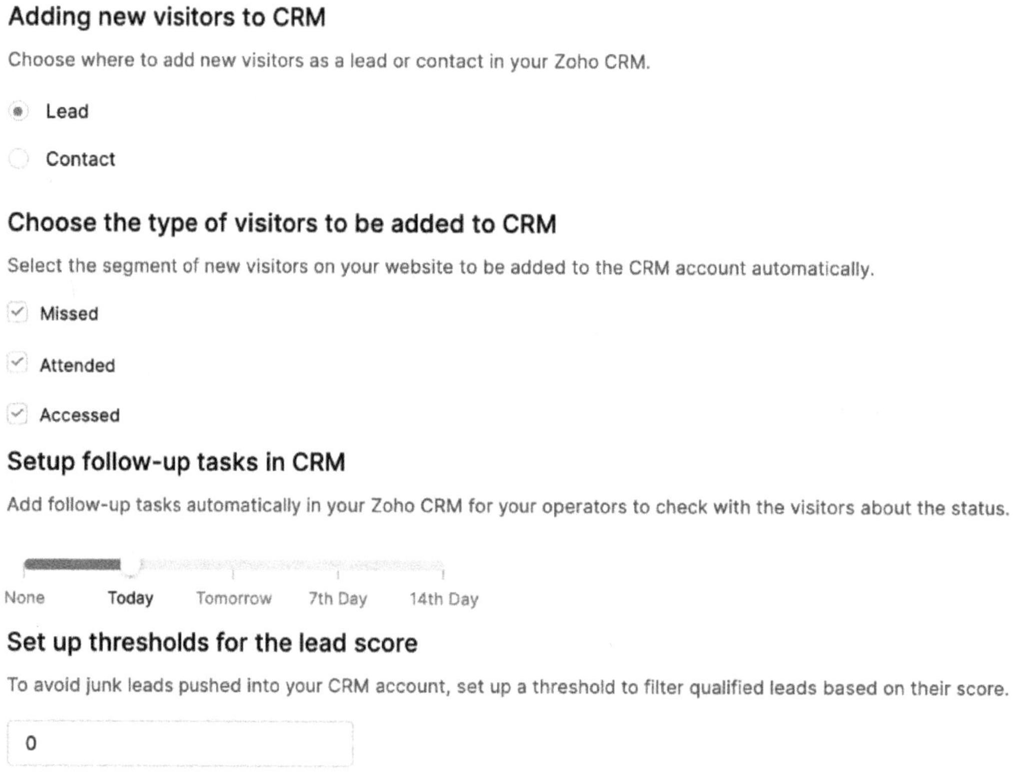

### Adding new visitors to CRM

Choose where to add new visitors as a lead or contact in your Zoho CRM.

⦿  Lead

◯  Contact

### Choose the type of visitors to be added to CRM

Select the segment of new visitors on your website to be added to the CRM account automatically.

☑  Missed

☑  Attended

☑  Accessed

### Setup follow-up tasks in CRM

Add follow-up tasks automatically in your Zoho CRM for your operators to check with the visitors about the status.

None      **Today**      Tomorrow      7th Day      14th Day

### Set up thresholds for the lead score

To avoid junk leads pushed into your CRM account, set up a threshold to filter qualified leads based on their score.

| 0 |
|---|

Figure 12.2 – Standard configuration for pushing data to CRM

9.   Return to the previous screen by clicking on the arrow pointing left next to settings.

10.  Now, you need to open CRM.

11. Navigate to the **Setup | Channels | Chat** section.

12. Select your account that should now appear within the **Choose Account** dropdown.

Congratulations, you will have now completed the basic SalesIQ and CRM integration.

> **Tip**
>
> After you have had the SalesIQ and Zoho CRM integration running for a few weeks, it is worthwhile reviewing with the team the settings you had selected and tweak any as required.

So, now you have completed the basic setup and integration. It's time to learn how you can get to know your visitors, which is the key to unlocking some of the powerful features you will explore later in the chapter.

# Getting to know your website visitors

The data that you capture in SalesIQ is useful in its own right to track visitor activities. However, when you know *who* these visitors are then this increases the value of this data exponentially. In this section, you will learn about integrating Campaigns, CRM (emails), and Forms with SalesIQ.

To get to know who these visitors are, they need to perform at least one of the following activities:

- Engage in a live chat.
- Click on an email campaign (integrated with SalesIQ).
- Click on a SalesIQ link from within an email sent manually or automatically from CRM.
- Submit a form (integrated with SalesIQ).

Upon the completion of one of the aforementioned activities, SalesIQ will match the **Internet Protocol** (**IP**) address to the email address. From this point onward, you will know the name and email of this visitor, and all the subsequent website visits will be captured in CRM. While engaging in a live chat is self-explanatory, let's look at the other three activities in turn in the upcoming sections.

# Integrating Campaigns to SalesIQ

The most effective way to integrate Campaigns to SalesIQ is to add some additional code (an identifier) to the link you insert into your email campaign. This can be achieved by following these steps:

1.  Open SalesIQ.

2.  Navigate to the **Setup | Integrations | Zoho Campaigns | Identifier Link** section.

3.  Paste the website link to which you want to add an identifier into the box provided and then click on the **Generate** button, as shown here:

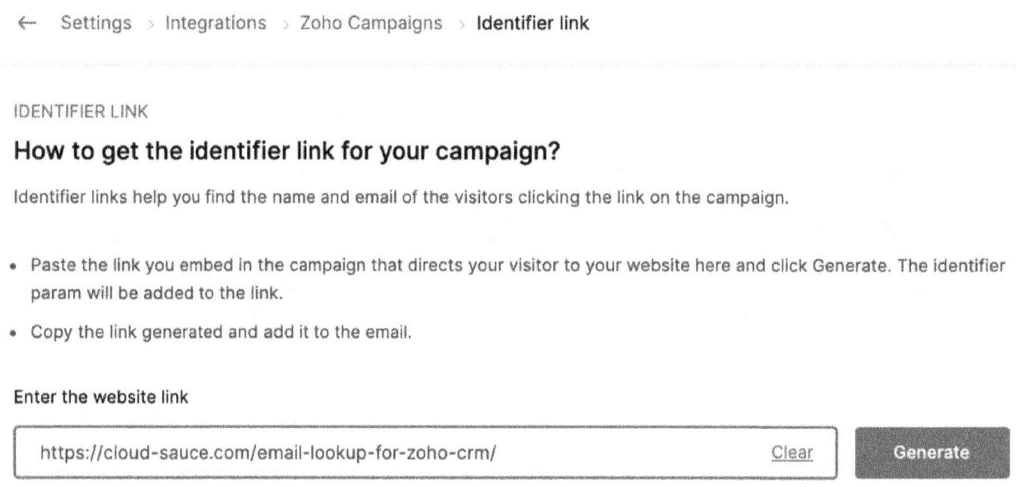

←    Settings  ›  Integrations  ›  Zoho Campaigns  ›  **Identifier link**

IDENTIFIER LINK

### How to get the identifier link for your campaign?

Identifier links help you find the name and email of the visitors clicking the link on the campaign.

*   Paste the link you embed in the campaign that directs your visitor to your website here and click Generate. The identifier param will be added to the link.

*   Copy the link generated and add it to the email.

**Enter the website link**

https://cloud-sauce.com/email-lookup-for-zoho-crm/          Clear          Generate

Figure 12.3 – Generating your link with an identifier

4.  You will now be presented with a box that contains your new link. Use this link in the body of your email or as a button link. Upon the recipient clicking on the link, SalesIQ will then be able to track this, and any subsequent website visits made and identify the visitor by their name and email address. The following screenshot demonstrates this:

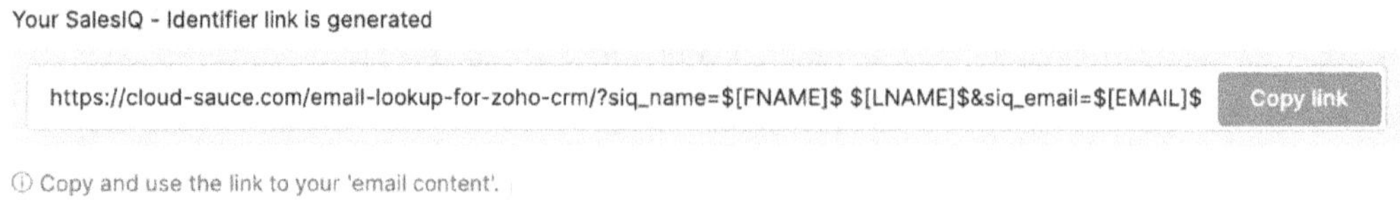

Your SalesIQ - Identifier link is generated

https://cloud-sauce.com/email-lookup-for-zoho-crm/?siq_name=$[FNAME]$ $[LNAME]$&siq_email=$[EMAIL]$     Copy link

ⓘ Copy and use the link to your 'email content'.

Figure 12.4 – An example identifier link ready to be used in your email campaign

In the next section, you will learn about integrating CRM email with SalesIQ.

## Integrating CRM email with SalesIQ

In a similar way to Campaigns, you can easily add an identifier to any email sent from Zoho CRM. We can achieve this by sending the email manually and following these steps:

1.  Open a **Lead** or **Contact** record in CRM then click on **Send Email**.

2.  Click on the **Insert SalesIQ Link** button as highlighted in the following screenshot:

Figure 12.5 – Inserting a SalesIQ link into a CRM email

3.  Now paste your link into the **Enter Web URL** field, as shown in the following screenshot, and then click **Save**:

Figure 12.6 – Pasting your link into an email template in CRM

Alternatively, we can also achieve this by inserting an identifier within an email notification, which could be linked to a workflow rule and sent to a **Lead/Contact** automatically, as explained in the following steps:

1. Navigate to the **Setup | Customization | Templates** section.

2. Open an existing template or create a new one and click on the insert link icon located on the toolbar at the top of the template editor window.

3. Paste your link into the **Enter Web URL** field, enter a title in the **Title** field, and check the box labeled **Include SalesIq identifiers**, as shown in the following screenshot, and then click **Save**:

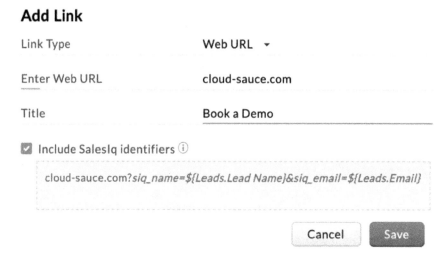

Figure 12.7 – Inserting your SalesIQ identifier into an automated email template

As email is increasingly the most common type of communication with prospects, knowing how to use this SalesIQ capability can be a very useful and valuable tool for your sales and marketing teams. Finally, let's conclude this section by looking at how we integrate Zoho Forms with SalesIQ.

## Integrating Forms with SalesIQ

The ability to link SalesIQ to Forms gives us lots of scope and reasons for creating a form. We can create a form for newsletter sign-up, for contacting us, to allow the visitor to download a PDF document, or any other activity whereby you are obtaining an email address in exchange for something of value to your prospect/contact.

We can achieve this integration by using the following steps:

1.  Navigate to `forms.zoho.com`.

2.  Click on **Settings** for the form you wish to integrate with (assuming you have already created your form).

3.  Select **Integrations** from the menu at the top.

4.  Then, select **SalesIQ** from the menu on the left.

5.  Click on the **Integrate** button, as shown in the following screenshot:

Integrate Zoho Forms with Zoho SalesIQ to track visitors when they submit a form.

Figure 12.8 – Enabling the integration between Forms and SalesIQ

6.  Now, select your portal and website from the respective drop-down fields.

7.  Select the fields you wish to map – note that you only have a maximum of three fields available within SalesIQ – **Email**, **Name**, and **Phone**.

8.  Click on the **Integrate** button, as shown here:

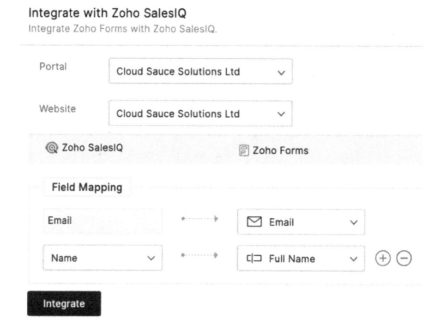

Figure 12.9 – Completing the Forms and SalesIQ integration

9.  Finally, click on **Integrate** (ignoring the visitor tracking code as you will have done that already).

> **Tip**
> You will still need to integrate your form with Zoho CRM to capture the form submission details, create/update your **Lead** or **Contact** records, and trigger any CRM automation.

In this section, you learned how to integrate SalesIQ with Campaigns, CRM (email), and Forms. So, with Campaigns, CRM emails, and Forms, you really do have lots of different ways in which you can find out exactly who your website visitors are. This will help you to maximize the value of visitor tracking and workflow automation triggered by your known website visitors, as described in the next section.

# Live chat, visitor tracking, and workflow automation

In this section, you will learn how to get started using the three key areas that may add the quickest value – live chat, visitor tracking, and workflow automation. The live chat feature is a great way to engage in real time with customers and prospects.

Visitor tracking features allow us to learn about visitor behavior, and workflow automation allows us to take action based on the types of behavior. Let's look at live chat first.

## Live chat

Open `salesiq.zoho.com` and click on the settings icon (the cog in the top right). This will take you to the settings menu as illustrated in the following screenshot:

| COMPANY | PERSONALIZE | CONTROLS | AUTOMATE | BOT | DEVELOPERS |
|---|---|---|---|---|---|
| Profile | Brands (Websites) | Chat Monitor | Triggers | Zobot | Integrations |
| Operators | Global Settings | Block IP | Visitor Routing | Answer Bot | Channels |
| Departments | Email Templates | | Chat Routing | | Webhooks |
| Usage statistics | Profanity Library | | Lead Scoring | | Widgets |
| | Apple TV | | Company Scoring | | Form Controllers |
| | | | Schedule Report | | Plugs |

Figure 12.10 – Settings menu within SalesIQ

To help you get to grips with the basics quickly, you can use this section as a quickstart guide. Once you've had a few weeks/months of experience with the application, it's worth reviewing these options and further refining your preferences based on your experience.

Updating the following settings will get you started:

- Navigate to **Company | Profile**: You can edit your company address, contact, profile, and logo details in this section.

- Navigate to **Company | Operators**: Click on the **Add** button (top right) to add the users you wish to give access to be able to chat with visitors.

- Navigate to **Personalize | Brands (Websites)**: Click on your brand/company name, then click on the **Personalization | Appearance** tabs, as shown in the following screenshot. On this screen, you can select one of four themes and a color, set the size of your chat window, and choose whether to display your company logo:

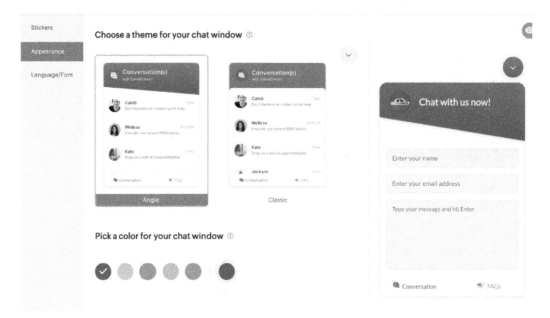

Figure 12.11 – Personalizing your chat window

- Navigate to **Personalize | Brands (Websites) | Flow Controls**: In this section, you can amend the fields to be displayed in the chat window and also personalize some of the standard messages that will be presented if operators are busy or unavailable. This screen is shown in the following screenshot:

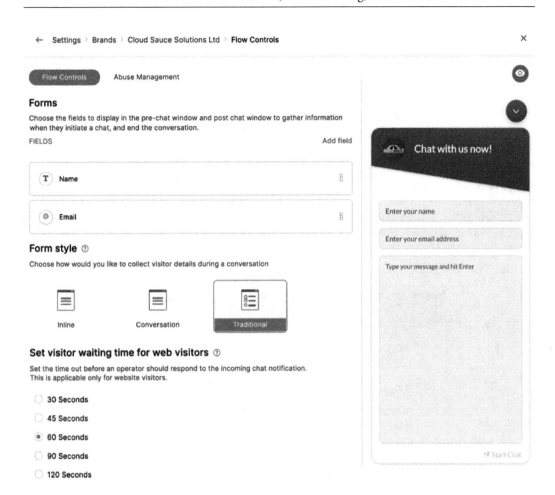

Figure 12.12 – Additional options to provide more personalization for settings and messages

Once you have personalized these settings, you are ready to use the chat tool. Open `salesiq.zoho.com` or download/open the SalesIQ mobile application to see when visitors are on your website. If a visitor initiates a chat with your user, you will hear a ringtone and upon clicking the **Answer** button you will be chatting with your visitor.

There are lots more settings you can adjust; however, you just need to get started with the basics, and then refine things as you learn and make progress. Now, it's time to see what happens inside CRM once we have integrated SalesIQ.

## Visitor tracking

The first difference you will notice inside CRM is that it pushes live data from SalesIQ into CRM. A pop-up window shows the number of current visitors, their names (if known), the time spent on the site, the number of pages visited, and the date they last visited toward the bottom right corner of the screen, as shown in the following screenshot:

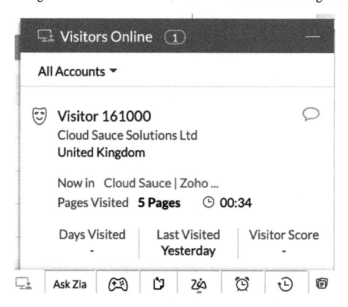

Figure 12.13 – Live website visitor details inside CRM

So, while that live data may be useful to prompt your sales team to engage in a chat, make a call, or send an email during or after the visit, we can also get some detailed information within a module called **Visits** accessible from the main menu. This will list all known visitors (**Leads/Contacts**) and their individual website visits, which we will explore in more detail later in the chapter.

However, information is summarized with the **Lead/Contact** module record in Zoho CRM in a section named **Visit Summary**. This displays summarized data including the dates of first/last visits, the first page visited, the average time spent on the site, and **Visitor Score** (see `https://www.zoho.com/salesiq/help/visitorhistory-leadscoring.html` for further details on **Lead Scoring** in SalesIQ). An example of how this will appear in CRM is as follows:

**Visit Summary**

| | | | |
|---|---|---|---|
| First Visit | 04/01/2021 15:22 | Visitor Score | 2670 |
| Referrer | https://cloud-sauce.com/wp-admin/admin.php?page=LD_dashboard | Average Time Spent (Minutes) | 33 mins 46 secs |
| Most Recent Visit | 08/05/2021 11:33 | First Page Visited | https://cloud-sauce.com/ |
| Number Of Chats | 3 | Days Visited | 33 |

Figure 12.14 – Visit Summary section within a Lead/Contact record in CRM

While this information can be really insightful for sales and marketing, being able to review and action that data in a timely manner is a challenge for many business owners and sales teams. It is for this reason that the workflow automation triggered by this data can often add the most value.

## Workflow automation

One of the best features of Zoho CRM is workflow automation, and one of the most insightful marketing tools in SalesIQ. So, when you put them together, they can really ignite your marketing efforts, especially when the prospect is at an advanced stage of the sales funnel.

The key to this is the **Visits** module in CRM. Once a *known* prospect makes a website visit, this creates a record in the **Visits** module. By *known*, we are referring to the fact that at some point the prospect has performed at least one of the activities discussed in the *Getting to know your website visitors* section.

So, let's look at an example of a visit record in CRM:

**General Information**

| | | | |
|---|---|---|---|
| Page Visited | B2B Leads - Help and Support - Cloud Sauce | Visited By | ▇▇▇▇▇▇▇▇ . |
| IP Address | ▇▇▇▇▇▇▇ | Time Spent (Minutes) | 2 hours 11 mins |
| Referrer | https://marketplace.zoho.com/ | Visited Page URL | https://cloud-sauce.com/prospector-for-zoho-crm-help-support/ |
| Created By | Dominic Harrington<br>Fri, 28 May 2021 15:17 | Modified By | Dominic Harrington<br>Fri, 28 May 2021 15:17 |
| Attended By | -- | User Details | Mozilla/5.0 (Macintosh; Intel Mac OS X 10_15_7) AppleWebKit/537.36 (KHTML, like Gecko) Chrome/90.0.4430.212 Safari/537.36 |
| Browser | Google Chrome | | |
| Visitor Type | Lead | Time Visited | 28/05/2021 13:05 |
| Number of Pages | 5 | Revenue | £ 0.00 |
| | | Portal Name | Cloud Sauce Solutions Ltd |

Figure 12.15 – A record in the Visits module in Zoho CRM

As seen in the preceding example, you can see the date, time, and actual URL of the page visited. Importantly, there is a link to the **Lead/Contact** record that will hold their email address.

So, looking at the page URL, you know that the user was looking at the help and support page for a specific product. So, you can assume by this that they are both aware of and interested in the product and most likely have one or two questions that they are searching for the answers to.

Based on this information, it is also very likely that if you were to reach out instantly and offer to help, then there is a good chance they will engage. Now, if you had an operator with SalesIQ open, they could try and initiate a live chat, or the prospect may use this themselves.

However, this technique will not work for everyone. So, using **CRM Workflow**, you can use this information to trigger sending an email to the prospect, which could contain a link to book a product demonstration.

The typical workflow in this situation will be triggered when a record is created in the **Visits** module. We can also add a condition that the action will be performed only when a specific website page is visited. Once this happens, our email will be sent using an email notification. A summary of this basic workflow can be seen in the following screenshot:

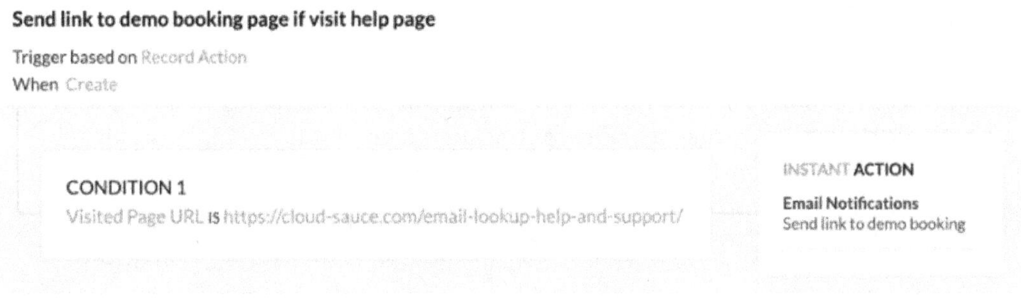

**Send link to demo booking page if visit help page**

Trigger based on Record Action
When Create

CONDITION 1

Visited Page URL IS https://cloud-sauce.com/email-lookup-help-and-support/

INSTANT **ACTION**

**Email Notifications**
Send link to demo booking

Figure 12.16 – Workflow example for sending an email upon a visitor landing on a specific website page

By creating this workflow, you are making the most of the insights provided by SalesIQ and the CRM automation and increasing the chances of progressing a lead through to the next stage of the buying process. Better still, by using this process you can easily identify similar workflows that can also be created to help warm up a lead and/or move them on to the next stage of the funnel. The following are some examples for this:

- Sending different emails based on landing on different website pages
- Creating a task for the sales team to follow up by phone or email
- Adding a tag to the **Lead/Contact**, which may push them to a different mailing list or automated workflow in Campaigns
- Scheduling a follow-up email at a later date, for example, inviting them to a webinar or other event
- Updating the status or another field of the related **Lead/Contact**

While the aforementioned examples are by no means exhaustive, it should be enough to inspire other ideas for you and the marketing team.

So, having understood how to link SalesIQ to CRM, you really are in a position to start tracking website visitors and also do something really useful with this information. Of course, it's really important to **build–measure–evolve** how you continue to use these tools, but one thing is for sure: the impact your marketing has on the successful growth of sales will get a real boost by putting these tools into action.

So, that brings us to the end of this chapter – let's have a quick recap.

# Summary

In this chapter, you have learned how to connect SalesIQ to your CRM, Campaigns, and Forms instances. You have also learned the various techniques we can use to find out who is on our website and create the capability for tracking them in future. You have gained an understanding of the key features of SalesIQ, including live chat, visitor tracking, and workflow automation.

As a result, your marketing and sales efforts will be boosted with real-time and historical data that can automatically prompt your sales team, ultimately helping your teams close more deals faster.

In the next chapter, you will learn about **Zoho Analytics** and discover some of the ways that you can build powerful dashboards and reports that will help you measure and manage the performance of your team and business growth.

# 13
# Zoho Analytics

**Zoho Analytics** is an enterprise-level **Business Intelligence** (**BI**) tool. It is also potentially one of the most under-utilized tools within the Zoho suite of applications. Partially, this may be due to the high quality of the native Reports and Analytics modules of the Zoho CRM, and perhaps it's a misconception that this tool is too complex to use.

In this chapter, we will bust this myth and provide some practical examples of how this tool can be used to gain insights that may otherwise be missed.

Topics covered within this chapter include the following:

- Connecting your CRM with Analytics
- Getting to grips with the basic tools
- Creating dashboards that can be shared automatically

By the end of this chapter, you will have learned how to configure your integration with Zoho CRM and Analytics. You will have developed skills with the basic report creation tools. You will also understand how to create powerful and insightful dashboards that can automatically be shared with peers.

So, let's start by connecting CRM with Analytics.

# Connecting your CRM with Analytics

To integrate CRM with Analytics, follow these steps from within Zoho CRM:

1.  Navigate to **Setup | Marketplace | Zoho | Advanced Analytics for CRM**.

2.  Click on **Get Started**.

3.  Select the fields from the modules that you wish to sync with Analytics.

4.  Select the frequency and time you wish to sync the data at using the **Sync Option** dropdown.

5.  Click **Save**. This configuration popup can be seen in the following screenshot:

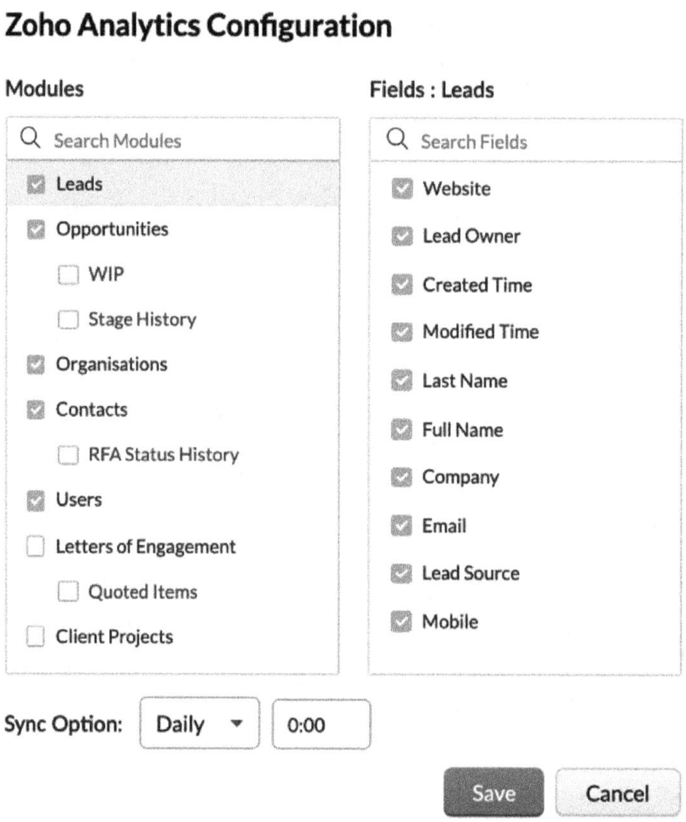

## Zoho Analytics Configuration

| Modules | Fields : Leads |
|---|---|
| 🔍 Search Modules | 🔍 Search Fields |
| ☑ Leads | ☑ Website |
| ☑ Opportunities | ☑ Lead Owner |
| ☐ WIP | ☑ Created Time |
| ☐ Stage History | ☑ Modified Time |
| ☑ Organisations | ☑ Last Name |
| ☑ Contacts | ☑ Full Name |
| ☐ RFA Status History | ☑ Company |
| ☑ Users | ☑ Email |
| ☐ Letters of Engagement | ☑ Lead Source |
| ☐ Quoted Items | ☑ Mobile |
| ☐ Client Projects | |

Sync Option:  [ Daily ▼ ]  [ 0:00 ]

[ Save ]  [ Cancel ]

Figure 13.1 – Zoho Analytics configuration screen

Upon clicking **Save**, the screen will change, and you will be presented with a summary of the sync you created.

Congratulations, you have just completed the integration between Analytics and CRM.

> **Tip**
>
> Only the fields that are checked will be synced with Analytics and available to build and/or filter reports. You can also come back and amend this configuration at any time if you wish to add or remove more fields.

So, now that the two applications, CRM, and Analytics, are integrated (synced), let's start with some basic orientation of the Analytics application itself.

Further information is available at `https://www.zoho.com/analytics/help/overview.html`.

# Getting to grips with the basic tools

In this section, we will look at basic navigation around the Analytics user interface and also where and how to start analyzing data. You will learn about navigation by completing the following steps:

1. Firstly, access `analytics.zoho.com` and then sign in using your Zoho account login.

2. Click on the box (known as a **workspace**) named **Zoho CRM Reports**, shown as follows:

Figure 13.2 – Zoho CRM Reports workspace as displayed on the Analytics home page

Next, you will see the workspace home page, shown as follows:

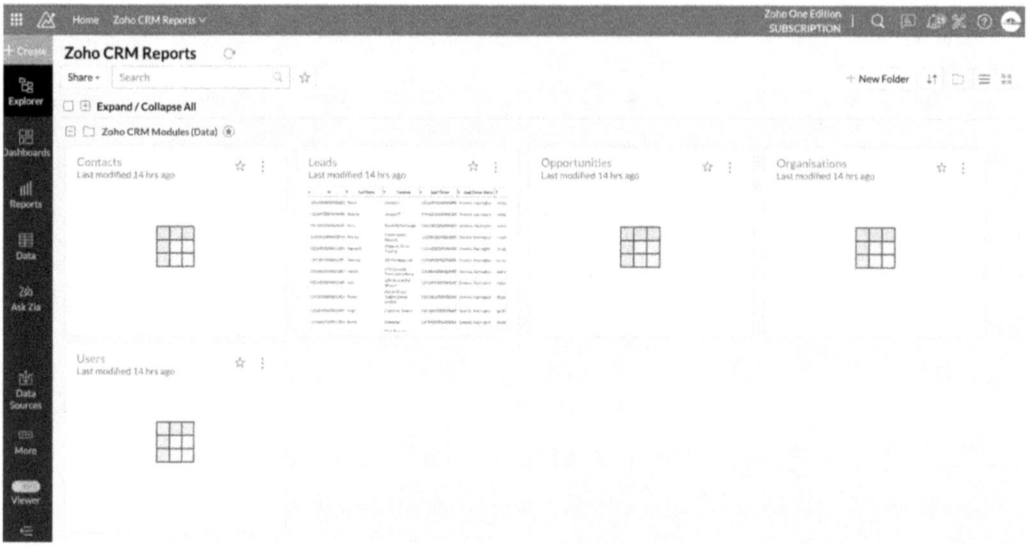

Figure 13.3 – The Zoho CRM Reports workspace home page within Analytics

On the screen shown in *Figure 13.3*, you will see the names of CRM modules displayed as boxes with grids. In this example, you will see **Contacts**, **Leads**, **Opportunities**, **Organizations**, and **Users**. These correspond with the (CRM) modules you selected to sync with earlier. Upon clicking on any of these boxes, you will be provided with a list of all records in the corresponding CRM module, including all the fields you synced. Each one of these grids is referred to as a table in the reporting database.

Let's have a look at an example table now – **Leads**:

Figure 13.4 – The Leads table in Zoho Analytics with some fields grayed out for anonymity

As seen in the preceding screenshot, the columns across the top correspond to field names in CRM, and within each row numbered sequentially on the left are individual records within the **Leads** module. As you will see, this very closely resembles a spreadsheet. For all the reports you create in Analytics, you will always start from here, that is, a table containing all the records you wish to analyze.

So, now you know how to integrate CRM into Analytics, how to sync the modules and fields, and finally, how to find this data within your Analytics reporting database. This is the first milestone to understanding Analytics.

The next milestone is learning how to use the most commonly used tools that will enable you to analyze your data. Within Analytics, we have four basic types of reports that we can use, which are named as follows:

- **Tabular view**
- **Summary view**
- **Chart**
- **Pivot table**

In the following sections, let's understand the definition of each report type and learn how you can generate a report using each one.

## Creating a tabular view

A tabular view allows you to display raw data in a tabular format similar to a spreadsheet. You may also easily summarize and group this data using this tool.

You can create a tabular view by executing the following steps:

1. Select one of your reporting tables. As seen in *Figure 13.3*, in this example, we will open **Leads**.
2. When the table opens, and you see a list of leads on the screen, click on the + towards the top right of the screen, shown as follows:

Figure 13.5 – Creating a new view

3. Now, select **New Tabular View** from the menu that appears, as shown in the following screenshot:

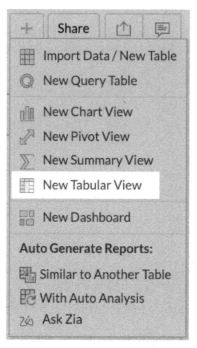

Figure 13.6 – Selecting New Tabular View from the create menu

4. Now, you will see all the data in that table set out in rows and columns. In the top-left corner, you will see a few buttons, as shown in the following screenshot:

Figure 13.7 – Options to customize our tabular view

These buttons provide options for configuring this report and are explained as follows:

a. **Sort**: Select the column you wish to sort by, then click **Sort**, and select the direction to sort by (A-Z or Z-A).

b. **Group**: This option will group records together by any field you wish. For example, if you want to group the **Lead** records by **Lead Source**, select the **Lead Source** column, then click on **Group**.

Now you will be presented with two options:

- **Group by Block** – This allows you to select a column and group it by unique values and display all records in a block.

- **Group By Section** – This allows you to select a column and group into sections

c. **Summary**: Select the column you wish to summarize by, then click on **Summary**. Now, if you check the **Count Records** box, you will see a sub-total at the bottom of each group, as shown in the following screenshot:

**Untitled-1**  📑Save  ⋮                                                                    +

| Sort | Group | Summary | More |

| | T | Lead Source | ↑ | # | Id | # | Lead Owner | T | Lead Owner Nam | T | Lead Status | 🗓 | Created Time | ⅞ | Is Converted? | 🗓 |
|---|---|---|---|---|---|---|---|---|---|---|---|---|---|---|---|---|
| | | COUNT = 33 | | | | | | | | | | | | | | |
| 34 | | Website - Consultation Page | | | 118168100001: | | 11816810000000680 | | Dominic Harrington | | Pre Qualified | | 05/02/2019 19:31 | | Yes | |
| | | COUNT = 1 | | | | | | | | | | | | | | |
| 35 | | Webform | | | 118168100004: | | 11816810000000680 | | Dominic Harrington | | Junk Lead | | 26/04/2021 07:26 | | No | |
| | | COUNT = 1 | | | | | | | | | | | | | | |
| 36 | | WebSite Visit | | | 118168100001! | | 11816810000000680 | | Dominic Harrington | | Pre Qualified | | 06/09/2019 14:56 | | Yes | |
| 37 | | | | | 118168100002; | | 11816810000000680 | | Dominic Harrington | | No for Now | | 18/05/2020 15:10 | | No | |
| 38 | | | | | 118168100004; | | 11816810000000680 | | Dominic Harrington | | Junk Lead | | 11/05/2021 00:41 | | No | |
| 39 | | | | | 118168100003{ | | 11816810000000680 | | Dominic Harrington | | Junk Lead | | 29/01/2021 16:52 | | No | |
| | | COUNT = 4 | | | | | | | | | | | | | | |

Figure 13.8 – Example tabular view report, grouped by Lead Source (by Section) and Summarized (records counted)

d. **More**: This option will allow you to show/hide a column and/or freeze a column. To utilize this, select a column, click on **More**, and check the appropriate box next to your preferred option.

Of the four reporting types, the tabular view is probably the least valuable and intuitive, so while it is useful to know what it does and how it works, the other report types will most likely be easier to interpret and gain more insight from.

So, let's have look at the next one now, a summary view.

# Creating a summary view

If you are working with very large datasets, then a tabular view will be difficult to interpret (imagine thousands of rows of data). In this scenario, a summary view will allow you to view only the summarized data in a table format.

Let's demonstrate how this works by using an example. We shall create a report summarizing the closed deals, grouped by **Type** and **Lead Source** in 2021:

1. Select one of your reporting tables (as seen in *Figure 13.3*). In this example, we will open **Opportunities**.

2. When the table opens and you see a list of leads on the screen, click on the + towards the top right of the screen.

3. Now, select **New Summary View** from the menu that appears.

4. Drag and drop columns (from the left) that you wish to be grouped by and compared into the **Group By** axis.

5. Next, select any numerical columns to be aggregated and drop them into the **Summary** axis, as shown in this screenshot:

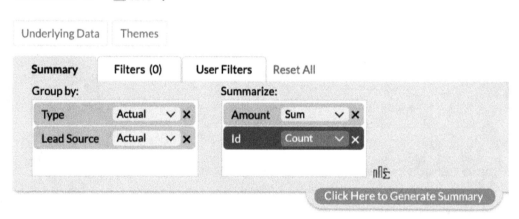

Figure 13.9 – Selecting fields for a Summary view

6. After that, for each field added in the **Summary** axis, click the drop-down menu and select which function you wish to apply, as shown here:

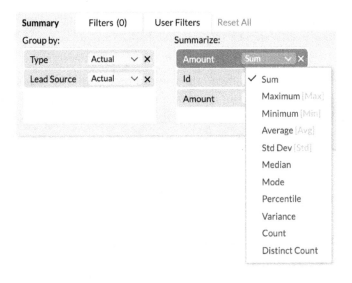

Figure 13.10 – Selecting the Sum of Amount from a list of available functions

7. Click on the **Filters** tab, then drag and drop the fields you wish to filter by and select the actual filters you require. For example, drop the **Stage** field and set the value to **Closed Won** and drop the **Closing Date** field and select **2021**.

8. Next, click on the **Click Here to Generate Summary** button. Upon which, you will be presented with the **Summary** view as it appears in the following screenshot:

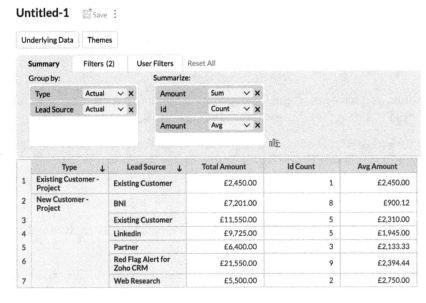

Figure 13.11 – Summary view when generated

9.  Creating a report is mostly an iterative process, so once you have reviewed your results, you may need to repeat *step 6* to *step 8*, then amend the fields and/or filters as required.

10. Sometimes you may need to amend the column header/title in your summary view. For example, we may want to rename **Id Count** to Number of Deals, which may be achieved by hovering over the **Id Count** column header, clicking the pencil, and then amending the name as desired.

11. Finally, when you're happy with everything, click on **Save**, then complete the **Name**, **Save in Folder**, and **Description** fields as required, followed by clicking on the **OK** button, as shown here:

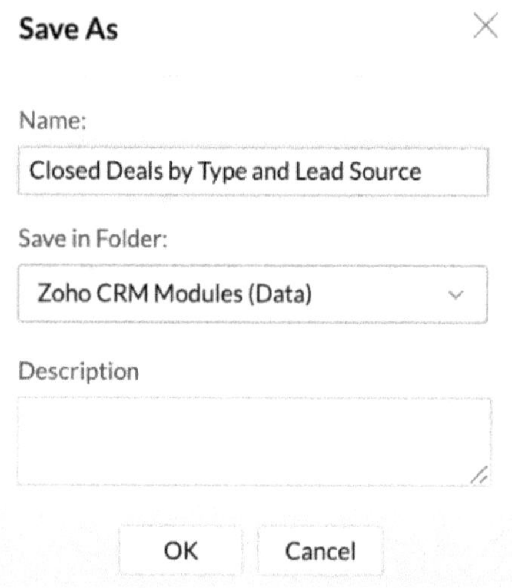

Save As                                              ✕

Name:

Closed Deals by Type and Lead Source

Save in Folder:

Zoho CRM Modules (Data)                          ⌄

Description

OK        Cancel

Figure 13.12 – Saving your report

Congratulations, you have now created a summary view report. As you will see, this is a lot more insightful than the tabular view and easier to analyze and understand.

Now, let's have a look at an even more intuitive and visual representation of our data by creating a chart.

## Creating a chart

A chart is a visual representation of data that provides an easy way to analyze and interpret data. There are over 25 chart types available within Analytics.

With over 25 chart types to select from, we really are spoilt for choice in this area. However, do not be overwhelmed by this if you only find yourself using a handful of them. The key objective is to select a type that is clear and easy to interpret for you and your team.

You can create a chart by executing the following steps:

1.  Select one of your reporting tables (as seen in *Figure 13.3*). In this example, we will open **Leads**.

2.  When the table opens and you see a list of leads on the screen, click on the + toward the top right of the screen.

3.  Now, select **New Chart View** from the menu that appears.

4.  Drag a column that you wish to measure (from the left pane) and drop it into the **X-Axis** or **Y-Axis** shelf at the top.

5.  For a more detailed view, drop columns to **Color**, **Text**, and **Tooltip** shelves.

6.  For each field that you have dropped, click the drop-down menu and select the required function. The following screenshot shows selecting fields that will display the number of leads created grouped by **Lead Source**:

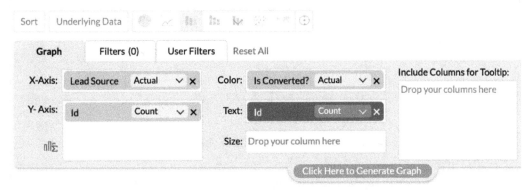

Figure 13.13 – Adding fields to create a chart

7.  Click on the **Filters** tab, then drag and drop fields you wish to filter by and select the actual filters you require. For example, **Created Time** is 2021 and **Lead Source** excludes or includes specific values.

8.  Next, click on the **Click Here to Generate Graph** button.

9. Repeat *step 4* to *step 6* until your results appear to be refined correctly as intended, then save your report, as shown here:

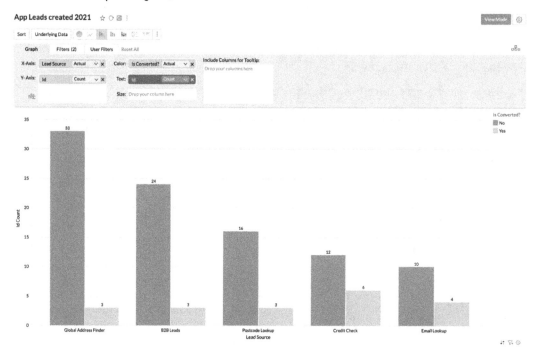

Figure 13.14 – Bar-chart comparing the number of leads generated across five lead sources (including whether converted or not)

10. Also, try removing the **Color** and **Text** fields and changing the visual appearance using the toolbar, as shown here:

Figure 13.15 – Changing the chart type using the toolbar

Reflecting on this chart, you can compare how much easier this is to interpret than the tabular view from earlier in this chapter. With charts, we have a summarized view displayed in a user-friendly format.

In time, you will find that most of the reports you create may be charts as they are intuitive for both creating and interpreting.

Finally, let's look at the fourth type of report, that is, a pivot table.

# Creating a pivot table

If you want to analyze large sets of data, then a pivot table may be the best option. This method allows you to summarize, group, and dynamically rearrange data while allowing you to filter, sort, and customize the appearance and content the way you want. Of the four report types, the pivot table is probably the most complex, yet powerful report type you can create, and it is worth investing the time to learn and then master this type.

You can create a pivot table by using these steps:

1.  Select one of your reporting tables (as seen in *Figure 13.3*). In this example, we will open **Opportunities**.

2.  When the table opens and you see a list of leads on the screen, click on the + towards the top right of the screen.

3.  Now, select **New Pivot View** from the menu that appears.

4.  Drag and drop a column from the left pane to the **Row** axis.

5.  Drag and drop a column to the **Column** axis.

6.  Drag and drop any numerical column to the **Data** axis.

7.  Click the drop-down menu within your dropped columns and select the required function for each of the fields.

8.  Click on the **Filters** tab, then add/drop the columns you wish to filter by, which will dictate which data should be included/excluded from your report.

9.  Click on the **Click Here to Generate Pivot** button, as shown here:

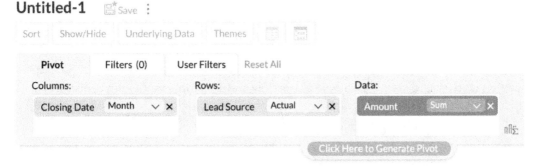

Figure 13.16 – Example of a pivot table including columns, rows, and data

10.  Repeat *step 4* to *step 7* until you have successfully refined the data that you are seeing in the pivot report before clicking **Save**, as shown here:

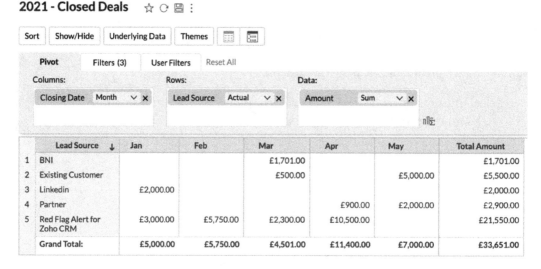

Figure13.17 – Example of pivot table showing sales by lead source grouped by month

Congratulations, you have created your first pivot report. With a little more practice, complex and large datasets will not be an insurmountable challenge for you/your team.

> **Tip**
> At first, it may seem difficult to understand whether a field needs to be dropped into **Columns** or **Rows**. Starting simply, with fewer columns and building your report in iterations, is usually a good technique. Also, keep generating the report as you go along. Build, test, and iterate!

As you have seen, each of the report types has different methods and outcomes. The best approach is to try and keep it as simple as possible and sometimes split your reporting requirements into smaller bitesize reports as opposed to trying to create one master report that has everything on it.

In this section, we learned about the basic tools in Analytics. We also learned about the different reporting types in detail. They are tabular view, summary view, chart, and pivot table.

To help with this approach, Zoho provides some additional functionality dashboards. So, let's conclude this chapter by exploring how we can create powerful and insightful dashboards.

# Creating dashboards that can be shared automatically

A **dashboard** provides a quick and easy way to display multiple reports on a single page that can be accessed and shared by your Analytics users. It is also possible to schedule sending a dashboard report to a list of users/other email addresses automatically on a daily, weekly, or monthly basis. This could be really valuable to managers that need to share reports with external stakeholders that do not have access to CRM.

The drag-and-drop interface provides an intuitive way to add your existing reports. You may also add **Key Performance Indicator** (**KPI**) Widgets, branding, and text, which will help you produce a functional and professional report. In this section, we will do the following:

- Create a new dashboard
- Create KPI Widgets
- Personalize the appearance of your dashboard
- Share your dashboard

So, let's begin by creating a dashboard.

# Creating a new dashboard

Starting from the **Zoho CRM Reports** workspace, you may create a dashboard by following these steps:

1. Click on **Dashboards** from the menu on the left of the screen, as shown here:

Figure 13.18 – Dashboards menu on the left

2. Next, locate and click on the **Create New Dashboards** link in the bottom-left corner of the screen, as shown here:

Figure 13.19 – Create New Dashboards link

3. On the next screen, you will notice that on the left-hand side is a list of reports. Locate the reports you wish to add and simply drag and drop them one by one into the middle of the window. Once you've added reports, the dashboard should resemble the following screenshot:

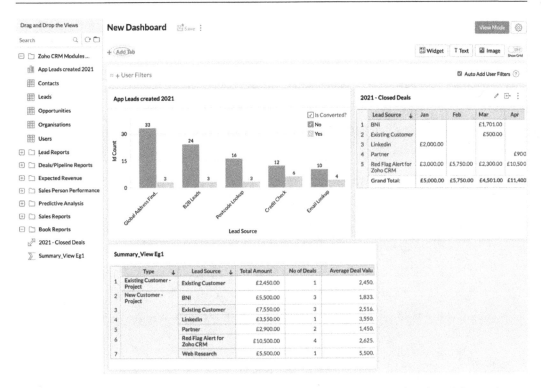

Figure 13.20 – A dashboard with three reports dragged into the main window from left to right

4.  Once you have added reports to the dashboard, you can rename, reposition, and resize them by hovering over a report using the toolbar in the top-right corner of your report, as shown in the following screenshot:

**Summary_View Eg1**

| | Type | | Lead Source | | Total Amount | No of Deals | Average Deal Va |
|---|---|---|---|---|---|---|---|
| 1 | Existing Customer - Project | | Existing Customer | | £2,450.00 | 1 | |
| 2 | New Customer - Project | | BNI | | £5,500.00 | 3 | |
| 3 | | | Existing Customer | | £7,550.00 | 3 | |
| 4 | | | Linkedin | | £3,550.00 | 1 | |
| 5 | | | Partner | | £2,900.00 | 2 | |
| 6 | | | Red Flag Alert for Zoho CRM | | £10,500.00 | 4 | |
| 7 | | | Web Research | | £5,500.00 | 1 | |

Figure 13.21 – Using the toolbar upon hovering over the report

Once you have added, amended, and repositioned the reports, it is often good to provide another dimension to the dashboard by adding one or more KPI Widgets.

## Creating KPI Widgets

Another great feature within Analytics is the ability to add what Zoho refers to as **KPI Widgets**. These widgets can be used to highlight any key metric in a dashboard in a visual and easy-to-understand format. You can display this metric with a comparison to highlight the trend or plotted against a target to show progression.

Let's take a look at an example KPI Widget now that will show the number of **Leads** created in the current month and compare this against the number created in the previous month:

1.  Within the menu, in the top-right corner of the dashboard window, locate the **Widget** toolbar, as shown here:

Figure 13.22 – Adding a widget to your dashboard

2.  Upon clicking **Widget**, you will be presented with the **KPI Widget Editor** box:

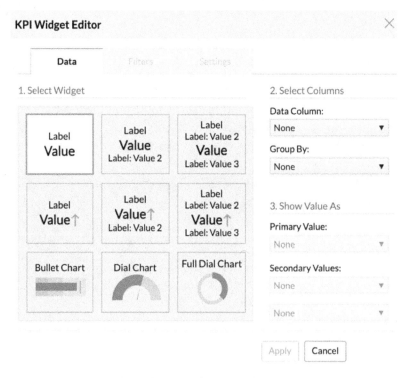

Figure 13.23 – KPI Widget Editor box displaying the nine different widget types

3.  In this example, we shall select the middle option (from the grid of nine types shown in *Figure 13.23*) and then complete the options within the **Data** tab as follows:

    a. Select the **Data Column** dropdown and select the field from the module we wish to measure, in this example, a count of **Lead ID**.

    b. Now, select the **Group By** dropdown and select how you wish to group the data. In this example, we will select **Created Time (Month)**:

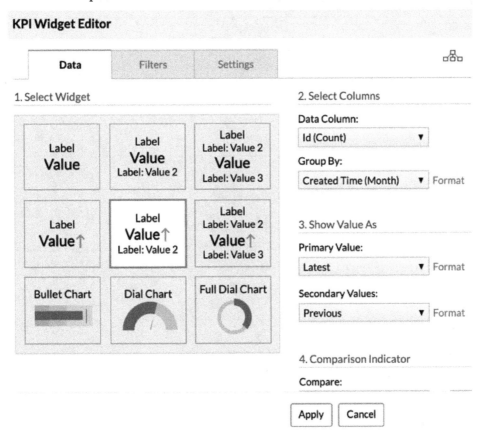

Figure 13.24 – Data tab in KPI Widget Editor

4.  Now, click on the **Filters** tab, drop the columns you wish to filter by, and select the values. In our example, we will select **Created Time**, as shown here:

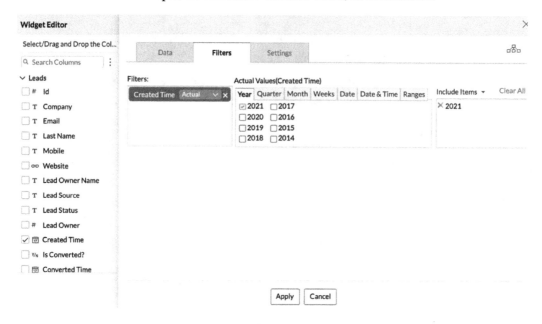

Figure 13.25 – Adding filters to your KPI Widget

5.  Finally, click on the **Settings** tab and apply some styling so that you may personalize the appearance of the widget, as shown in the following screenshot, then click **Apply**:

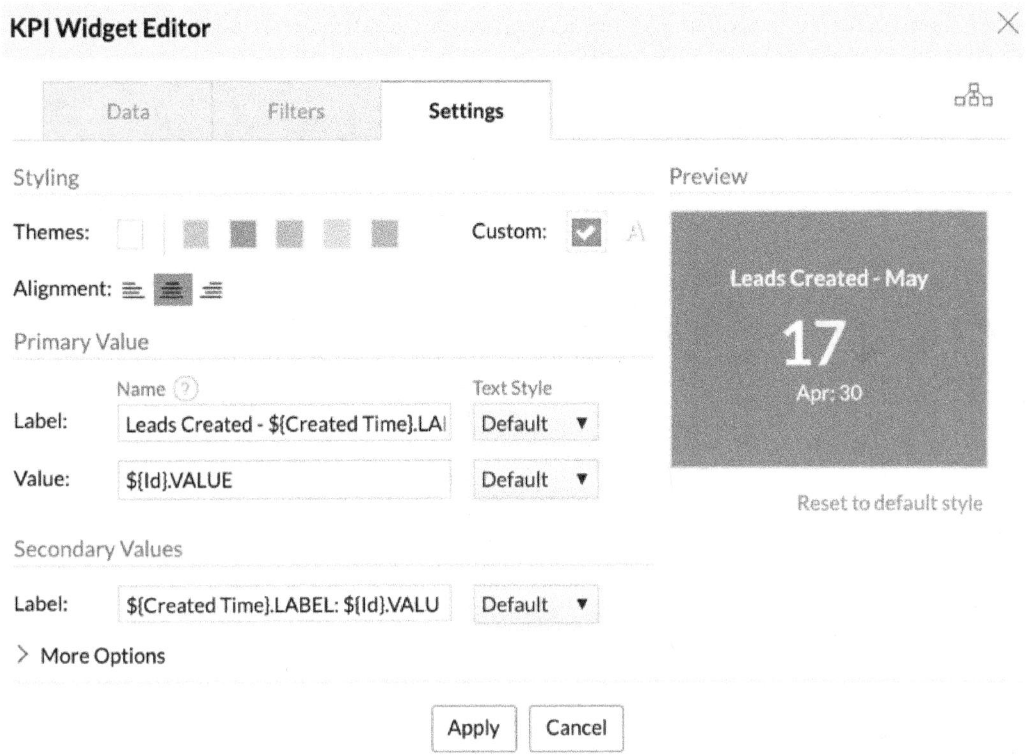

**KPI Widget Editor**                                                          ✕

| Data | Filters | **Settings** |

Styling                                                    Preview

Themes:   ☐  ◼ ◼ ◼ ◼ ◼        Custom:  ☑  A

Alignment: ☰  ☰  ☰

Primary Value

|  | Name ⑦ | Text Style |
|---|---|---|
| Label: | Leads Created - ${Created Time}.LAI | Default ▾ |
| Value: | ${Id}.VALUE | Default ▾ |

Secondary Values

| Label: | ${Created Time}.LABEL: ${Id}.VALU | Default ▾ |

> More Options

Leads Created - May

**17**

Apr: 30

Reset to default style

[ Apply ]  [ Cancel ]

Figure 13.26 – Updating the settings to personalize the appearance of the widget

You can add more widgets as required. If you create one, it triggers ideas for a few more. Next, let's have a look at the last stage and work on the appearance.

# Personalizing the appearance of your dashboard

You can also add images and/or text to your dashboard using the toolbar at the top right, as shown in *Figure 13.22* previously, which will provide your dashboard with more structure and color. Once you select those buttons, simply add your text/images to the intuitive editor, then click **Save**.

Finally, navigate to **View Mode | Themes** to pick an existing theme (or customize your own) as shown in the following example:

# 2021 SALES DASHBOARD

CLOUDSAUCE

| Leads Created - May | 2021 Leads Generated v Target | 2021 Average Deal Value |
|---|---|---|
| **17** Apr: 30 | 222    400 | **£3,008.39** |

**2021 - Closed Deals**

| | Lead Source | Jan | Feb | Mar | Apr | May | Total Amount |
|---|---|---|---|---|---|---|---|
| 1 | BNI | | | £1,701.00 | | | £1,701.00 |
| 2 | Existing Customer | | £500.00 | | | £5,000.00 | £5,500.00 |
| 3 | Linkedin | £2,000.00 | | | | | £2,000.00 |
| 4 | Partner | | | | £900.00 | £2,000.00 | £2,900.00 |
| 5 | Red Flag Alert for Zoho CRM | £3,000.00 | £5,750.00 | £2,300.00 | £10,500.00 | | £21,550.00 |
| | Grand Total: | £5,000.00 | £5,750.00 | £4,501.00 | £11,400.00 | £7,000.00 | £33,651.00 |

**App Leads created 2021**

| | Is Converted? |
|---|---|
| 33 | No |
| 30 | Yes |

**2021 Sales Summary**

| | Type | Lead Source | Total Amount | No of Deals | Average Deal Value |
|---|---|---|---|---|---|
| 1 | Existing Customer - Project | Existing Customer | £2,450.00 | 1 | 2,450.00 |
| 2 | New Customer - | | | | |

Figure 13.27 – A dashboard with a theme, text, KPI Widgets, and reports

Once you are happy with your dashboard, then you will most likely want to share it, so let's finish this section by looking at how to achieve this.

## Sharing your dashboard

Zoho Analytics offers a wide range of publishing options to enable easy sharing of your dashboard. For example, you can publish the reports and dashboards that you create as live embedded reports in your websites/web pages or share them as easy-to-access URLs. However, the quickest and easiest method is to share them by email as a PDF, for which the simple instructions are listed as follows:

1. Open your dashboard: **Home | Dashboards**.

2. Click on the **Share** button in the top-right corner.

3. Select the **Email | Layout as in Dashboard - PDF** options, as shown here:

Edit Design
Share
Themes
Email as HTML
Layout as in Dashboard - PDF
Each Report in a New Page - PDF
Edit Email Schedules
Share this View
Make this View Public
Edit Shared Details
Email
</> Embed
URL/Permalink
Slideshow

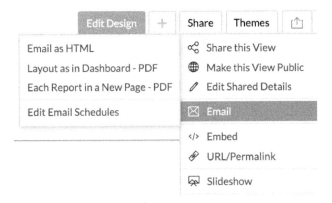

Figure 13.28 – Sharing your dashboard by email as a PDF

4. Set and amend the email recipients, subject, and message before clicking **Send** on the screen, shown as follows:

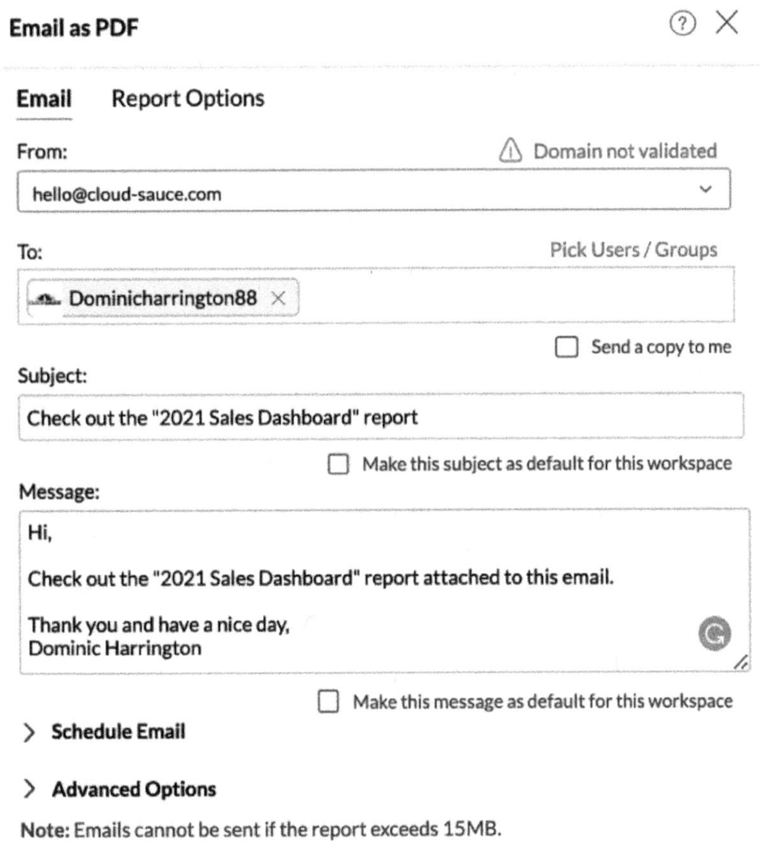

Email as PDF
Email
Report Options
From:
Domain not validated
hello@cloud-sauce.com
To:
Pick Users / Groups
Dominicharrington88
Send a copy to me
Subject:
Check out the "2021 Sales Dashboard" report
Make this subject as default for this workspace
Message:
Hi,
Check out the "2021 Sales Dashboard" report attached to this email.
Thank you and have a nice day,
Dominic Harrington
Make this message as default for this workspace
Schedule Email
Advanced Options
Note: Emails cannot be sent if the report exceeds 15MB.

Figure 13.29 – Sending the PDF by email

5. Alternatively, instead of sending the email immediately, we can schedule the dashboard to be sent automatically by clicking on **Schedule Email**, as shown in the preceding screenshot. Complete the settings as required, then click **Save Email Schedule**, as shown in the following screenshot:

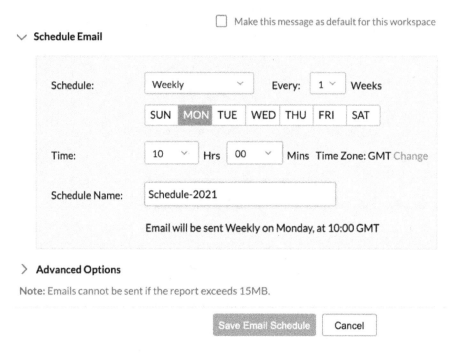

Figure 13.30 – Scheduling an automated email of your dashboard

Congratulations, you have now created and shared your first dashboard in Analytics. The ability to schedule automatically is not something that can be achieved within CRM. So, by completing this step, you have taken your reporting capability to the next level.

You can rest assured that your team and colleagues are now being presented with the information they need when they need it. This will improve collaboration and help ensure that everyone is up to date with performance and key performance indicators. So, this brings us to the end of this chapter; let's have a quick recap on what we have learned.

# Summary

In this chapter, you have learned how to configure the integration between Zoho CRM and Analytics. You have developed the basic skills required for working with the four report creation tools. You have created a dashboard that pulls multiple reports together and learned how to add widgets, images, and texts to it. Finally, you now know how to share these dashboards manually or automatically with peers and colleagues.

In the next chapter, we will conclude *Section 3, Six of the Best Zoho Apps to Integrate with Your CRM*, with another powerful application, **Zoho Creator**. Zoho Creator is an exciting low-code development platform that allows you to create custom applications to further improve your digital transformation.

# 14
# Zoho Creator

Zoho Creator is another excellent application developed by Zoho that can further contribute toward the digital transformation of your business.

In this chapter, we will provide an introduction to how you can create custom applications on your own with minimal coding experience or IT expertise using Zoho Creator's low-code platform.

The concept of low-code/no-code automation is rapidly gaining traction across just about every industry. In fact, Gartner (a leading global research and advisory firm) forecasts that 75% of large enterprises will be using not just one but at least four low-code development tools by as early as 2024.

So now is the time to discover this growing trend and see what it could possibly do to help your future business.

Topics covered within this chapter include the following:

- Creating your first application
- Customizing the web form to capture the right information
- Pushing data into CRM
- Publishing your application
- Further reading and training courses

By the end of this chapter, you will understand the basic concepts of Zoho Creator. You will have practiced creating your first application and customized the web form to capture information. You will have also learned how to push this data into your CRM. Finally, you will gain knowledge of the types and locations of additional training and further reading.

So, let's get started with how to create your first application.

# Creating your first application

The best way to understand the basic functions and capabilities of Creator is to create a simple example. In this working example, we will create a web form that can be shared with your referral partners for them to submit referrals to your business. We shall also push this data automatically into your CRM **Leads** module so that your team may follow up and engage with the prospective client from there.

Let's start at the beginning, accessing Creator at `creator.zoho.com`:

1. Complete the sign-up form to create your account. You will be able to build this app within the Free Trial version and either link to your Zoho One account (if you have one) or sign up to one of three available plans at a later date if required.

2. Click on the **New Application** button toward the top right of the page.

3. Click on the **Create from scratch** icon as shown next:

Figure 14.1 – The Create from scratch icon to start building your application

4. Now enter your application name in the pop-up box that appears, as shown; for example, `Partner Referral App`:

Figure 14.2 – Naming your application

5. Click on the blue **Create New Form** button.

6. Next, you'll be presented with a screen as shown in the following figure. Click on the **Blank** option on the left of the screen:

## How would you like to create your form?

| Blank | Import with data | From a template | Integrations |

Figure 14.3 – Creating a new form

7. Now give your form a name, for example, Referral, then click on the **Create Form** button:

## Create from Scratch

Figure 14.4 – Naming your form

So now that the application creation has been started, next, we need to customize the fields and appearance of our web form.

# Customizing the web form

Customizing your web form is important to make sure that we are collecting the data we need, in the correct format. In this section, you will learn how to add fields and set their properties.

Upon creating your new form in *step 7* in the previous section, you will be presented with the following screen:

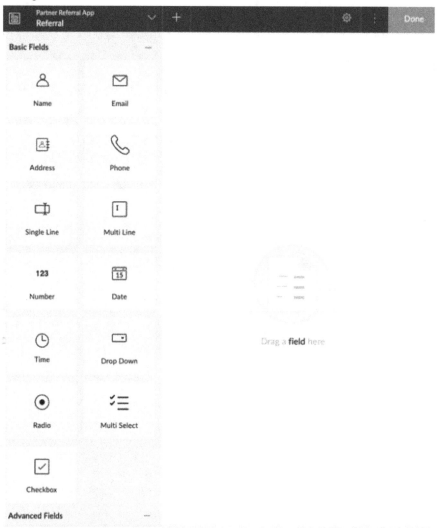

Figure 14.5 – A simple drag-and-drop user interface for creating your new form

Bearing in mind that we will be pushing this data into CRM later, we need to ensure that we only use the field types that are also present in CRM.

Now, let's go on to create our web form as follows:

1. Drag a **Single Line** field from the **Basic Fields** pane on the left to the blank section on the right.

2. Next, create the **First Name** field by completing **Field Properties** as follows:

Figure 14.6 – Setting the field properties for our First Name field

3.  Now add the remaining fields to your form with the field name/types as follows:

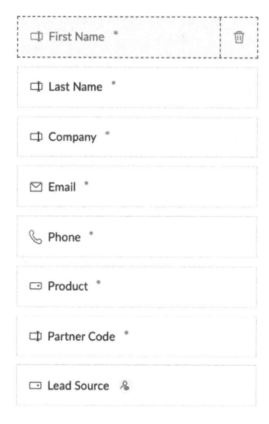

Figure 14.7 – A form with the basic form fields added

4.  Once we have added all the basic fields that we need the user to complete, we need to also add a hidden and pre-populated field to capture that the **Lead Source** is **Referral - Partner**.

5.  You can achieve this by selecting the **Referral - Partner** field from the **Choices** dropdown. (This will be the only option in the dropdown.) Next, set the **Show field to** option to **Admin Only**. Refer to the following screenshot for an illustration of this step:

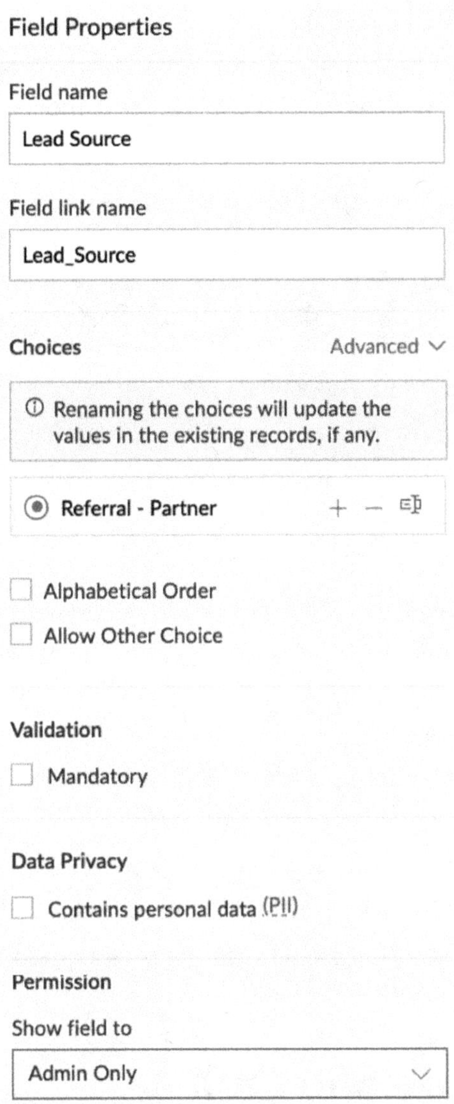

**Field Properties**

Field name

Lead Source

Field link name

Lead_Source

Choices                              Advanced ⌄

ⓘ Renaming the choices will update the
values in the existing records, if any.

⦿ Referral - Partner          +  —  ⅗

☐ Alphabetical Order
☐ Allow Other Choice

**Validation**

☐ Mandatory

**Data Privacy**

☐ Contains personal data (PII)

**Permission**

Show field to

Admin Only                              ⌄

Figure 14.8 – Adding a hidden field with a value pre-selected

6.    Upon adding the **Lead Source** field, click on the **Done** button in the top-right corner.

Congratulations, you have achieved the first milestone by completing the web form! At this stage, while only basic, you have taken the first step toward understanding how Creator works. Next, let's explore how we can make changes to the appearance of the form.

# Designing your web form

In this section, you will learn how to change the appearance of your web form. You will see how your form will appear across multiple devices and understand where to change themes and sections as follows:

1.  From within the app, click on the **Design** tab on the menu at the top of the screen, as shown next:

Figure 14.9 – Amend the appearance of your form using the Design menu

2.  Use the following icons to make changes to the appearance of the form on desktop, mobile, and tablet devices:

Figure 14.10 – Desktop, mobile, and tablet icons

Click from left to right to use these icons to amend the web form's appearance.

3.  Upon selecting a device, use the following icons to make changes to the theme and sections of your web form:

Figure 14.11 –Theme and sections icons (from left to right)

These icons allow you to change the theme and personalize the sections.

Once you have experimented with these settings and personalized the appearance, it is time to set up the integration with Zoho CRM.

# Pushing data to Zoho CRM

One of the main benefits of using Zoho Creator is the ease with which we can push a submitted web form to Zoho CRM.

While there is native integration with Zoho CRM that allows us to push data into any module using a simple mapping function, unfortunately, it does not support custom fields (at the time of writing). Until such time that this becomes available, you may use a function with a script as provided. Here's how you push the data to Zoho CRM:

1.  From within the app, click on the **Workflow** tab on the menu at the top of the screen:

Figure 14.12 – Click Workflow to enter the Workflow menu

2. Click on the **Create Workflow** button in the center of the screen.

3. Now complete the form that appears subsequently, as illustrated in the following screenshot. Next, click on the **Create Workflow** button:

## Run workflow on any event in the form

| | |
|---|---|
| Choose form | Referral ⌄ |
| Run when a record is ( Record Event ) | ⦿ Created    ○ Edited    ○ Created or Edited    ○ Deleted |
| When to trigger workflow ( Form Event ) | Successful form submission ⌄ |
| Name the workflow | Push to CRM |

Create Workflow

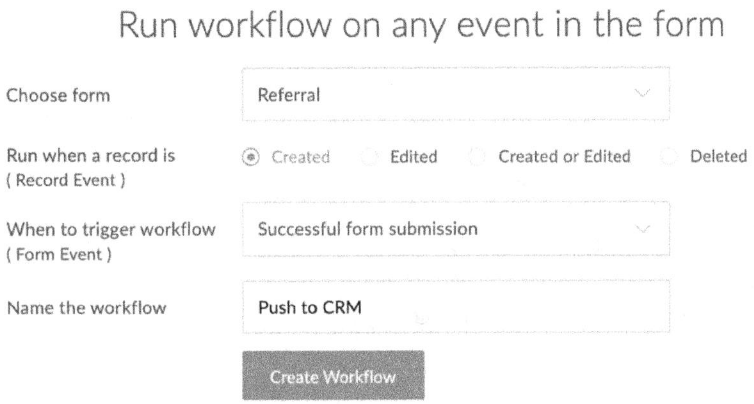

Figure 14.13 – Selecting the triggers for the workflow

4. Click on the **Add New Action** button on the next screen that appears.

5. Click on the **Deluge Script** button, then add the following code into the **Deluge script** screen that appears:

```
leadinfo = {"Company":input.Company,"Last_Name":input.
Last_Name,"First_Name":input.First_Name,"Phone":input.
Phone_Number,"Email":input.Email,"Product":input.
Product,"Partner_Code":input.Partner_Code,"Lead_
Source":input.Lead_Source};
response = zoho.crm.createRecord("Leads",leadinfo);
```

To understand this code, let's consider the first part of it as follows:

```
"Company":input.Company
```

In the preceding code, `"Company"` is the API **Field Name** within the CRM **Leads** module and `.Company` is the field name within our Creator application.

If you need to check your API field names in Zoho CRM, navigate to the following page:

**Setup | Developer Space | APIs | API Names | Leads**

6.  Once you have copied in the code and checked/updated all the CRM API names, click on the **Update** button at the bottom of the screen and then on **X** in the top-right corner, which can be seen in the following screenshot:

Figure 14.14 – Adding/editing your Deluge script

7.  Next, you should test your form and integration by first clicking **Done**, followed by the **Share this Application** button, both located in the top-right corner of the screen.

8.  You will now see your web form as a referral partner would see it, so complete the form with some sample data and click **Submit**:

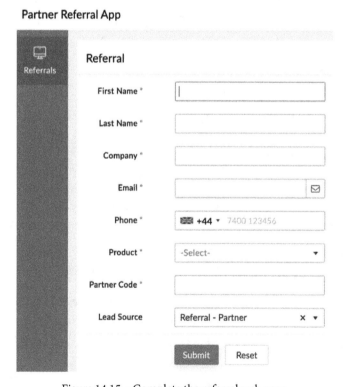

Figure 14.15 – Complete the referral web page

9. Finally, log in to your CRM and view the **Leads** module – where you should see a new record, created by your script, which was triggered when the form was submitted.

> **Tip**
> If some fields have not pulled through into CRM correctly, recheck your Creator field names and CRM API names as per *step 6*.

Congratulations, you have now built, customized, and integrated your first application! This is a significant milestone toward understanding the scope and flexibility that Creator integrated with CRM has to offer.

Let's take a look at how we complete the final step and publish our application.

# Publishing your application

Once you've built and tested the application, it is time to publish it, which can be achieved by completing the following steps:

1. From within the **Edit Application** screen, click on the **Settings** tab from the main menu:

Figure 14.16 – Accessing Settings from the main menu

2. Click on **Publish** within the sub-menu named **Users and Control**.

3. On the next screen, click **Publish** again to display the following options:

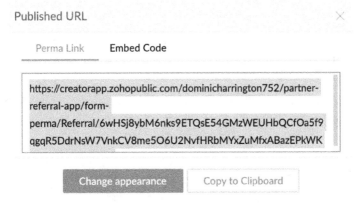

Figure 14.17 – Publishing options for your application

4. Use the required options described in the following list and displayed in *Figure 14.17*:

   - **Change appearance**: Use this option to further customize the appearance of the web form.

   - **Perma Link**: Copy this link to share it by email or as a button-click URL.

   - **Embed Code**: Provide this code to a web developer for them to insert the code (form) into a web page.

5. Finally, click on **X** to the right of the text **Published URL** and click on the **Publish Component** button in the top-right corner of the screen.

So now you have published your first application using Zoho Creator, you may possibly be considering possibilities for extending the functionality of this one. Perhaps you have other ideas you wish to try out. Either way, there are many resources available.

Let's now consider additional reading and training that is available on the internet to help you with the next steps using Creator.

# Further reading and training courses

While you should appreciate that you have achieved an important first milestone by completing the steps in this chapter, you should also realize there is a lot more to learn and achieve with Creator.

As such, it is highly recommended that to further develop your basic skills in this application, you should consider exploring the following resources:

- *Zoho Creator User Guide*: This is the official user guide provided by Zoho, which will cement what you have learned so far and allow you to build upon this example. Visit `https://www.zoho.com/creator/newhelp/user-guides.html`.

- *Zoho Creator Training and Certifications*: These are a range of online training courses provided by Zoho. Visit `https://www.zoho.com/creator/training/online.html` for further details.

- *Zoho Creator Application Gallery*: This is a range of pre-built applications, providing some ready-to-use solutions for certain industries. See `https://www.zoho.com/creator/apps/?src=hdd` for further details.

- *Zoho Creator Community*: This is an online community managed by Zoho that enables Zoho enthusiasts to connect, engage, and learn from each other, accessible at `https://help.zoho.com/portal/en/community/zoho-creator`.

Every one of these resources will help you to learn and gain more value from Zoho Creator and, most importantly, make you realize that Zoho is so much more than a CRM solution – it is a platform with which you can grow, evolve, and scale your business.

Finally, let's have a brief recap of what we have learned from this chapter.

# Summary

In this chapter, you have gained an understanding of the basic concepts of Zoho Creator. You have created your first application and customized the web form to capture information. You have also learned how to push this data into CRM. You now know the best sources of further reading and additional training so that you can build upon these skills and improve your knowledge of this app-building software. The skills gained will help you extend the capability of your Zoho solution, providing you with more control and flexibility. Your digital transformation potential now has fewer bounds.

This chapter concludes *Section 3* of this book. We'll now move on to *Section 4, Measure, Learn, Evolve,* with the next chapter. In the next chapter, you will learn how to create powerful and insightful reports and dashboards within Zoho CRM.

# Section 4: Measure, Learn, Evolve

Once you have built your very own system on the Zoho CRM platform, you should see immediate benefits.

In this section, you will learn how to measure the performance of your CRM so that you can maximize your investment and ensure that the system continues to enable your business to thrive and grow as you start to achieve the success you defined.

This section comprises the following chapters:

- *Chapter 15, Building Actionable Reports and Dashboards (CRM)*
- *Chapter 16, Best Practices to Adopt and Evolve Your CRM*

# 15
# Building Actionable Reports and Dashboards (CRM)

The reporting and dashboard capability within **Zoho Customer Relationship Management** (**Zoho CRM**) is first class. There is a common saying/cliché in business: *Whatever gets measured, gets done*. Whether or not you believe this to be completely true, it is difficult to argue against the fact that measuring performance is an essential undertaking for every business that wants to become successful.

Every business at some stage sets goals, followed by targets to help it achieve these goals. Therefore, it follows that we need to measure how we are performing against such targets. Zoho CRM facilitates this by allowing a majority of fields in every module to be used within a report as a measure or as a filter. Also, many numerical and statistical functions (similar to those in Excel) are built into the software. As Zoho users, we have in our hands the tools to create actionable, insightful, intuitive, and visual dashboards with relative ease and speed.

In this chapter, you will learn about the different types of dashboards available in Zoho CRM and how to create a report. You will have guided practical examples to complete and will also gain an insight into some of the best reports and dashboards successful businesses around the world are using.

The following topics are covered in this chapter:

- Creating a report
- Scheduling a report to send automatically
- Creating dashboards
- Example dashboards to accelerate a successful **customer relationship management (CRM)** experience

By the end of this chapter, you will have learned how to create a basic report. You will have discovered how and why we should automate the distribution of reports, and you will have learned how to create a visual dashboard as well as gaining insight into some of the best dashboards used by Zoho users.

Let's start with report writing!

# Creating a report

In this section, you will learn how to create a report using the UI (User Interface) released by Zoho in July 2021. We can create a report as follows:

1. Starting from the **Home** page, click **Reports | Create Report**.
2. Select the primary module you wish to base your report upon. In this example, we will select **Leads** then click **Continue** as shown:

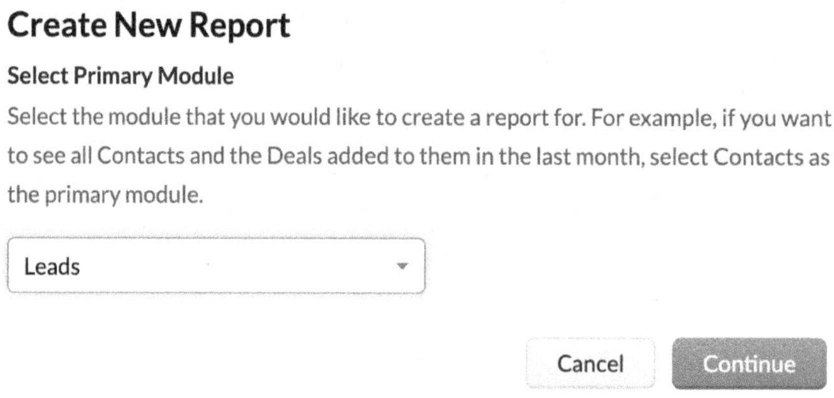

## Create New Report

### Select Primary Module

Select the module that you would like to create a report for. For example, if you want to see all Contacts and the Deals added to them in the last month, select Contacts as the primary module.

| Leads |
| --- |

Cancel    Continue

Figure 15.1 – Creating a new report based upon the Leads module

3.  You will now see the following screen:

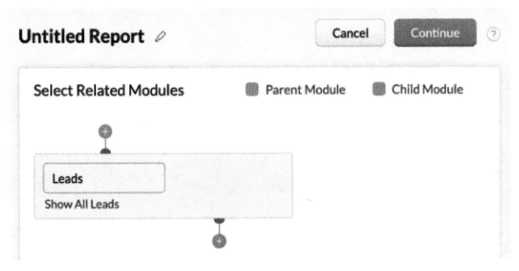

Figure 15.2 – Adding related Child or Parent Modules

You can add additional related child modules by clicking on the blue + and/or parent modules by clicking on the green + button. In this example, we will click **Continue** without adding any related modules.

> Tip
>
> When reporting on **Leads** you most likely will not need any related modules. When reporting on the **Deals** module, you may wish to include **Contacts** and **Accounts** as child modules. By doing so, you will be able to select any field from the parent and child modules in your report.

4. Next, select the columns you wish to add/remove from the report using the + next to **Columns** as shown in the following image. In this example, select **Created Time** and then click **Done**.

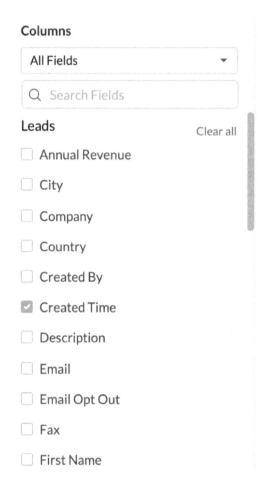

Figure 15.3 – Select the columns you wish to include within your report

5. Now select the fields you wish to **Group By** (or summarize by) by clicking on the + next to **Row Groups**. In this example, select **Lead Source** and **Country** (or any other picklist you wish to summarize by) then click **Done**.

6. Once you have added the columns and the rows to group by, you will see a preview appear in the center of the screen showing how your report will look:

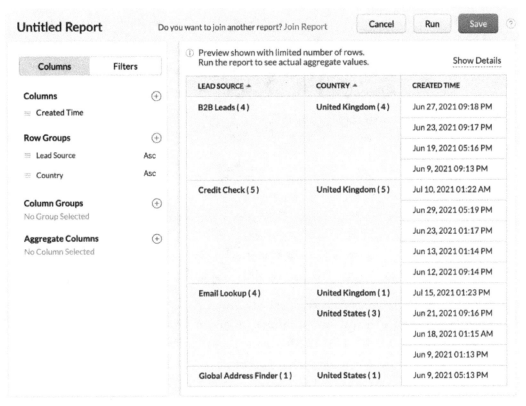

Figure 15.4 – A preview of the report once columns and row groups have been added

> **Tip**
>
> When you start creating reports, you will not be sure whether your fields need to be selected in **Columns**, **Row Groups**, **Column Groups**, or **Aggregate Columns**. Do not worry about that – just experiment and iterate until you achieve the desired result.

7.  Using the same menu on the left as shown in *Figure 15.4,* you may also add columns to **Group By** or **Aggregate By** as desired.

8. Once you are happy with the preview, click on the **Filters** tab followed by the +
as shown:

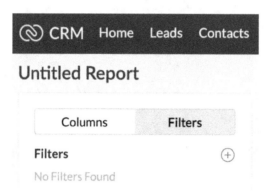

Figure 15.5 – Selecting the Filters tab

9. Now select the fields you wish to filter your report on.

If your filter is based on a date, use the **Date Filter**. if you wish to filter using any
other field, then use the **Advanced Filters**. In this first example, we will filter
**Created Time** within the **Last 12 Months** as shown in the image, then click **Save**:

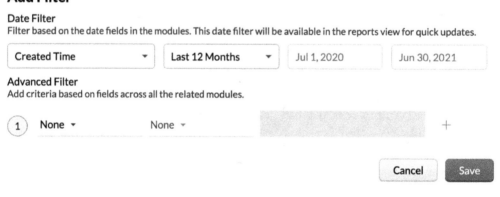

Figure 15.6 – Adding filters to your report

10. Click the **Save** button in the top-right corner once more.

11. Give your report a **Name**, **Description** (optional) and select the **Folder** you wish to
add the report to. Then click **Save**:

## Save Report

Report Name    | 2021 - Leads by Source and Country |

Description    | |

Folder    | Lead Reports    ▾ |

Cancel    Save

Figure 15.7 – Saving your report

12. Once you have saved your report, you will be presented with your report, consisting of the **Columns**, **Groupings**, and **Filters** selected. An example of this can be seen in the following screenshot:

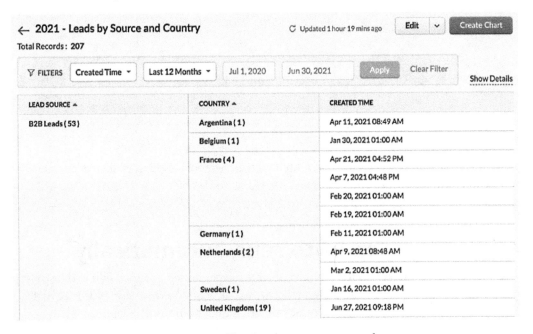

Figure 15.8 – Viewing the report once saved

13. Finally, there are a few options remaining to use in the top right:

   - **Edit**: This allows you to amend any of the columns, groupings, and filters.

   - **Clone:** This allows you to clone (copy) your report and then amend any of the columns, groupings, and filters as required. This is a time-saving way for creating multiple, similar reports.

   - **Export**: Export our report into Excel, CSV, or PDF format.

   - **Send Mail**: Email our report to a single or group of recipients.

   - **Create Chart**: Create a visual representation of this filtered data (which we will consider in the next section, *Creating Dashboards*).

   You can see these options by clicking the drop-down menu next to **Edit**:

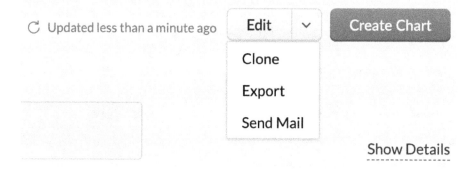

Figure 15.9 – Additional options once you have saved your report

Congratulations! You have created and edited your first report and have taken a key step toward using one of the most powerful and beneficial tools of Zoho CRM. Next, we will look at how we can schedule reports automatically.

# Scheduling a report to send automatically

In the previous section, we created a report of all leads generated grouped by **Lead Source** and **Country**. In this section, you will learn how we can schedule a version of this report to send automatically. Automating reports, while making you more efficient, is a great way of making sure that you and your team are constantly aware of some of the **key performance indicators** (**KPIs**) that are helping to fuel your business growth.

It might be useful to send an amended version of this report to a colleague(s) monthly. That report should only contain leads created the previous month. This can be achieved in the following way:

1.  With the report open, click on the dropdown next to the **Edit** option, as shown in *Figure 15.9* earlier, and click on **Clone**.

2.  Now click on the **Filters** tab and change the **Standard Filter** to **Leads Created Time** to **Last Month**.

3.  Click on the pencil next to the report name in the top left then amend the name of the report to Leads Created Last Month.

4.  Click **Done**.

5.  Click **Save**.

6.  Click on **Reports** (module) on the main CRM menu, then locate and select a folder from the list on the left named **Scheduled Reports** to reveal the following screen:

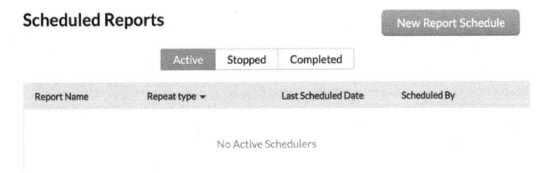

Figure 15.10 – Scheduled Reports folder

7.  Click on the **New Report Schedule** button (top right).

8.  Complete the **New Report Schedule** screen that appears now, selecting all the options, with a typical example shown in the following screenshot:

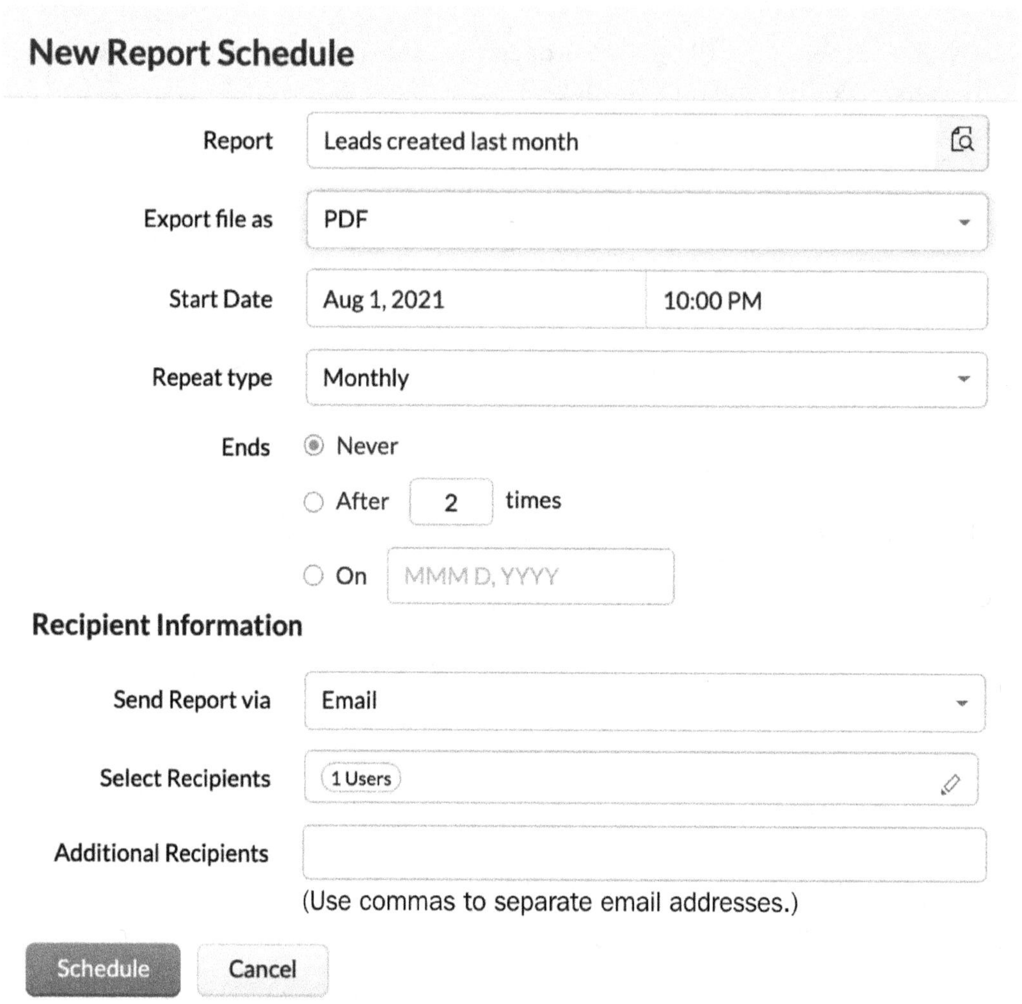

## New Report Schedule

| | |
|---|---|
| Report | Leads created last month |
| Export file as | PDF |
| Start Date | Aug 1, 2021     10:00 PM |
| Repeat type | Monthly |
| Ends | ● Never |
| | ○ After   2   times |
| | ○ On   MMM D, YYYY |

### Recipient Information

| | |
|---|---|
| Send Report via | Email |
| Select Recipients | ( 1 Users ) |
| Additional Recipients | |

(Use commas to separate email addresses.)

Schedule    Cancel

Figure 15.11 – Creating a new report schedule

9.  Finally, click **Schedule**.

By completing the process of scheduling automated reports, we have achieved another milestone—one that will add a lot of value to your CRM system overall by providing the performance data that management needs. Receiving this information consistently will often serve as a prompt for managers/users to improve accuracy and consistency when updating the system. So, as you now have some experience with how the reporting module in Zoho CRM works, let's take a look at another great performance management module: **Analytics**.

# Creating dashboards

A **dashboard** in a CRM system is a summarized view of a custom CRM report. It provides real-time analysis of the activities performed by users in addition to analysis of how the business development function of a business is performing.

There are two ways to create a dashboard: from an existing report and/or by using the **Quick Chart** tool. Let's explore the first method—creating a dashboard from an existing report.

## Creating a dashboard from a report

There are two scenarios in which you will need to create a dashboard from a report—firstly, if you want your dashboard to be located within the **Dashboard/Analytics** module alongside other dashboards, and secondly, if you cannot create a chart using the **Quick Chart** tool so must first create a report, followed by a chart (for example, a summary of notes).

You can create a dashboard from a report in the following way:

1. From the CRM **Home** page, navigate to the **Dashboards** or **Analytics** module on the main menu (Zoho CRM accounts created circa 2019 onward should be named as **Analytics**).

2. Click on the + sign in the top left of the screen, just next to the word **Dashboards**.

3.    Input a name for your dashboard—for example, `Your Company Name -` `Dashboard`, as shown in the following screenshot:

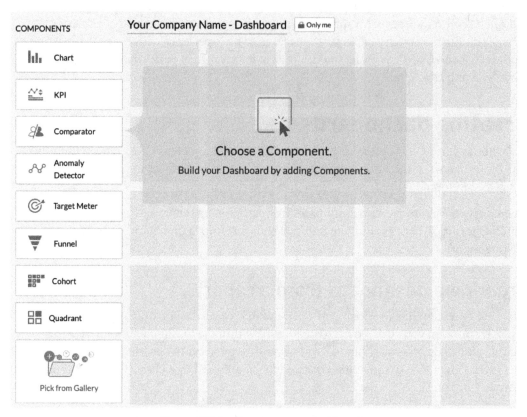

Figure 15.12 – Creating a new dashboard

4.    Click on the **Chart** component at the top of the list on the left, then select **From Existing**.

Now, complete the popup that appears subsequently, as follows:

a) Input a suitable name in the **Component Name** field (which is often the same as the report you are creating a chart from).

b) Select a report from the **Report** list that you wish to use to represent the data.

c) Leave the **Measure (y-axis)** field at the **Record Count** setting.

d) Select **Lead Source** as the **Grouping** option.

e) Select a chart type using the dropdown next to the **Column chart** (**Column chart** or **Pie chart** is recommended for this type of component).

f) Click **Done** as shown in the following screenshot:

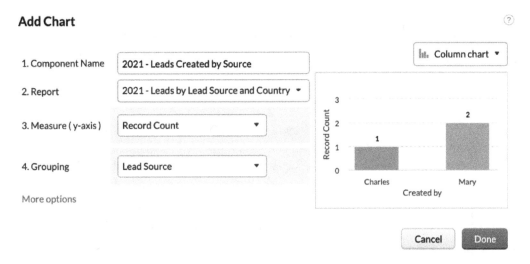

Figure 15.13 – Adding a new chart (component) to the dashboard

You will now be presented with your chart, at which point it is a good time to click **Save**. Your chart should now resemble the following one:

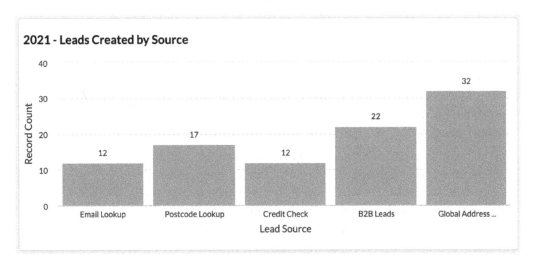

Figure 15.14 – Our report now represented visually on the dashboard

Congratulations – you have now created your first dashboard! Adding dashboards such as this really brings a CRM system to life and helps get users and managers to engage with performance measures. Now, let's look at a second way to create a dashboard: using the dashboard creation tool.

## Creating a dashboard using the Quick Chart tool

The dashboard building tool in Zoho CRM is very intuitive and powerful, and dashboards can be created quickly, often without needing to create a report in the first instance. There are several different types of dashboard components we can use, summarized as follows:

- **Chart**: A chart is a graphical representation of the data. Analysis with this component is easy and quick. Types of charts supported include bar chart, horizontal chart, line chart, stacked chart, pie chart, donut chart, table chart, funnel chart, and area chart.

- **KPI**: KPIs allow simple measurement of the performance of a team. Types of KPI supported include **Standard**, **Growth Index**, **Basic**, **Scorecard**, and **Rankings** KPIs.

- **Comparator**: Comparator gives users a comparative overview of any data, including user performance, lead source, and more.

- **Anomaly Detector**: Anomaly Detector detects any type of discrepancy in a user's usual business process. This is most effective when you have been using Zoho for over 12 months or are working with large volumes of data.

- **Target Meter**: A target meter is an easy way to set and monitor targets.

- **Funnel**: A funnel provides a visual representation of different stages in a business. Types of funnel supported include **Standard**, **Compact**, **Segment**, **Classic**, and **Path**.

- **Cohort**: Cohort analysis helps us to understand customer behavior across the sales life cycle or buying trends and patterns.

- **Quadrant**: Quadrant analysis scatters the data you wish to analyze into four quadrants. It is possible to analyze data, such as types of campaigns versus revenue generated to identify the campaign that was the most effective, or leads created versus lead source to identify the source and other information.

So, with that basic understanding of the types of dashboards, let's take a look at a couple of simple examples to get you started.

## KPI

We will create a KPI that measures the number of leads in the current month versus the previous month. This can be achieved as follows:

1. Open the dashboard you used in the previous section and click **Add Component**.

2. Click on **KPI**, as shown in the following screenshot:

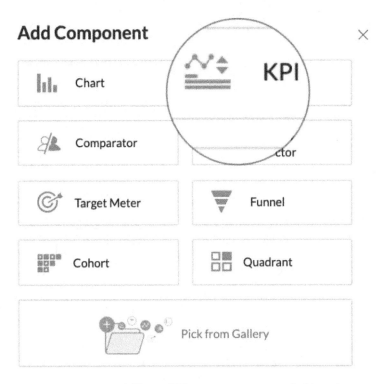

Figure 15.15 – Adding a KPI component to your dashboard

3. Select the **Standard KPI** option, then complete the parameters as displayed in the following screenshot. Note the graphic on the left is illustrative only and does not change when setting the parameters on the right:

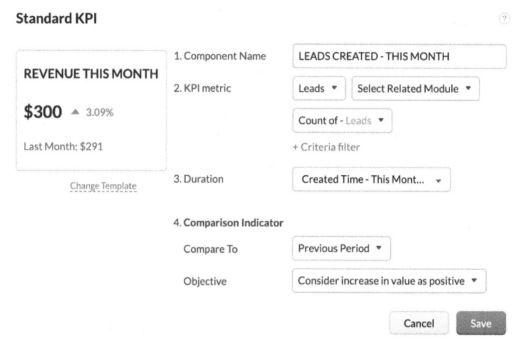

Figure 15.16 – Defining the parameters of a KPI component

4. Click **Save**.

You will now see this KPI component appear on your dashboard, similar to the one shown in the following screenshot:

Figure 15.17 – A KPI dashboard component showing the number of leads created this month versus last month

Next, let's have a look at an example of another popular component type—a **Target Meter** component.

## Target Meter

In this example, we will create a component that will show the amount of **Closed won** revenue against a target over a three-month period. This can be achieved as follows:

1.  Click on **Add Component**.

2.  Select **Target Meter**.

3.  Click on the **Bar** target type, as shown in the following screenshot:

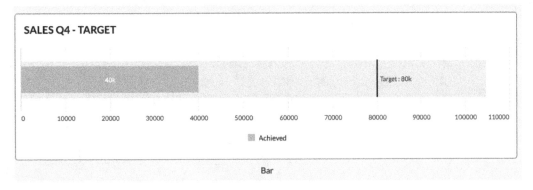

Figure 15.18 – A Bar target

4.  Complete the subsequent screen that appears with the values shown in the following screenshot (or similar values to these):

Figure 15.19 – Defining the parameters of a Bar target – Target Meter

You should now see this component appear on your dashboard, similar to the one shown in the following screenshot:

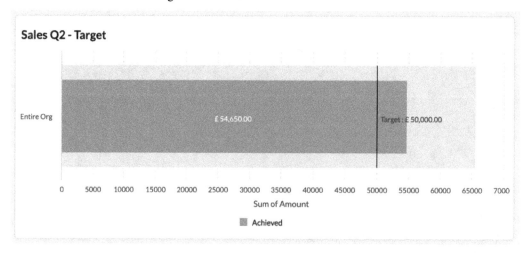

Figure 15.20 – An example target meter once configured

Once you have completed these couple of examples, experiment with a few other component types – you will notice that the process is always similar.

More information on creating dashboards can be found at `https://help.zoho.com/portal/en/kb/crm/analytics-and-dashboards/dashboards/articles/analytical-components`.

Once you grasp the basic principle of creating dashboards, it's quite common to seek inspiration for others. So, let's now look at some further examples to help you with this.

# Example dashboards to accelerate a successful CRM experience

Many Zoho users have common objectives from their CRM system, and thus similar reporting requirements. For this reason, Zoho has provided a gallery of dashboards to select from and tweak slightly to fit your solution. Using this gallery will serve two purposes: it will inspire you and also help you develop the dashboards much more quickly—win-win!

To access the gallery from your own dashboard created earlier, click on **Add Component |
Pick From Gallery**. You will now be presented with the gallery, as shown in the
following screenshot:

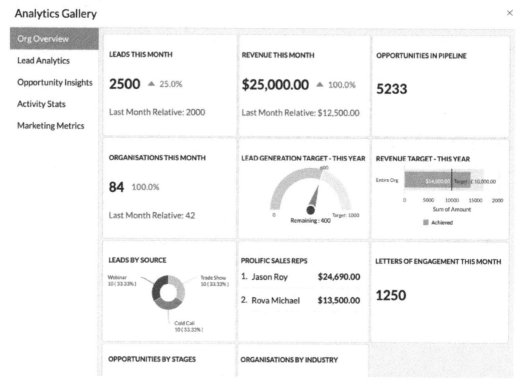

Figure 15.21 – Analytics Gallery, grouped into five categories displayed on the left

Within the gallery, the reports have been grouped into five types, as follows:

- **Org Overview**: This set of dashboards contains the type of summaries that would be
  reviewed during regular management meetings. You will recognize some of the **KPI**
  and **Target Meter** charts discussed in the previous section. However, if you scroll to
  the bottom, there are a couple of really useful **Comparator** charts that allow you to
  measure multiple metrics over a period of time, which is great for identifying trends
  and better/worse performers in your team.

- **Lead Analytics**: New leads are often described as the lifeblood of any business. Therefore, it is crucial that you can measure the performance of your marketing and lead-generation activities. Using this will help you identify how many leads become qualified and the status of those yet to qualify, and also gives you a detailed view of which sources of leads convert at a higher rate than others. The standout dashboard in this set is the **Sales Funnel** dashboard toward the bottom. This is arguably the most valuable dashboard you can ever have—be sure to utilize this one.

- **Deal Insights**: Once you have qualified a lead, it becomes a deal. The dashboards in this section will provide you with easy-to-interpret insights into overall revenue, performance by salesperson, the value of a pipeline, and many similar related metrics.

- **Activity Stats**: Do not overlook this section, for it is the activities that are completed by you and your team that will contribute to achieving those revenue and other performance targets. Use these dashboards to help you measure how many tasks, meetings, and calls have been completed.

- **Marketing Metrics**: If you are using Zoho Campaigns and/or the **Campaigns** module within Zoho CRM, then these dashboards will provide you with a great way to measure expected and actual revenue generated from each campaign. This will give you and your marketing team insight into which campaigns to continue, which to increase, and which to change or stop altogether.

The dashboards you adapt from these five sections will give you a great head start toward having a suite of dashboards that will help you to report on multiple aspects of your Zoho CRM and ultimately toward your growth and retention goals as a business. Be sure to review the usage and value of these dashboards every 3 to 6 months, especially if your business is experiencing growth or change.

That brings us to the end of this chapter—let's finish with a quick recap.

# Summary

In this chapter, you have learned about creating a basic report, as well as discovering how and why we should automate the distribution of reports. In addition to this, you have learned how to create a visual dashboard and gained insight into some of the best dashboards used by Zoho users.

The skills and knowledge gained in this chapter will help you gain insight into which users are working with the CRM system and how it is being used. However, the main benefit of having good reports and dashboards is to enable you to measure, learn, and evolve. Measure current performance, learn from this, and use it to help make decisions on how to evolve not only the CRM system but the marketing, sales, and account management functions within your business.

In the next chapter, we will consider best practices to adopt in order to evolve your CRM system.

# 16

# Best Practices to Adopt and Evolve Your CRM

As good as your CRM may be, if it is not adopted by your team successfully, you will never fully realize the potential it has to transform your business. It is often cited that slow user adoption is frequently the main cause of a CRM project's failure. In this chapter, you will learn how to avoid common mistakes and set three early adoption milestones that will set you on the right path. The topics covered in this chapter include the following:

- The importance of successful user and business CRM adoption
- Three early adoption milestones to focus on
- Great habits for you and your team to develop
- Future-proofing your CRM for continued success

By the end of this chapter, you will have a good understanding of why successful CRM adoption is important for you, your team, and your business. You will have discovered the best ways to hit the ground running with your CRM adoption. You will have learned the habits you must develop and maintain and why they are important. Finally, you will gain insight into how to keep your CRM fit for the future to achieve continuous improvement.

# The importance of successful user and business adoption

Since a Gartner study in 2001 showed that 50% of CRM implementations failed, much has subsequently been written for the last two decades about the high rate of failure of CRM adoption. While no definitive overall figures are available, most estimates put this figure somewhere in the 40-70% range in 2021.

So, for all your efforts in selecting, designing, and building the CRM solution for your business, you statistically have around a 50% chance of it being successful. How do you beat this trend? What steps can you take to avoid being yet another failure statistic?

The most common reason cited for such failures is that the CRM is not successfully adopted by the user(s) and/or the management. Therefore, the most important thing you can do to improve the success of your CRM is to ensure that your users and management adopt the solution well.

While there is no single solution or magic wand that will achieve this, there are several tips and techniques that, once actioned, will improve the successful adoption of your CRM immensely. Let's explore these tips and techniques as follows.

## Revisit and share why you need a CRM

Revisit the reasons why you invested in (needed) a CRM and make sure that these are now established as goals for the CRM implementation. If you are a solopreneur, write down these goals and check them off as you achieve them. If you have a team supporting you, then share these goals and make sure everyone is aware of each one, why they are important, and what impact achieving them will have on the business. This should obtain buy-in at the top level. Some of these reasons were described in *Chapter 1, The Foundation Modules – Understanding the Building Blocks to Success*; however, a summary of some of the main ones is given here:

- You are experiencing growth and need this growth to be scalable and more profitable.

- To improve how customer data is collected, managed, and used within your business.

- To increase sales from new customers and repeat customers by nurturing and following up more often.

- To hold and process all customer data in a single place.

- If one single system is not possible across the whole business, then you need to ensure that the CRM integrates with the other system(s).

- To replace a previous CRM that was no longer fit for purpose or was out of date.

## Agree CRM success measures with key stakeholders

Following on from the reasons mentioned in the preceding point, in *Chapter 1*, *The Foundation Modules – Understanding the Building Blocks of Success*, you will also have listed some ways in which you will measure the success of the CRM. This is different to the reasons *why*; think of these measures as the benchmark that will confirm that you have achieved the goals. Again, sharing these measures with key stakeholders and other users will help give them a common goal and purpose. If all these measures are hit, the CRM adoption will have been a resounding success.

Some of the example measures cited by successful Zoho users include the following:

- Increase the conversion rate of lead to deal by 50% within 3 months.

- Be able to measure your **return on investment** (**ROI**) on marketing.

- Know how many times per year you have communicated with existing clients.

- Understand how many/which products each of your clients have.

- The business will replace *all* paperwork for orders and jobs by using the CRM.

- Your operations team will be reminded whenever a service is due in advance so this can be scheduled and completed.

- Increase first-year retention of members/retained/contracts from 40% (current level) to 60% within 2 years.

- Ability to measure where leads have come from.

- Ability to measure conversion rates (from inquiry to customer).

- Provide the sales management with complete visibility of the pipeline.

- Provide senior management with a weighted forecast of the pipeline.

- Be able to break down sales performance by territory/area and target areas for improvement.

- Replace several spreadsheets and Outlook contact directories that are used in the business with a single, central database accessible by all the team.

# Involve stakeholders and/or key users in the implementation process

Identify who the key people will be who will drive the users/lead by example as you strive to achieve your goals. Involve them in the design and build (evaluation) stages of implementation as well as in the training. This will help obtain their buy-in early on and they will naturally adopt the role of CRM champion among their peers. When the CRM is for a team, then successful implementation project teams often include representatives from each department of the business: marketing, sales, operations, customer service, and finance.

# Process, process, process

Successful, scalable businesses are always highly process-driven. Every business function has a clear, structured, and well-documented process. For example, marketing will have a clear lead-nurturing process and automated workflows that follow a specific process of attracting new customers.

The team that follows up on new leads will have a clear follow-up and qualification process. The sales team will follow a well-defined sales process until the deal has been won or lost. The operations team will have a clear process of delivering the products/services and for managing customer service and aftercare.

The CRM system should be viewed as the vehicle by which these teams will complete the processes. By welding the business process to the CRM, you will be ensuring that the solution is always used and will become paramount to the success of the business.

In addition to this, it is vital to ensure that when any of the business processes are changed, the changes are applied to the CRM as required. This will ensure that the CRM remains up to date with processes, which will increase the longevity of a successful CRM adoption.

# Keep it simple and avoid jargon – imagine someone new to your business and industry is going to use it

One of the tips for a good CRM design in earlier chapters was to avoid jargon. Keep the field names simple and conversational and you will make it more intuitive for users to follow. Using the same terminology that is used within your business will be good enough for now. However, if you wish to try and future-proof this, then a useful exercise is to review from the perspective of someone who is new to your business and/or sector. If they can understand the field names, picklist values, and dashboards, then this will also have a significant impact on future-proofing this success.

# Create a crib sheet/quick-start or how-to guide

There is a popular theory that is often discussed in the world of training called the **Forgetting curve**. This theory was formed by a German psychologist, Hermann Ebbinghaus, back in the early 19th century, and the fact that it has stood the test of time for over 100 years shows that it is a theory not to be ignored. This theory concluded that 90% of new learning is forgotten within 7 days! Imagine that! You can give the best training you can deliver and 90% of it may be lost within a week. So, bearing this in mind, it is no surprise that some of the most successful CRM adoptions happen when the business documents some of the training materials. While there are a few ways to do this, a popular and successful method is to create a short series of how-to guides.

This will be mainly used in the early weeks and by future new starters; however, it will help user adoption a great deal and so is a worthwhile investment of time.

# Training – the rule of a third

This is something observed personally over 20 years of training users in the software domain. Regardless of the application, location, and group size, you can almost always split delegates/users into three groups after receiving initial training on new software.

A third of users will pick it up straight away, without the need for reiterating, and will be implementing their skills immediately and successfully. In fact, most of these will be adding to the skills themselves proactively and be ready, willing, and able to train and coach others.

The second group retains a good level of information and with a little time and support will reach the level of the first group within the first few weeks.

The third group, however, may struggle. They will find it difficult to retain much information and, generally, change is not easy for them. Not all is lost, however; with additional training, support, and encouragement, most of them will get to the level of competence required but at different times, sometimes taking weeks and months.

So, a great tip is to identify which of these groups each member of your team comes under and act accordingly. In doing so, you will be taking a big step toward successful CRM adoption.

## Focus on quick wins

Another great tactic that has been deployed successfully is delivering quick wins for you and your team. In other words, implement something early on in adoption that will deliver value, something that was not provided before. This shows everyone that this is a good system, better than the last one, and opens their eyes to its potential and starts to win them over. When people want something to work, they often adapt quickly and make more effort to help make it work.

There are several examples of this, but some of the most popular include these:

- Configuring a good home page for each user – showing what they need to do today/ this week and how they or the team are currently performing

- A workflow that sends an automated email and creates a reminder task

- A marketplace extension that provides integration to another tool that the business uses (for example, Dropbox, Google Drive, WorkDrive, Zoho Sign, or Global Email Finder)

There are many more examples of quick wins; however, in this context, think in terms of this: *what can I set up quickly that adds value immediately and is better than what we had in place before*?

Add three or four of these for *Day 1* and your users will start to enjoy and enthuse about this new CRM – it's a simple yet powerful technique that helps achieve successful adoption.

## Measure–Learn–Evolve

The final technique to help you with a successful user and business adoption is to apply the **Lean Startup methodology**. For background information on this, an internet search will provide numerous links to this topic, and one book that would be very useful reading is *Lean Startup* by Eric Ries. Out of the many learnings and concepts we can take away from this book, the methodology that is most suitable for CRM adoption is the **Measure–Learn–Evolve** loop.

Applied to our CRM adoption, we must measure feedback from our team on how they are finding the new system. Asking a few short questions of yourself and/or your team frequently will allow you to measure how the new CRM is perceived by the users. Once we have captured the feedback, you must learn from it. What are the common factors and general consensus? It is fair to say that while everyone will have their own opinion, when a specific feeling/observation is shared by more than 20% of users, it may be that there is something we can learn from this and take action upon. Finally, when we do learn something, we should seek to address it – by making a change. In the CRM, it could mean we tweak some terminology, add a report, amend a workflow, deliver more training – it could relate to any of the elements from any of the chapters in this book.

Be sure to obtain feedback from users in the first few weeks and then set up a process of gaining regular feedback (Zoho Survey), perhaps quarterly thereafter.

Taking the **Measure-Learn–Evolve** approach to user and business adoption will certainly have a positive and significant impact on the successful adoption of your CRM. This may be illustrated as follows:

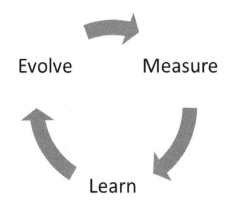

Figure 16.1 – The Measure-Learn-Evolve loop

To summarize, you now have several tips and techniques to consider and deploy. The more of these you implement, the more successful your CRM adoption will be. You will see a greater ROI and more quickly and ultimately you will see an increase in sales from new and existing customers. Win, win, win!

Now let's take a look at another way that will be sure to help accelerate the successful adoption process – understanding three milestones to aim for.

# Three early milestones to focus on

In this section, you will learn about three milestones that you must aim for when starting to use the CRM. Pay attention to these and it is pretty much guaranteed to speed up the successful adoption and you will experience a quicker ROI. Let's start with the first milestone.

# Milestone 1 – all users are using the system – every day

While this may sound straightforward and glaringly obvious, it is often overlooked, and you would be surprised by how many new users of Zoho (or indeed any CRM) will trip over at this first hurdle. There are a few reasons for this, which you need to be aware of yourself and especially for other users.

### Old habits die hard

If you are new to CRMs, then it is hard to change habits overnight, so you must make sure that each user makes a conscious effort to use the new CRM every day. According to many studies, it takes an average person between 18 and 28 days to change a habit. So, you need to ensure that users are logging in and using the system for all their customer-related activities. You may need to police and enforce this for at least this period.

*I am too busy, but don't worry, I've penciled in some time on Friday to catch up with my CRM updates.* You would be amazed at how many times this saying is heard when a new CRM is implemented – sometimes by the business owner themselves, even if they are the only user! Hard to believe? Well, it is true. When this statement is followed up with the question, *Oh really, what have you been doing to prevent you from using the CRM? What are the things stopping you?*, amazingly, most of the responses will involve being busy speaking to and visiting clients, prospects, suppliers, and partners. Yes, indeed, all of the activities that we should be using the CRM to manage!

The solution to this is simple: users must update the CRM every day that they are undertaking these activities. They should use the CRM mobile app if they are mobile workers and the desktop app when working from the office or home. There should be no excuses.

### People resist or do not like change

This should not be an issue if you are the business owner and sole user, as you will want to get a return on your investment and improve your business performance and growth. However, if you have additional users, then you need to be aware of the people who do not like change. You will need to support, encourage, and motivate these people, but as long as you know who they are, you can and should drive them accordingly. Failure to follow a new business process is after all a performance management issue, and you should treat the CRM adoption as such. However, if you adopt the techniques discussed earlier in this chapter, you should not encounter resistance – in fact, your users should be excited and eager to see the benefits.

So, be aware of and proactively manage these reasons why users may not use the CRM and you will reach that first milestone much more quickly. Now let's take a look at the next milestone.

## Milestone 2 – all users are using the system correctly, in the way that was intended

Firstly, understand that if you do not achieve the first milestone, then you will never achieve this second one. The most effective way of measuring whether all users are using the system correctly is to generate activity-based reports and dashboards. For example, there are several activity-based dashboards and reports you can create quite easily, such as these:

- Leads created
- Notes added
- Tasks completed
- Meetings booked
- Opportunities created
- Contacts added

When you create these charts, including some comparison per user and/or over time (weeks at first), you will be able to easily identify who is using/not using the system in the way you intended.

Focus on activities completed, not the results, in these first few weeks and you will get there quicker. The performance-related charts can come later (month 2).

If you refer to *Chapter 15, Building Actionable Reports and Dashboards (CRM)*, you will find a reference to the gallery of dashboards, one of which is related to activities, so use this for examples of the charts that will help with these measures. Once you have achieved this milestone, you are ready to strive for the next one.

## Milestone 3 – you start to achieve your goals and experience a return on your investment

Understand that if you do not hit the previous milestone, then this one will take much longer to achieve and the success will only be partial. Evidence of reaching this milestone will be seen in both the reports and dashboards you created (using your success measures) and also from the positive feedback you will be receiving from your team and customers.

The important thing here is to make sure that from month 2 (Go Live + 1 month), you have in place some measures (reports) that show you how you/your teams are performing. The success measures discussed earlier in this chapter should be written down, and you should review how you are performing against each one. Depending on the scale and size of these measures, some may take weeks or even months. However, tracking where you are in the pursuit of these goals, and defining any related actions that need to be undertaken, will without a doubt help you to achieve these goals much quicker.

When this happens, you will have reached milestone three and will be starting to achieve your goals and get a return on your CRM investment. So, when you focus on those milestones, you will achieve them much quicker. However, once you have achieved them, you do not want to stop there; you will need to make sure you build on such a positive start. In the next section, we will explore some great habits that, when developed, will help you to enjoy ongoing success with your solution.

The following diagram illustrates the three milestones to focus on for a faster and more successful CRM adoption:

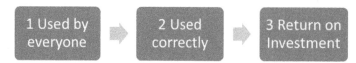

Figure 16.2 – The three milestones to aim for early in your adoption

Next, let's have a look at some of the good practices that should be turned into a habit.

# Great habits for you and your team to develop

In this section, you will learn about some of the actions you and your team need to practice daily and develop into habits. Doing so will ensure that the users remain completely engaged with the system and you continue to enjoy an increasing return on your investment. We will look into these habits in the following subsections.

## Become habitual note-takers

The notes users add correlate directly with the sales they make. Developing the habit of adding a short note to summarize a conversation and agreed next steps will work wonders when it comes to both attracting, delighting, and retaining customers. Notes do not need to be an essay, but simply a succinct summary of the communication, outcome, and next steps. Notes are automatically user, date, and time stamped and it only takes seconds to add one, so there can be no excuses.

## Become task masters

The amount of tasks completed also has a direct bearing on the success of customer relationships and of the CRM overall. Tasks may be created manually and/or created automatically using workflow rules. A user that habitually adds and completes tasks is following a process. They are not missing things, they are proactive, and they will succeed.

## Cut the Outlook/Gmail cord

The more time your team spends with Outlook/Gmail emails and calendars, the less time they will be spending in the CRM. While Zoho does not replace either of these platforms, it works nicely alongside them, and when integrated correctly they complement each other. Making sure your emails and calendar are synced with either platform means that you really can make Zoho the master for all emails and meetings. This is where people sometimes fail, and as a result, it weakens the potential success of the CRM due to less time being spent on it. There are also great plugins for Office 365/Gmail that allow users to add leads and contacts from within their email inbox – which is also a beneficial tool to have.

## Use Notebook for everything else

Within CRM, you now have a **Notebook** app that is also available to download to your Android/Apple mobile devices. While the functionality is very similar to Evernote, OneNote, and iOS Notes, the benefit of using this one is that it gets you completely working within the CRM environment. The more time we spend inside Zoho, the more we see our charts, tasks, and pipeline reports, and the more we use it. Access Notebook within Zoho CRM by clicking on the following icon in the bottom-right corner:

Figure 16.3 – Notebook icon within Zoho CRM

## Use the Deals Kanban to manage your pipeline

This view of your pipeline, provided by Zoho, is one of the most intuitive and powerful reports within Zoho CRM. At a glance, it will show the sales team, how many deals are at each stage of your sales process, and the individual and total values of them. From this view, you can access any **Deal** record, so it is the easiest way to stay focused on the deals that are open and being worked on. If you want your team to be proactively managing these deals and closing more business, they need to get into the habit of working from this view. An example Kanban view can be seen in the following screenshot:

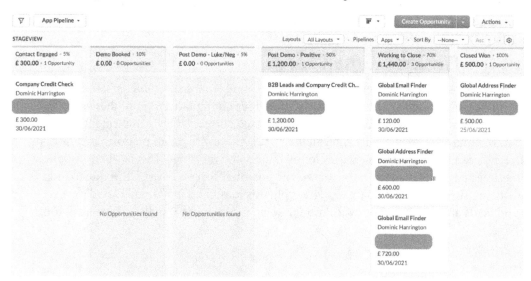

Figure 16.4 – Example of a Kanban view

So, now that you understand some of the key habits that will help make your CRM users more effective, let's turn our attention now to how you can future-proof your CRM for continued success.

# Future-proofing your CRM for continued success

Once you have built and customized your CRM, integrated with one or more Zoho applications, and achieved successful user adoption, does your work in terms of the CRM stop there? No, of course not. Ideally, your business will be growing; however, it will be evolving too, and for the CRM to continue to support this evolution and growth, the CRM must evolve also.

While every Zoho user's journey will be different, there are some things that you can and should do to help ensure that the CRM remains a vital and valuable tool for your future business.

In this section, you will gain an understanding of some of the techniques to deploy and guidelines to follow that will help future-proof your CRM for continued success.

## Remain focused on the success measures

This is critical, for if you do not maintain this focus, you will lose sight of the goals. Also, once you have achieved them, it is important to set new goals and subsequently new measures of success for the CRM and users. It is often said that to stand still is to move backward, and this is true within a CRM too. We must always be striving toward existing or new goals to help drive the business, employees, and CRM forward.

## Contact and company fields

In earlier chapters of this book, you will have learned that we should adhere to standard company and contact fields, especially when it comes to address and contact details. By doing so, you will be future-proofing your CRM so that it will be able to integrate with third-party applications, integrations, and APIs in the future.

# Audit the data

If you consider the database you are building in your CRM as an asset, you must treat it as such and carry out 6-monthly/annual data audits. This activity is probably one that most small businesses overlook; however, if you consider the data within your CRM as an asset, understand that this asset will be worth much less if the results of a data audit are poor.

There is no definitive way to complete these audits, as your CRM database is unique to your business. While there are third-party data analysis tools available to purchase, the quickest and most cost-effective method would be to back up your CRM database to CSV and conduct your analysis within Excel. It would be advisable to focus these audits on your four foundation modules: **Leads**, **Deals**, **Accounts**, and **Contacts**. Some of the questions you should seek the answers to include the following:

- Last Modified Date – using a data comparison. For example, what percentage of records was last modified within 3, 6, 12, 18, and 24 months?

- What percentage of **Leads** and **Contacts** records contain email and mobile fields?

- How many records in each module are completed in full, and what gaps do we have in the data?

- Which fields are not being used at all/seldom used/used frequently/always used?

- Do we have any duplicate/similar field names?

- Are users using the fields correctly?

This list is by no means exhaustive; add your own questions that are specifically important to the integrity of your database.

# Collect user feedback (quarterly)

To achieve long-term success with your CRM, it needs to continue to work for and be constantly used well by the users. They will be the ones to highlight any areas that could help them achieve results more effectively and provide you with a barometer of how they feel about the CRM overall. You should devise a process of capturing feedback from them at least quarterly, even if it's just a handful of questions.

## Check the CRM marketplace (quarterly)

As referred to in *Chapter 8, Supercharge CRM with Marketplace Extensions, Custom Functions, and Integrations,* the marketplace is a treasure trove of new functionality and integrations. While you will receive monthly emails and see social media updates from Zoho about new extensions, it is worthwhile checking the marketplace on a regular basis. If you have a challenge or want to integrate Zoho with a new third-party application or API, then if it exists on the marketplace, this will save you a lot of time, effort, and money.

## When business evolves, ensure that your CRM is ready and aligned

Make sure that when you make a change to the business, for example, by launching a new product, service, market, or channel, do not make the change and then implement the CRM change after the event. Instead, you should view the CRM changes as a crucial part of any customer-facing/impacting change within your business. Ideally, you will make the change to the CRM before the new business initiative is implemented. Failure to do so may confuse or alienate some users and could lead to a *the CRM is out of date, so it does not need to be used* mentality. This is an easy mindset to avoid, provided you are proactive with your CRM changes.

Now let's conclude this chapter with a quick recap.

# Summary

In this chapter, you have learned why it is important that the users and business must successfully adopt your CRM. You have gained insight into some tips and techniques that will increase the probability of your CRM being adopted successfully.

To boost your chances of a quicker, more successful adoption, you have learned about the three milestones that you should focus on from Go Live. From this great start, you now know some great habits that you and your team should develop to continue this success. Finally, you learned some techniques and guidelines that will help future-proof your CRM for continued and ongoing success.

Congratulations! You have reached the end of the book. Implement as many of the practical lessons learned within and you will enjoy a more successful journey with Zoho CRM.

Thank you for reading, and I wish you the very best for your CRM experience and your future business growth and success. If you'd like to share any feedback or write to me with your success stories, then I'd love to hear from you.

Dominic Harrington

Packt.com

Subscribe to our online digital library for full access to over 7,000 books and videos, as well as industry leading tools to help you plan your personal development and advance your career. For more information, please visit our website.

## Why subscribe?

- Spend less time learning and more time coding with practical eBooks and Videos from over 4,000 industry professionals

- Improve your learning with Skill Plans built especially for you

- Get a free eBook or video every month

- Fully searchable for easy access to vital information

- Copy and paste, print, and bookmark content

Did you know that Packt offers eBook versions of every book published, with PDF and ePub files available? You can upgrade to the eBook version at packt.com and as a print book customer, you are entitled to a discount on the eBook copy. Get in touch with us at customercare@packtpub.com for more details.

At www.packt.com, you can also read a collection of free technical articles, sign up for a range of free newsletters, and receive exclusive discounts and offers on Packt books and eBooks.

# Other Books You May Enjoy

If you enjoyed this book, you may be interested in these other books by Packt:

**The Art of CRM**

Max Fatouretchi

ISBN: 978-1-78953-892-2

- Deliver CRM systems that are on time, on budget, and bring lasting value to organizations
- Build CRM that excels at operations, analytics, and collaboration
- Gather requirements effectively: identify key pain points, objectives, and functional requirements
- Develop customer insight through 360-degree client view and client profiling
- Turn customer requirements into a CRM design spec
- Architect your CRM platform
- Bring machine learning and artificial intelligence into your CRM system
- Ensure compliance with GDPR and other critical regulations
- Choose between on-premise, cloud, and hybrid hosting solutions

# Packt is searching for authors like you

If you're interested in becoming an author for Packt, please visit `authors.packtpub.com` and apply today. We have worked with thousands of developers and tech professionals, just like you, to help them share their insight with the global tech community. You can make a general application, apply for a specific hot topic that we are recruiting an author for, or submit your own idea.

# Share your thoughts

Now you've finished *Building Expert Business Solutions with Zoho CRM*, we'd love to hear your thoughts! Scan the QR code below to go straight to the Amazon review page for this book and share your feedback or leave a review on the site that you purchased it from.

`https://packt.link/r/1-800-56466-X`

Your review is important to us and the tech community and will help us make sure we're delivering excellent quality content.

# Index

# D

www.ingramcontent.com/pod-product-compliance
Lightning Source LLC
LaVergne TN
LVHW081332050326
832903LV00024B/1125

* 9 7 8 1 8 0 0 5 6 4 6 6 4 *